There's a Worm in the Apple

There's a Worm in the Apple

Lea McClure

Blessed are you who care about children and the future of our country.

Lea McClure

CREATIVE ARTS BOOK COMPANY

Berkeley ∾ California

There's a Worm in the Apple is published by Donald S. Ellis
and distributed by Creative Arts Book Company

For information contact:
Creative Arts Book Company
833 Bancroft Way
Berkeley, California 94710
1-800-848-7789

ISBN 0-88739-445-0
Library of Congress Catalog Number 2003102098
Printed in the United States of America

Acknowledgments

To my editor Lynn Park, who cut and tailored my work, always giving me freedom and encouragement. I learned from your expertise.

To my dear family and friends who always showed interest, read, praised, advised and never lost faith in me. A special thanks to fellow members of Hawaii Island Writers Group.

To my dear students through the years; you were of every color, nationality and religion. I learned as much from you beautiful young Americans, and from you wonderful newcomers to America, as you learned from me.

My thanks to the writers who have given their permission for me to incorporate their words and wisdom into this novel.

This novel is dedicated to my husband Lerre, my partner, my love, my cushion against the challenges and triumphs in life. I thank you from my heart for always being there for me.

Preface

I had looked forward to my retirement in 1992. There were so many things I intended to do, activities that motherhood and a career had not left time for. Surely, I would soon adjust to the leisure of retirement, but instead of enjoyment, I spent my time combing the news about education, its disheartening results, and who was being blamed.

During my thirty years of work in education, almost every semester I was assigned either a new subject, or a more advanced level of those subjects. My preparation required on-going graduate courses, study at night and during vacations. The time needed to raise my own children was in short supply. Student and class responsibilities became my priorities. Like other parents with demanding careers, I buried myself in books and paper work. Many teachers miss much of their families' lives.

As a retiree, questions I didn't find time to consider while I was teaching were haunting me. I read about the subject, especially public education. I read the philosophies of educators from the times of Confucius, Plato and Socrates. I devoured biographies of Helen Keller's teacher Anne Sullivan Macy and John Dewey. I reviewed the history of education.

I read works by current educators, Dorothy Fink Ungerleider,[1] and a 479 page volume, edited by Francis A. J. Ianni, with more than fifty contributors.[2] Mr. Ianni says, ". . . We see the role of education not as presenting [the education major] students an arsenal of ready-made solutions to any problem they encounter, but rather as preparing people to make increasingly more accurate judgments about values and the social issues they generate."

I read letters and viewpoints published in the media, and I wrote a few to the editors. Teachers I knew shared their problems with me. Some of those experiences are scattered through the novel. I withheld some that were too unpleasant or unbelievable to be plausible, even in fiction.

So much had changed in my own lifetime as well as in all of written history. Social and family patterns, parenting and children's behavior, and multiple societal problems. Each generation of parents had their own ideas of how to rear their children. At some point in time parents decided they would reason with their children. It takes time to acquire both education and experience to be able to reason. Parents overlooked that as they sought to be their child's "pal". It was inevitable that schools would change, in fact they should continually evolve. But, children were changing faster than the schools were.

Families and schools discovered that the tail was wagging the dog. The ones in charge were often the kids. Some parents and children continually staged protests when the staff invoked rules to improve behavior. Administrators spent more time at meetings and less time in their school grounds, halls and office. Students became frustrated with school. They avoided study. They passed in spite of that. "Discipline? Not my kid!" parents said. Teachers and principals were the source of derision on television sitcoms, and in schools. Principals became the bullseye on everybody's target.

The conditions I speak of were common in the mainland schools and those in Hawaii, USA.

For comparison, here is a description of a classroom in an article by Joseph Coleman:

In philosophy teacher Tsuiji's class one morning, students shouted across the room to their friends. A couple slept at their desks, and one in the back row read a comic book amid the chatter. Tsuiji plodded through Descartes.

"I was hardly paying attention," said one student who hopes to study interior design after graduating. She spent the hour talking with friends in the back of the room.

In class after class, students chat, giggle or snooze through lectures. Teachers and school officials are surprisingly tolerant, attributing the unruly behavior in part to large class size—a standard 40 students—or the increasingly restless younger generation.

"We're trying not to be too strict about discipline," said Hirata, the vice principal. "Some students simply cannot follow the class, and some are just tired."

Of course, some students do pay attention, and it's because of those students and their education-conscious parents—that Tsuiji and other teachers race to get through all the material.[3]

Mr. Tsuiji's classroom was in Japan. And we thought it was only in America that schools were out of control. Not true. Children have changed worldwide. How to play catch-up with education then? How to narrow it down?

I thought of the students I felt most sorry for in my classes. As some classrooms became more like zoos, my heart went out to the dutiful few, perhaps 20 to 25 percent who struggled to hear, concentrate, study and accomplish in spite of the environment.

Conditions in the required classes were the worst. It was so unfair to those who wanted to learn. They were often uncomfortable, frustrated, and embarrassed by the behavior of those few who initiated ways to disrupt, and the majority who urged them on rather than to be an outcast. An "outcast" was anyone who conformed to school rules and authorities. Those who did their work and followed rules would not go that extra step to criticize their wayward classmates. It's hard to be in a minority.

With the facts I had accumulated, I began to write—to pour it all out. First, I wrote nonfiction, then finally I incorporated much of it into this novel.

There's a Worm in the Apple presents ideas that may be a start toward providing, a practical educational system for a new era. As parents and educators, we must plan for these children who are of a different mind than those in the past, and they are not like the defiant rebels in most of today's schools. As educators added more and more subjects, sports and miscellaneous requirements, the basic studies have been progressively watered down. We were provided less and less of the fruit of education. There was indeed a worm in the apple eating it away.

My guess is that about one-fourth of our middle to high school students are capable, and would welcome the opportunity to take responsibility for their own education, given teachers and other mentors to guide them. A favorable reaction to this schooling would be contagious. Their younger siblings would notice a change of attitude, and some of these ideas might gradually be introduced into the lower grades.

An examination of current public schools is a reminder of how much time and money is wasted. It is obvious that we cannot teach everything. We can't teach as much as we are attempting to, if we are to do it well.

In 1957, the Russians had succeeded in getting the first satellite, Sputnik, into space. Americans began to question our educational system in earnest. It was compared unfavorably with that of the USSR. Our pride was wounded. We had assumed that the first victory in space would be ours. Since even in the whirlpool of anxiety, neither government nor education moves fast, it was 1963 before the schools paid attention to public demand for more and more effective provision and teaching of foreign languages.

Then the schools went bonkers with technology. Manufacturers and publishers of teaching materials saw the opening, and the government willingly paid the bill for every new method, material and varied teaching technology that flooded the market. From that magical world of exaggerated promises generated by the publishing and manufacturing industries, everyone expected miracles. In due time schools discarded equipment that the government had poured millions of dollars into. Schools could not afford to maintain and repair it. There was not enough money to pay people to monitor the equipment and to prevent vandalism. And it had not lived up to the claims of distributors.

Will the current frenzy to supply schools with computers be worthwhile? Can we afford repairs and replacement of equipment that becomes antiquated overnight? With normal wear plus vandalism will this end the same way as the language lab equipment? Will students use it more as a toy than an aid to learning? Or will we realize that technology's tools are best used after a child's brain has improved his or her necessary skills and broadened interests?

We have given our children choices in almost every aspect of their lives. How then can the public schools force-feed them the same diet. We must prepare a repast that gives them some choices. My premise is that pleasure amounting to joy will result from our children's freedom, within reason, to choose when and how much they want to study of any given subject, even those studies we consider "basic". Their choices will be governed by exposure and need. Then the expectations, encouragement, faith and appreciation of their accomplishment by teachers and parents will spur them on to fulfillment and growth.

We cannot make our children conform to the ways of the past. So we must make education palatable to the "new breed" for they are what we have made them, resistant to, and vocal about the plate they are being served. We are schooling the rebellious ones in the same classes as those wanting, or at least willing to learn. The cooperative students have been short-changed as we have provided special education to every other group.

Here are questions we might ask ourselves:

—What are the characteristics of our children?

—What are society's major problems?

—What are the needs within ourselves, our society and in the world at large?

—What can we do as individuals to improve negative conditions that affect us?

—Where can we find facts and wisdom to answer significant questions?

—When can we cease our search and reexamination to answer the preceding questions?

Where to find information? The sources are endless. We must learn and teach how to organize and evaluate information; to decide what is and what is not true, what is acceptable, and how to use it constructively. There is an information explosion. We need general knowledge of most of the information we are flooded with. Most of us do not become experts in many areas of study. Our own needs, time and interests determine how much of that information we care to study in depth. These are times of worldwide inter-dependency, ease of travel and communication. A curriculum must be planned with all of this in mind.

The answer to the last question: When can we cease our search and study? "Never". It is a lifetime task. To learn, to evaluate and reevaluate and continually to ask questions.

Any study is a failure if the books and the teachers ask all of the questions. The best students are those who are constantly questioning as they learn.

Following is the description and expectations of Hawaii's first charter school begun in 1994. It was an optional program within the only high school on the Kona Coast at that time. Only a small number of students qualified. It reflects the needs of an island in the mid-Pacific ocean, and any other similar community worldwide.

"An academically challenging, hands-on learning environment ideal for scientifically curious and self-motivated students tenth through twelfth grade. Students self-select and self-direct research projects according to their area of interest, with teachers lending guidance and support."

The academy has since become a New Century Public Charter School. Like the school in my novel, they say, "The program works best for students who are academically ready to manage their own learning experiences, and want freedom to explore new challenges."

This is now a public school that operates independently of the State Board of Education, with a local school board made up of educators, students, parents and community members from West Hawaii. Put another way, the school belongs to Kona, and is operated by parents, relatives and friends. The focus is on marine science, agriculture, aquaculture and technology.

The grading, recording, and responsibilities of students is similar to that of the school in my novel.[4]

Charter schools are becoming popular. Some are a part of the public school system. They may give emphasis to one major interest. This echoes the pattern for schools dating back to the early twentieth century. Some cities then had separate high schools, each dedicated to either the college bound, business, or manual arts oriented students. In each pursuit, they required students to read and write.

While charter schools are increasing in number, there are not enough to fill the demands and expectations. They differ in emphasis and quality. There are many inferior ones among the successes. Some parents are so frightened to have their children in public school that they are not using good judgment in selecting an alternative. Some schools last a short time then fail and close. Arizona has the most charters in America, 416.[5] School boards are approving some charter schools. We need more.

I hope that the readers of this novel see something of value in the story, but my initial and overwhelming intention is to open our eyes, ears and creativity as we seek better ways to guide our youth toward a lifetime of expanding their education. I hope readers will enjoy the characters, and their adventures in *There's a Worm in the Apple*, but may you also see education for what it is, and what it could be if we become creative instead of continuing in the lock-step pattern we have fallen into.

Whichever kind of education you choose for your children, may you be guided to help them use, and enjoy, a most carefree and fulfilling time of their lives. As they seek answers to their questions, it is imperative they learn to communicate effectively. As they become aware of the world around them may they become COMPETENT, CONFIDENT and CREATIVE.

---

[1] Dorothy Fink Ungerleider, M.A., *Reading, Writing, and Rage,* The terrible price paid by victims of school failure, Jalmar Press, Rolling Hills Estates, California, 1987.

[2] Francis A. J. Ianni, Editor, *Teachers College,* Columbia University *Conflict and Change in Education, Scott Foresman and Company, Glenview, Illinois, 1975.*

[3] Joseph Coleman, Associated Press Writer, Tokyo, *West Hawaii Today,* November 17, 1996

[4] West Hawaii Explorations Academy, Public Charter School, 73-4460 Queen Kaahumanu Hwy #105, Kailua-Kona, Hawaii 96740. Ph. (808) 327-4751. Email: explorations@whea.net. Applications Available at: www.whea.net

[5] Jodie Morse, *Do Charter Schools Pass the Test?, Time Magazine.* (June 4, 2001), 60

There's a Worm in the Apple

Chapter 1

Sleepless

When I die the time on the digital clock will read 2:34, 3:33, or maybe 11:11. When I awaken in the middle of the night, I squint to read those orderly numerals. I wonder if the numbers are prophetic, a sign from somewhere, an answer. It is becoming a nuisance. I snort, change my position, and think of Amy, the love of my life, the mother of our son Barry, who should be sleeping soundly on the pillow next to mine, and is not.

What is it my mind seeks to explore at this hour? And why? I am not obsessed with my death, and I am not controlled by time. That is, not any more than any other father juggling responsibilities of parenthood, work, and a faltering marriage.

When Amy left me, it seemed like a rug was pulled out from under me. I had to regain my balance and find solid ground, or I must learn to fly. That was why I started tutoring students who were struggling in school.

Volunteering at the public library filled my lonely evening hours. It energized me to make friends with other tutors. The kids needed special help, but they weren't dumb. Some were even bright. That's when I became furious with the public school system. Why didn't these kids have basic skills?

These are the nagging thoughts I wrestle with, posed by this thief who keeps me awake. I am troubled by people who underestimate the seriousness of turning these kids out into a world they are not equipped to deal with. We are planting seeds for the future that are unlikely to produce a bountiful harvest.

Why in hell I chose to work with the kids who were having trouble with math, I will never know. I wasn't the brightest math student myself, but I could get good grades by memorizing formulas, and remembering them long enough to pass tests. Then I promptly forgot the formulas and retained only enough math to get by in my world. That's as it should be. Anything is easier to learn when we have a need for it, and it's also easier to relearn.

I toss and turn. Those first children I tutored had such limited skills that I could not assume they knew even the most basic arithmetic. I began teaching them as though they had never sat in a classroom. In fact, I began as though they had never seen numbers.

Something in the way I was taught math was wrong. Other classes were a joy, but I thought anything numerical unworthy of my attention. I wanted to show my students how math helps us in daily life. I wanted them to feel awe at the magic of numbers. I did not use any terminology that they could not explain to me. No one showed me the relationship between fractions, decimals, and whole numbers. I couldn't remember how I had learned, but I knew that rote learning gave me no sense of purpose.

I had to teach myself first. Now I'm the one who is fascinated with numbers, how they interact, how they serve our needs. Nightly they swirl in my head. They challenge and entertain me. They keep out other more disturbing thoughts as I examine them on the clock face.

Much changed for me, after I forgot my own problems long enough to pay attention to the kids. Much changed for the good, yet I still search in the darkness to figure out ways to help my charges understand concepts, not just memorize methods. I go over lesson plans in my mind. I anticipate how I might unlock the prisons of closed minds and let the light in. I encourage those who have been told that they can't do math . . . or anything else either.

My father's passion for learning was contagious. He inspired me. I liked school. Unlike my students, I experienced the exhilaration one feels when a light goes on. They need to know that knowledge is connected, and that like a chain one discovery is a link to the next.

So, I lie here night after night, while ideas jump around inside my head like droplets of water sizzling on a hot skillet. If I don't give my attention to the ideas, they disappear into a vapor. I must wake up and examine them.

This immersion into education has been my salvation for the moment. It crowds out the threat of divorce, but the loss of sleep endangers my health. I keep adding more and more responsibilities. I am trying to win back my wife, to maintain a stable home for Barry, and to work full time in a real estate management business. On top of that I'm reading reams of material in my search for answers to problems that plague our schools.

Tutoring showed me how much we need to update. But educators, our government, indeed our whole society, is either apathetic or blind to solutions that could strengthen, and save, one of our most necessary institutions. The name of the game is blame. Political factions, confused parents and overwhelmed teachers all try to blame someone else, which keeps us from seeing that today's children need drastically different approaches to learning.

Our educational institutions need a massive infusion of creativity. No wonder parents who can pay for private schools are doing so, while the masses are doomed to ever-increasing mediocrity. The effect on the country will be disastrous.

I kept having a recurring dream. I handed a shiny, red apple to Mrs. Price, my third-grade teacher. An ugly caterpillar that oozed out of a hole in the seemingly delectable apple was gnawing away all that was good to leave a hollow shell where once had been substance. Finally, I couldn't ignore the dream, and the inevitable end of an institution that would lead to diminished power of our great country. After what seemed hours, a ray of sunlight pierced the gray dawn. I watched the shadows of gently swaying leaves dance on the wall in the light of a new day. I stared at the emptiness of Amy's pillow, as I have done every morning since she left. Then, I found a sense of purpose. I swung my legs over the side of the bed eager to begin. I would start an organization called "Apple A Day" to pursue constructive changes in public education. Together with the like-minded people I would gather around me, we would make a difference.

Chapter 2

Evolution or Revolution?

Yes, I had moments when I questioned my sanity. Why me? But, never had I been closer to quitting than when I envisioned myself standing alone before my peers under the all-revealing spotlight. The hollow place that should contain my guts would be filled with hot air . . . Bang! And I could then rest in peace.

Tonight though, I was far from that moment but, already I felt that gut-wrenching desire to escape. I knew I'd have to face the battle again and again. I'd need intestinal fortitude to conquer it, or to concede defeat. The result would be either peace or self-destruction.

I could not accept mediocrity in public education. It would be a crucial threat to the future of my son, his peers, and in fact to the future of humankind. Pretty heavy stuff. Until I could conquer my self-deprecation I was stuck. Otherwise I would settle for defeat, when in my heart I knew the battle could be won.

"Ladies and Gentlemen of the King County School Board, thank you for letting me speak. We are concerned about the future of all American children, but tonight I speak for the children referred to as 'gifted and talented'. Children at the bottom of the scholastic ladder rightly receive necessary attention. Our future depends on their schooling, and the contributions they will make to our society if they are well prepared. However, the high grades that many students receive gives the impression that they are well educated. To the contrary, they are receiving a mediocre education. The future of our country is threatened if we do not do as well, or better, by all our students than other countries do.

"Even if the most capable students do their assignments, even if they get 'A's' or 'B's', they will be severely challenged by private school students when they are ready to begin careers, or job training.

"Students who supplement their education through reading of worthwhile literature, or exposure to stimulating activities, broaden their interests and knowledge. They go beyond the level of their peers who may have moved through current public schools in lockstep. Unfortunately, there are few dedicated readers in this television era.

"Literary zeal, plus completion of class assignments, and report cards boasting 'A's' or 'B's' may attest to a child's superior ability, but has that child reached his full potential? Are letter grades indicative of that? Teachers, parents, and society in general seem satisfied with that method of evaluating them. We, to the contrary, question whether standard grading is meaningful.

"It is human nature to fulfill expectations, yet not exceed them. It is unlikely that students put more effort into their education than teachers and guardians require of them. It is our low expectations that allow them to graduate even though they may have fulfilled meager requirements. Our graduates are often unprepared for college or employment. Thus, we are graduating students who have a limited preparation for life. Colleges or employers are forced to provide remedial training or turn such applicants away.

"A common cry in the schools is 'Dad, Mom, it is so boring.' Of course, people often blame the teachers for the child's 'boredom,' claiming that they should make school interesting. Here is their intelligent child who is not being challenged, or entertained, they assume. 'Why don't they make school fun?' our society asks.

"The organization I represent, Apple-A-Day Inc., has developed just such a plan. We present it to you. Much thought, work, and creativity have gone into our findings and our proposed solutions. Public education is in a slump. We are buried in tradition without favorable results. New ways are continually introduced. Then we find that the only thing new is the terminology. Public education has been deteriorating for more than fifty years.

"Yes, ladies and gentlemen, I did say, 'for more than fifty years,' and that is a conservative estimate. Research shows conflicting philosophies of established educators who disagreed throughout that period and preceding it. And yes, that time includes the period of my public school experience, and perhaps yours as well.

"The fact is that unless you and I had read voraciously to entertain and educate ourselves, we would not have been sufficiently educated to fit into our various careers, nor into the social stratum we are accustomed to. Likely, we did read.

"Since the advent of television, however, the illiteracy rate has been steadily rising. Why? Because a large and growing number in our country have never acquired the joy of reading. They do not have that worthy experience to pass on to their children. For many years we have been turning out graduates who were taught to read, and they did learn. It is only necessary to learn once. However, it is then necessary to use the skill. Lack of use negates development. Any skill that is not used regularly is lost. That is the most common reason 'Johnny' can't read.

"Today a person without reading skills is likely to have limited vocabulary, therefore less ability to comprehend what he sees or hears. He will likely be weak in other communication skills also. Opportunity for increasing or improving occupational skills is barred to the illiterate, and the semi-illiterate. Likewise, there is less opportunity to interact, to discuss major concepts, and to gain confidence. The dire consequences resulting from citizens who are poorly educated affect national and world conditions.

"Please read our findings and reports with an open mind. Our children are different from any American or foreign children of the past. Their education must differ therefore from that of children of other times and places. We must be willing to alter our public education. We must tailor it to fit the children of today. There must be drastic change. A bandage does not solve a problem that requires surgery.

"First we must give our most capable and cooperative students a chance to soar whereas they have previously been forced to march in lock-step. When there is proof that it works, those same changes must be applied to others in the secondary schools. Gradually, some elementary students may be capable of more choices and more responsibility in their education.

"We must have a virtual evolution, or revolution if need be. The future of our country depends on our courage to meet these problems head-on.

"Thank you for your time. Well?" Guy Benson looked at his friends sprawled around his small living room. Noah lay stretched out on the couch with his eyes closed. Sandy leaned against large pillows on the floor. Ike sat in a straight chair at the small dining table clutching a bottle of Coors. This did not include the entire group of members in the corporation they had formed, but these were the ones who had given birth to the ideas contained in the words Guy had just read to them. "Well? Tell me the best and the worst. How does it sound? Will they buy it?"

"I don't know. It's hard to know what to include and what to save for later. It seemed long. Even if they show interest we'll be expected to present constructive ideas to them later on." Gail Sanders, better known as Sandy, sounded noncommittal.

Noah stretched. The light played on his biceps. Such muscles were not meant for lounging, but for action.

"It's ten minutes long. I timed it," a voice said. "Will they give us ten minutes at the School Board meeting?" someone asked.

No one replied. Noah cleared his throat, ready now to comment. "The part about education having gone downhill for over fifty years includes all teachers, administrators, and school board members who attended public schools. They will resent that, but fifty years is a conservative estimate of how long public schools have shortchanged kids seeking an education. It might make them more receptive if they don't feel that we are blaming the school board members for the failure of public school education." Noah demonstrated his usual concern for the importance of reading audience reactions if we are to win them over to our cause.

Sandy had watched his muscular display with appreciation. "I disagree. They'll take it as an insult, that allusion to the weakness of education reaching as far back as during their own years of schooling," Sandy said. She jumped to her feet. "Yes, our research shows that to be true, but people probably all think that public schools were good when they were attending. They usually had no opportunity, or experience, to make comparisons.

"They don't care to know that they also were shortchanged by a system that was constantly experimenting with new, often impractical, ideas about how to educate." Sandy was always teaching, even when she wasn't in the classroom. She always carried herself with a regal presence as if she were in the spotlight front and center. Hurriedly, she continued, so as not to yield the limelight. "The more education became institutionalized, the more cumbersome it became. First, lots of homework and teach the classics. Then, go easy on the homework and modernize the curriculum. Then, add more and more subjects until everything has to be watered down to allow its inclusion. And sports getting priority over all, of course."

Sandy had majored in the history of public education in the United States. She shook her head at the complexity of it all. She wavered between the unlikelihood that they could alert their community to an awareness of "How bad is it?" And her drive to "Do what we must to save what is good, and to replace what is ludicrous about the system." "The fact is," she reminded them, "that the strength of education has always been determined by how much outside reading students did, and the content and quality of what they read. That was what educated them, whether it was assigned or their own choice. Good readers resulted from reading extensively. Good writing came from an endless amount of writing practiced throughout the school years. Speakers developed from speaking experience. Once upon a time there were polite, attentive students who listened quietly and learned. Once upon a time there was a pride in being learn-ed." Sandy slapped the table top for emphasis.

Everyone was silent. If the Board acknowledged them, the community would assume they were accepted. They needed that, or all of their work would amount to nothing. Would Guy's presentation achieve that? That was the question they now asked themselves.

Ike, the eldest of their group, downed the last gulp of beer and set the bottle down as if he were wielding a gavel. "Too wordy, Guy. Too long. Keeps 'em guessin' while you speak. Too much included and they'll be thinkin' a reasons to say no to everything you suggest. People being what they are, which is 'set in their ways,' they will be lookin' for points that agree with their prejudices. When they hear otherwise, they won't be wantin' facts. Their minds are made up." Ike was brief and to the point voicing his reaction, after which another long silence reigned.

Ike was probably the least educated of all of them, as to formal education anyhow. But he was as dedicated as the others to their cause. He was one of them, and highly respected.

Ike Epstein was encouraged to join them after they realized the depth of his interest in kids, therefore in education. As a custodian, he knew more about the kids and the politics of school than most of the teaching staff. He was likely more of a role model accepted by the kids than the teachers were.

He knew a lot about the teachers, too. When he cleaned rooms he observed little things such as bulletin boards and the kids' work posted on them. The same few students always had their work on display.

There were clues to a teacher's personality in each room. Even evidence of incompetence or capability. Ike had some sound ideas about what was wrong with the schools.

Guy Benson had done his best to write the treatise they felt they must submit to the School Board. The intention, that is the hoped-for reaction, was that the School Board would want to know more about the ideas of these people who claimed to have answers that their Board would profit from. If the Board rejected their petition to share their wealth of ideas, then what? Well, their group efforts would have to about-face toward a different source of influence and power.

The silence following their comments about Guy's reading of the proposed presentation clearly rejected it as the way to go. Ike was right, Guy thought. "We're not ready yet to even approach the School Board. We need backing. We must build the organization and beef up the membership. Influential people," Guy admitted. "If we jump the gun we'll surely fail."

"We need to know more about the people on that school board, too. Everything depends on knowing what they want to hear and what they'll reject." Sandy was emphatic.

Guy ran a hand through his sun-bleached hair, a gesture of impatience and nervous energy. "Sorry, everybody. I thought we were ready. Sorry to take your evening."

"Nonsense, we're a step closer," Noah said. "I enjoyed the evening, the people, and the pizza and beer." He grabbed his jacket, tossed some dollar bills in the bowl on the table as his share of the food. "G'night all," and he was out the door.

The others were also stirring, then gone, and Guy was alone. It was a condition he was trying to get used to. Being alone meant thoughts of Amy crowding out all else in his life. The pain of his marital problems became too much to bear at this hour. The main reason Guy was getting so involved in education was Barry, his six-year-old son.

Guy wanted to send his son to a private school. Financially impossible now with grasping, expensive lawyers and counselors to pay. Anyway, even if he could afford it, how could he abandon a sinking ship leaving behind those who had no option but public education? Guy felt that he had gotten a good education in public schools. Of course his early grades were in a private school where his father taught in Sweden.

If he had expressed indications of boredom, his Swedish dad would have said, "When you are taking more responsibility for your own needs and helping others, you don't have time to even think about boredom." However, Guy could not ever remember having been bored. Life and learning had always been fulfilling.

Why, then, were today's kids, who had so many more material benefits, such frustrated whiners? What did they want, for God's sake?

Guy had been given a fair balance of responsibility from an early age. His schoolwork was his responsibility. He couldn't remember his parents ever having to be involved directly with his education. That concern was his and his teachers. His parents didn't have to check on his homework or give him gold stars for household duties. He knew his responsibilities, and he accepted them.

He knew the consequences if he didn't share the work of the household. He knew the consequences if he didn't do his homework. It instilled pride in him that he was respected and appreciated as well as loved in his family. He was productive, and he was proud that the people in his community respected him, also. That's what it's all about, Guy thought. Respect and responsibility, not usually in that order.

Chapter 3

Life's Lessons

Happiness is a talent, one that immunizes you against being bored.
Boredom is sinful.
—George Will

Boredom is the shriek of unused capacities.
—Saul Bellow

"Hello," Ben called, pushing open the door. He stepped into the room, and called again. From his grandson's room Ben heard giggling and roughhousing. Quite different, Guy's relationship with Barry, like day and night compared to the relationship Ben had with his own children. How could a father maintain his dignity and respect rolling around on the floor with a child? Never mind. Keep out of it. It was Guy's turn now to raise the perfect children.

"Papa!" Barry shouted, wriggling away to race to his grandfather. This first grandchild made his first sounds six years ago. "Papa" was the first recognizable sound the baby repeated every time he saw the white-haired old fellow with the moustache. It was love at first sight for both of them.

"Are you ready, boy? We're going to play bocci in the park. If we get there a little early, then we'll decide where we want to go for lunch, and afterward . . . well, we'll jump that fence when we come to it."

"We're gonna jump fences, and play in the park, Daddy." Barry's dark eyes flashed with excitement.

"Yeah. Well, don't let your grandfather jump too high."

"He's ready, Dad. We were waiting for you." Guy gathered up the jacket and cap. "Thanks for taking him today. It will help me to get caught up with my work, and to see my lawyer."

"Still going to go through with it?"

"What choice do I have?"

"Then, why aren't you looking for solutions? Why aren't you and Amy talking about your differences? I don't understand."

"I'll talk with you about it one of these days. It's too complicated to cover right now." Guy turned to help Barry get his arm through the sleeve, plopped the cap on the boy's dark curls, and gently pushed him toward the door. "On your way, you two. I want to hear all about it when you get back. Call if you're running late, and I'll wait dinner for you."

The door closed on their backs. Guy watched his father's limp. How much force he used to set his cane. Each step was a gauge of how indignant he was at that moment. The old man had no patience with divorces.

After a few steps, Barry was chattering with delight, and Ben was already losing some of his rigidity. The grandson could wrap him around one small finger and pull the strings like a master puppeteer.

At the park, Ben saw that his friend was there to provide the bocci balls for the Italian variety of lawn bowling. Good, the three of them could play before the regulars arrived. In their prime of life they had given themselves totally to their life's work, whatever their proficiency or expertise. Now in their retirement years, they could not settle for inactivity, or seclusion. Bocci became their passion for life. Ben and a few others were not Italian, unlike the men who long ago had started playing bocci in this park.

And in other parks the elders from France had introduced Apetanque, or "Aboule." The scoring was identical. The balls were of different size and material. The French used metal balls; the Italian wooden.

The men of each culture played their games with an intensity they had transferred from work they had dedicated their lives to while rearing children. Pride still ruffled their feathers when opponents pointed, and placed the balls to shoot the contestants out of the way. They could be scornful, even volatile. These were good signs really, indicating that the men were viable regardless of age and changes they must accept with advanced age.

Alf Benson and his parents had emigrated from Sweden. Most of the bocci players were immigrants from Italy, where the game originated, or they were descendants of immigrants. Each of them, occasionally, brought a child or grandchild to show off.

Parents and grandfather had schooled Barry early to the courtesies of language. Barry had learned fast how "please" and "thank you", "yes, sir", or "no, ma'am" worked magic in dealing with adults. Ben loved to show him off. The manners and attitudes of so many of today's children grated on him. He would not allow Barry to be uncouth, not with a grandfather from the old school.

After the regular group of men arrived, Ben allowed Barry to be roughed up and teased by loving old hands. The boy loved it. At first he had been wide-eyed and leery of the booming voices. Soon though, he sensed their approval and basked in their attention.

Barry liked how they laughed, shouted, and joked the way kids do. They were free now of the labor or professions that had consumed their lifetimes. They no longer experienced the prejudice suffered in the early years in their new country. In the park, they found refuge, peace, and camaraderie.

The sun warmed their old bones. A gentle breeze cooled their bodies, but never their ardor. "Hey, boy. Roll it like-a dis," and one would bend painfully, gently take Barry's arm, and help him to direct the ball. Then, they would applaud Barry, who jumped up and down, gleefully clapping his hands.

The sun moved overhead. Its heat sapped their energy. They tired, and waved their goodbyes promising to meet next week. "Addio professore." It was the bocci players who had begun to call him Ben or professor, instead of Alf.

"Well, well, my boy," Ben wheezed. "You did a fine job in the bocci game. How did you like it?"

"It was boring, Papa."

"Boring?" Ben stared, open-mouthed. The boy had seemed to enjoy it. "Boring, eh? What does boring mean, Barry?"

Barry hesitated, sensing that Papa was not pleased. "I don't exactly know, Papa. It's just something kids say."

"Oh, they do, do they? Well, I suggest that you make this the last time you ever say it, and that you never say anything again that you don't understand."

"Okay, Papa. Is it a dirty word?" His eyes widened, recalling how excited grownups get when they hear a "dirty" word. Usually Barry couldn't understand how a word could have dirt on it, but he knew he'd better not say that word again, ever.

"No, son," and Ben nearly laughed aloud, in spite of his alarm at the boy's reaction. "It's offensive, but not dirty. Maybe it is worse than dirty. You see, boy, what we put into our minds, by thinking or saying it, can be harmful or helpful to us. Where did you hear the word? Who uses it?"

"Kids, Papa. All the time they say it. It's something they don't like, I guess."

Ben envisioned the looks on the faces of adolescents lazing about in the shopping malls. It was an outward expression of attitude, a negative attitude. They appeared to be scarcely alive, or wanted that look to suggest they didn't want to be. Why not, and the negative attitude toward what, he wondered? This most exciting time to be living. What was on their minds to be talking of boredom?

Wondering if he had made too much of this issue, considering it came from a six-year-old, Ben softened his approach. "Did you like playing the bocci game, Barry?"

"Yes sir, I did. I really did." Anxious to please Papa, Barry's eyes were glassy, ready to spill tears, although he had no idea how they had arrived at this moment of Papa's disfavor.

"Never mind, son. I want to explain to you what I mean by offensive, and why I growled at you like an angry old bear. I understand now why you said it. We'll just talk about it a minute. You were just trying out a word that you hear so often, because other kids say it.

"Those kids just say it out of habit. A habit is something that is hard to stop. Sometimes you don't even know you are saying it, or why. It's copying someone without thinking. Habits are fine if they are good for you. But bad habits should be stopped. They rob you of the joys of life."

Ben sat down on a bench, under a shade tree near the lake. His emotional outburst had taken a toll. He exhaled forcefully. A mallard duck, followed by its mate, hurried over to them, and then waddled away as though miffed that it was offered no food. Barry watched them, wanting to touch the iridescent feathers, or play with the escaping pair.

Ben's words were pouring out faster and faster, and with emphasis. Something about people feeding ducks, Barry heard that it was a bad thing. Something about Sir Vaivul. Barry wondered who that knight could be. Maybe like the Knights in Armor in stories his Dad read to him. Must be important, since Papa said that the parents of the ducks taught their ducklings all about him.

"Sir Vaivul. Sir Vaivul." Barry was repeating over, and over to himself, liking the sound of it.

Barry curled up at his grandfather's feet, wanting so much to be in the old fellow's good graces again. The boy was drifting off. Ben stood up, stretched, and reached for the boy's hand to begin the walk home.

"Boring, huh?" Ben persisted in a calmer tone of voice. "Life can only be boring if we put that thought in our minds, my boy. Bored people pretend superiority, but do nothing, while the adventurers in life are never bored and enjoy life's bounty."

Ben's voice droned on. His grandson's mind had tuned out from fatigue, or overload.

"I learned a lot today, Barry. It's hard for an old man to understand younger people. If your father had told me something was 'boring' I would probably have smacked him."

"Smacked? What's that?"

"It means 'hit', Barry, in a way that makes a loud noise."

"Hit? You'd have hit him, Papa? Why? Are you going to hit me?" He looked worried.

"No, m'boy. A smack sounds worse than it feels. I just did it to get him to pay attention. Grandfathers behave differently than we did as fathers. My, my!" Ben shook his head in astonishment that parents were raising children without ever giving them a loud smack on the bottom. "My father would have smacked me too, Barry, if I had ever said I was bored. And you're wondering why, lad." Whatever the child had understood, Barry knew this was serious.

Ben could not cease the lecture. He had always spoken to his own son and students on an adult level. "When you were a baby," he continued, "and first opened your eyes to the world, even without knowing words yet to say it, you thought the world was enticing, magnificent, exciting, interesting. Because you had those feelings, you were eager and craved to know more and more. You did not sample the world and think to yourself, 'Boring.' If you had, you might never have taken your first step. Such foolish words block us."

The old man had worked himself into a lather at the very idea. He looked at the dark, bright eyes staring back at him, and wondered what, if anything, the boy had understood. Well, Ben decided, the boy understood the intensity of it. That was enough for now. Ben had a few good years left to repeat that lecture in endless ways, and he would.

No grandson of his was going to saddle himself with such nonsense. So much to see and do, to study and learn, to know and understand, to use as guidelines on the path of a full life. To the Bensons boredom was a false idea placed in an idle, weak mind, until it poisoned all initiative. "Bah! Humbug!" snorted Ben as Barry raced up the apartment house steps.

"We're back, Daddy," Barry shouted as they reached the apartment. His dad opened the door and swept him up into his arms.

"How did it go, partner? Did you learn anything besides bocci?"

"I learned to never say 'bored,' because life is wonderful, and no one should ever, ever be bored, and if they say it, they might be it, and if they are, it is their own fault if it ruins their whole life. What does bounty mean, Dad?"

Papa's gaze dropped to the floor. When he looked up, he saw an amused look in his son's eyes.

"Bounty, son? Well, it is something good, like a reward you get."

Guy in fact recalled many such lectures when he was small. Boring, eh? Interesting that the education group he had formed was concerned with the excessive use of that word, and the attitude it provoked in and outside of school. Well, his Dad was already on the path to turn a new generation toward optimism, and damn the negativity of the world.

Guy had considered getting his father involved in their group's struggle. Why not? Would he be too conservative? Would he be able to understand today's youth?

"Dad, a group of people, frustrated about public education are meeting here tomorrow night. We need people like you. Would you come?"

The smile on Ben's face was answer enough. His questions poured forth. They lost all count of time in their discussion.

When he and Barry drove Papa home, there was a gleam in his father's eyes, a lightness in his step that Guy had not seen for some time. By damn, was that steam coming out of the old fire horse's nostrils?

Chapter 4

Brainstorming

Guy counted heads. Everyone was there except Amy. "We'll start on time," he said and thanked them for coming. "We all know a lot about education, if only from our own experience. We'll have a lot to share, and we must agree on some rules. A rough agenda, some guidelines, not necessarily Robert's Rules, or comparable. Informality is fine in a group this size, but we're going to grow in numbers. There'll be more confusion, but also our creativity will expand.

"Excuse me, Dad, but I want to introduce you. Folks, my dad Alf Benson is a retired educator from the old school in Sweden. Later he was an administrator in a private school in Minnesota. I asked him to visit, and, if he likes what he hears, to join us."

"Just call me Ben," he called out, and waved a hand to indicate Guy should continue with business.

"As we progress with our plans, it is going to be hard for some people to accept what we propose. It was hard for some of you, and that is why I suggest the following pattern in our meeting.

"Number 1. We are brainstorming. This demands sharing . . . as briefly as possible. If anyone of us rambles or repeats . . . well, give us some suggestions. I may be the one running on at the mouth, so don't throw tomatoes or rotten eggs, but we need a way to tip the speaker off that he has exceeded his time allowance."

"Just wave a hand back and forth till the speaker catches on, summarizes, and yields the floor. The more people waving their hands, the faster Guy will catch on," Noah said.

"Thanks, Noah. Just wait until you're the one sounding off. You're targeted, buddy. We need as much information as possible, but let's not generalize too much based on our own limited unique experience as students, teachers, or parents. If our information applies to others, as well as our own, it is then valid. Agreed so far?" asked Guy.

Ben had never seen his son in this role. He wanted to laugh at the audacity of these few people intent on changing an institution that had stood rigid, unchanged for centuries. But he would reserve judgment.

There was some discussion; other rules and ideas were offered, added or rejected. Someone spoke for agreement. Everyone accepted these first suggestions. They listed and approved the following:

"**Number 2.** To share information heard or read in the media or elsewhere. Cut out articles that show what our government, administrators, teachers, and students are saying, doing . . . or not doing. To compose letters to editors and call talk shows, especially if they are handing out the same bureaucratic bunk that has gotten us nowhere.

"**Number 3.** Keep alert for more people to join us. Encourage positive people who will not tear us apart, or divide us before we get started. We need information on the school board members. There must be at least one who is impatient with the status quo.

"**Number 4.** What about PTO, PTA, SCBM, or other such groups? They serve a need. They unite parents, students, community, and businesses. When we have a clear mission statement we'll approach them. We can't have them rejecting us before that time."

"Anything else you can think of? Ike?"

Sandy was scribbling notes as fast as she could.

"Everyone, for the next meeting, please write about your own experiences with education, personal or family related. List the good and the bad as you see it. Give examples. Tell why you are with us in this. I'd like to know, and I'd like to tell you what I see in the schools every day so you'll know."

Ben stood up to speak. "Excuse me, but I have so many questions. I don't yet know what this is all about. I'd like to write what you suggest, and visit the next meeting. So far, this takes on the air of a bunch who are planning to overturn the government. I'll corner my son so that I'll know more before the next time we meet. I want to suggest that this not be based on negativity, or generalizations. Our youth have to be recognized for their strengths, as well as what they need strengthened."

"Hear! Hear!" shouted Noah, and the others joined in.

Ben smiled and continued. "I would like to give an assignment also. Everyone write what you think education should accomplish. May I ask that? We won't know how to change it if we don't agree on what education should be."

"Absolutely. Good idea." People nodded, and the meeting was over.

Guy wasted no time getting on the phone to call his wife. "Amy, where the hell were you?"

Amy knew that missing the meeting would provoke questions and attack. How to explain to Guy that it was still difficult to be around him? And meetings! As if teachers didn't already have too many endless meetings to attend.

Enough. She would tell Guy that agreeing to take part in his meetings was a mistake. What was this sudden interest in education anyhow?

He tuned out as she argued the point. He reviewed the meeting. So much to be changed. The public didn't even realize the extent of deterioration in the schools. They wouldn't accept new ideas.

Guy closed his eyes and ears to her protests. When he did not reply, Amy hung up. The dial tone jarred him awake. He rang her number again.

It was some comfort when he assured her that the meetings were to be kept as short as possible.

"Sorry, Amy. Guess I fell asleep. So, can we count on you?"

"Good grief. You never can take no for an answer. All right, I'm in for awhile."

"Don't fail me, Amy. It's going to be a tough fight to get our ideas across."

"I said I'd be there." She hung up with the words "Don't fail Me" echoing in her ears. If he had only been that passionate expressing a need for her as a wife, perhaps they would not be on the verge of a divorce.

She would invite a friend to the next meeting. That would avoid any discussion of their marital differences afterward.

Chapter 5

Warning

Words spread fast in a small community. The local newspaper ran announcements of meetings. Their mission was not yet explained in depth. There was only enough information to attract people of like thinking to join them. They wanted to reach others who were disturbed by the negligible results of public schools. They were still in the planning stage. Some were prepared to revise the system completely to save it. Some wanted to eliminate all but the basic studies. Some were in favor of minimal changes.

The latter did not yet agree as to which changes should be made. To cease sports participation and competition? To eliminate the arts? Apple A Day had never openly proposed such things, but readers made such suggestions in letters and phone calls to members. The idea aroused anger in advocates of sports, art, and music. Many people profited from those interests. They were ready to fight to retain their income.

The members of Apple A Day were surprised, also pleased, at the attention they were getting. Letters to the editors featured them daily. A reporter tried to get interviews. Until group members were in accord, they would not speak to the press, or to others. Let them attend the meetings, and be involved in decisions, if they were really interested.

Guy awakened to the sound of a cardinal's unmistakable chirp, then felt something pressing against him, crowding him to the edge of the bed. He smiled to see Barry's tousled head sharing his pillow, the boy's small frame snuggled close. Sometime during the night he had left his own bed in Guy's study, where he slept during weekend visits, and crawled into bed with Daddy.

Guy tried to wiggle out of the cramped position he was in, without awakening his son. No such luck. Barry, unlike most children, always woke up bright as a new silver dollar, ever eager to start a new day.

"Hi, Dad." Like a puppy Barry was all over him, hugging and kissing Guy out of his drowsiness.

"Holy hamburgers!" Guy groaned, substituting a more appropriate noun for his usual exclamation.

"Hamburgers! That sounds great. I'm hungry as a bear."

A glance at the clock elicited a pained groan from Guy. "Barry, don't you want to go back to sleep? Saturday isn't supposed to have a 6:00 A.M."

"Why, Daddy?"

"Because I say so, that's why." He reached to tickle Barry's ribs, but as if his legs were on springs Barry bounced to his feet and raced to the bathroom.

Guy wasn't so energetic. "Ah, youth!" he exclaimed. "So what are you fixing me for breakfast?"

"I only know how to fix one breakfast. Post Toasties. I pour them in a bowl, and put milk and sugar on them."

"OK, go get breakfast. Time you earned your keep. I'll tidy up while you do that."

"Daddy, what's this paper?"

"Paper? Where did you get that, Barry?"

"On the floor." The boy ran to carry it to his father.

The yellow piece of paper, standard letter size, had letters and words cut out of a newspaper and pasted on it. "Warning!" Guy read it to himself wondering, Is this a joke? "Barry, show me where you got it."

"It was coming under the door, Daddy."

Guy, leaped at the door, turned the latch, and opened it in one motion. He looked right and left down the hall, and listened as the downstairs door slammed shut. In an instant, he was racing the three flights down to the street outside. All was quiet. Not a soul in sight. Guy stood wondering, confused. He couldn't continue the chase. Which way? Barry was upstairs alone. Maybe the person was still in the building. He took the stairs up two at a time to his open apartment door, and locked it behind him. He leaned back against it, breathing hard. Barry was holding the note as if trying to read it. Guy reached for it, patted the boy's head, and knelt beside him.

"Is it a letter, Daddy? Who wrote it?"

"Something like that, son. Got that breakfast ready? Can you use some help?"

"Yeah. Can't reach the bowls."

The rest of the morning was uneventful. Guy kept rereading the yellow note. If this was somebody's idea of a joke, it had already gone too far. He dialed his father's number. "Dad, Barry and I are coming over if you don't have plans . . . OK. See you in a few minutes."

Ben thought he detected a nervous stammer in his son's voice. He was at the open door waiting as they walked up the steps.

"Is Tiger out in the back yard?" A nod. "Barry, go play with Tiger while your grandfather and I talk?"

Barry hesitated, noting something different in his father's order.

"Go, Barry . . . Then, we'll all go to the park and play some ball." Overjoyed at the prospect, Barry ran to hug and play with the landlord's old dog. The dog was so old that he was willing to allow kids to climb all over him. Anything, as long as he didn't have to move.

As soon as Barry was out of earshot, Guy gave the paper to Ben.

"Warning! You liberal dogs go to far. Stop while you are ahead Better to fail than be dead. Do not mess with our tradishuns. School was good enouf for us. Leave it alone."

"Someone slid it under our door from the hallway this morning, then ran like hell. I couldn't see who it was."

"That one line threatening death . . . mm. That isn't to be taken lightly. Are you taking it to the police, or shall I? We don't want to scare Barry. Leave him here with me while you go. It's probably from some jokester."

It was the first threat that seemed connected to the Apple A Day activities. In a way the first caused the most concern until the police recognized the note as the doings of a young man in Guy's neighborhood, a mental case, but considered harmless. The people involved with Apple A Day let down their guard. They shouldn't have. Other threats they received, called them rednecks, Jews, haters, the establishment, reds. It seemed there were whole nests of paranoid people out there.

Chapter 6

Where to Turn

"We should get involved with one of the established parent-teacher organizations," a mousy little woman in the corner said.

Since they needed everyone they could get in their group effort, Guy was careful not to say what came to mind, such as "Are you out of your mind, woman! Haven't you ever been to one of their meetings?"

Instead, he held his tongue, smiled at the lady, and said, "We considered that, Mrs. Gallup. We discounted it for now because they have proven to be very conservative." She looked puzzled, so he continued, "They want everything to proceed as usual. Unless someone with a Ph.D. in the field of math, language, or reading is selling another new, effortless way he has devised to teach those disciplines, they are not interested.

"You'll all recall many of the detours the public schools have taken in the past. Many so-called solutions came from educators with the title 'doctor,' so many I can't remember their names anymore. But you'll find them in the textbooks that university students majoring in education must memorize to pass their tests for certification."

"That's about right. If a guy has a Ph.D., even in garbage collecting, everyone is perking up their ears to see what he's got to say about everything." A quiet man in well-worn jeans volunteered this.

Hands went up. Heads shaking in dismay upon recall. "Yes, it would seem that we've been through every possible innovation, but there'll be more."

Guy sensed that he'd better sit back and let them get their frustrations out in the open. They were on a roll.

"That's right." Ed DeBoer spoke up. There was the 'New Math', then the language labs were going to work miracles in foreign language learning. Don't forget that they threw out phonics. Now they are bringing phonics back . . . after, I may add, we had several years of graduates who could not read."

"Yes, and the schools with no partitions to separate classes—that was a great innovation! So the classes, all in one huge room, could 'interact', they claimed. What a farce that was. Total bedlam and constant distractions, with three teachers speaking to their classes, a video going, and almost a hundred kids struggling to hear, or be heard . . ."

"Or getting into mischief," someone interrupted. "Usually they gave up trying to concentrate on what their own teacher was saying."

"Yes, I recall those school buildings. Some architect who had never gone to a public school designed them."

"Now computers are going to save the world. Just put the kids on a computer and they'll learn everything without effort by playing games," another voice volunteered.

"We have to face the fact that many people side with the conservatives who don't want change. They think the only answers to the problems with schools is that they need more money, more buildings, better trained teachers . . ." This comment came from a newcomer, a mustached fellow wearing a baseball cap. "I'm Rod Holcombe. I'm here because I've heard that you folks have new ideas for promoting change. Do you plan to throw out everything in public education, and start over?"

Guy chose to ignore the last question and call for a break. He wasn't ready to answer that. What to keep, what to minimize, and what to discard were tough choices. He didn't want the group to split on an issue that had not been fully explored. The discussion was going well and gaining momentum. Let them mingle now to share, and get acquainted. He had his own opinions.

As others munched on snacks, he circulated. He had lost interest in food. It seemed he only ate when Barry was with him on alternating weekends. He didn't notice that he was losing weight. His job, preoccupation with Apple A Day, and tutoring crowded out everything except Barry, and Amy. He never knew what to expect from her, or how to win her back. She said one thing, and did another. Didn't level with him. Why?

Some of the discussions did seem more like a protest. He smiled, recalling his father's words. Ben had said that the last meeting seemed to take on the air of rebels ready to overturn their government. Guy had not known how emotional people would become as they initiate, or oppose, change in the schools.

Mrs. Gallup was cornered by a man whose size and bass voice threatened to intimidate her. "We'll never be accepted by the parent-teacher organizations. They think they have their hands on the pulse of the schools. They don't even know what the problems are. Their own kids aren't ever in trouble."

Mrs. Gallup wondered whether they just have good kids or the kids can't get away with anything, because the teacher knows their parents.

Ike Epstein was recalling how the PTO people behaved toward him. "Some of those officers are so uppity, they wouldn't give us the time of day, let alone allow us to use any of their precious meeting time to present our ideas. All I see them do at their meetings is to read what they did at the last meeting, minutes that no one listens to. Cake eating time is a big part of their meetings, too. And raising money. All-a time," Ike added and just shook his head, discouraged at the thought of getting them to cooperate, venting his anger over rebuffs the prissy PTA president had directed toward him, the school custodian.

When they resumed the meeting, Ike brought out his trump card. "I got a friend. Like to bring him to a meeting if you're agreed." Those still standing moved in closer, squatted on the floor, or pulled up a chair. "Don't know if you're aware that there are small radio stations out there just big enough to reach a small radius. My friend's name is Igor Connifer. He operates out of his garage, a 50-watt station."

"You talking about a pirate station?" Noah said. His eyes were wide with interest.

"The FCC is cracking down on them."

"Yeah. You got it, Noah. We wouldn't want to operate without a license. We'd have to pray for an angel to help support it. And maybe we'd need more wattage. But, keep it small—that's the ticket. Most radio operators are just average citizens wanting to serve the community. What better way to serve than to save the public school system and turn it into an educational organ we can be proud of?"

"Those stations sometimes interfere with FM stations, or air traffic control."

"Well, this Connifer guy was shut down. The Federal Communications Commission moved in and nabbed him. He operated out of his garage, played some rock music, and had political documentaries and programs by and for homeless people.

"The FCC knows that hundreds of radio stations nationwide try to operate without licenses. Technology makes it easy to set one up. Igor says that we could do it. Since so many stations are ignoring the law, the government is looking for ways to open the airways to new voices. The FCC proposed issuing very low-power licenses to help churches, schools, and other community groups get on the air legally."

Guy sat up to take notice of this idea. "Well, why the hell didn't you say that first, Ike? We thought you were about to suggest we stick our necks out to do something illegal. Can we arrange a conference with Mr.

Connifer to learn more about it?"

"He'll be in town before our next meeting. I'll take care of it."

"Thanks, folks. We'll adjourn. Pick up duplicates we've made of what our members are writing. Views as to what a good education should include, or omit. Read them, circle, underline, whatever, show what you agree or disagree with, questions you have. Give them thought, and we'll be prepared to move forward at the next meeting. We should be able to write a first draft of what we want public education to provide, as well as what we expect of students in their search for knowledge and wisdom."

Ben stretched his legs to relieve the aches, and as if he were a member of British Parliament, he raised his hand to get formal recognition from his son.

Guy smiled. "Dad, you don't have to be so formal here. What is it you have to say?"

Ben almost stood up to speak, then changed his mind. Habit was a hard thing to break. He smiled. "I just want to thank Ike for his input about radio transmission to spread our mission. It's an excellent idea which, of course, will depend on the outcome of the FCC decisions and getting someone willing to finance it."

Some people were nodding in agreement. Some were looking bewildered, perhaps reticent about the whole idea. Others were leaving.

Guy was elated. This meeting had tripled attendance. Then he sobered recalling that Amy had again broken her promise to be here. Why could he not just let Amy go her way?

"Because I need her," he answered himself aloud. He looked up sheepishly hoping no one had heard him. Well, she was making it as clear as possible that she did not need him.

"I think we have something here, son." His father's voice startled him. He was sitting in the wing chair, smiling, his small expressive hands held with fingers laced resting on his chest.

"Good Lord, I thought everyone had left, Dad."

"Would I leave without a hug?" Guy was grateful that even the men in their family were appreciative of hugs. He needed one tonight. Father and son were becoming closer since his separation. It would make the divorce easier to have Dad to turn to.

Ben stood up, a bit shaky in spite of having his cane to steady him.

"I'm so glad, Dad, that we have you in this group. We need all ages, economic levels, and educational backgrounds. I don't expect many of your generation to show an interest."

"Don't be too sure, Guy. You may be surprised."

It was not a late hour, but Guy insisted on walking him home. They didn't talk other than to comment on the balmy weather, and the pleasant aroma of night-blooming jasmine. Being together in a worthwhile cause . . . just being together was enough to provide pleasure for the moment.

Chapter 7

Mister Ota

Friday morning Guy opened the office door at 5:30 A.M. He wanted to catch up on the work piled on his desk. Other thoughts had hampered his ability to focus.

Must get Amy out of my head. How? Must get work on my desk cleared. The boss has been eyeing my production. Guy crammed some of the backlog into a drawer so it wouldn't be so obvious, then gave free rein to his thoughts: The Apple A Day organization to improve public schools is progressing. Except for some hotheaded implausible diehards, the general public seems to welcome our approach.

That's on my mind whenever Amy is not. Barry's weekend visits help. Thank God Amy didn't get hardheaded, or mean about sharing our parenting. But it isn't the same now. Barry feels it, too. What a kid!

"Good morning Guy. You're here early." Ross Ota stretched his body to his full five feet, while noting that his employee's absorption in writing did not seem to be related to business.

Guy could not hide the fact that he was startled and ill at ease. He hastened to stuff a journal into an overcrowded drawer, while stammering, "Morning Mr. Ota. Yes sir, decided to get some work done early before the phones start ringing." It was now 6:30, still early. Apparently, he had spent more time in thought than getting his work done.

"How are you doing, Guy? I've been wanting to have a talk with you. Maybe this is a good time before the office starts humming. Let me get my daily plan laid out, fifteen minutes at most, then come into the office."

"Sure, Mr. Ota." He had never been invited to call his boss Ross, so he didn't. Damn, he thought, there goes more time I needed to get caught up. "I'll be there at quarter to seven," he replied. Time was becoming his worst enemy. Not enough of it . . . then too much of it. Couldn't sleep when he should be . . . his efficiency was shot to hell. His mind was a jumble of confusion. His brain was turning to jelly. He made the effort to follow Ota's example and to organize his day with a written plan, and too soon it was 6:45. He took some deep breaths as he strode, with a confidence and vigor he didn't feel, and opened the boss's office door.

Ross Ota was a third-generation American. He was one of the many descended from Japanese immigrants brought to Hawaii for labor in pineapple, sugar cane fields, or other needs of the rapidly growing island communities in the late nineteenth century. He and his family had experienced poverty, but had no contrasting comparisons in their background to recognize it as such, so they did not resent it. They never felt they were poor, as long as they were equal to the tests of survival. Survival was the only thing they sought, and survival was everything. What else could they ask for? Life was not easy, but with each year, each generation found it easier. They acquired skills to adjust to the demands of their new and ever-changing island home. They bent as the willow bends with the winds of change, and became ever more capable to fight the elements and adversities life dealt them.

Ross's grandmother was a mail-order bride. She was sent to the islands by the two sets of parents: hers and those of the groom to be. The dowry, due her parents, was paid for with money earned by her groom's daily backbreaking labor. His initiative brought in more money on the side. Even a bit of gambling produced large sums to send back to Japan. His gambling paid off because he was shrewd and depended more on wisdom than chance.

The man his grandmother sailed to the islands to marry was not handsome. He was kind, and he was clever, and from the first moment she met him she thanked the Shinto gods for her good fortune in winning such a man.

Never would she indicate that to him, except by the respect and honor she showed. Admire and cherish him, do his bidding, bear and rear his children, yes. She had been schooled by the women in her family before she set sail. She well knew how to be a worthy life-long partner to serve this man. Respect carried with it much more than our over-worked English noun/verb "love," but it certainly included everything that two hundred years later should still be contained in that word.

The third generation seemed far removed from the peasant forebears who migrated here. Ross Ota, his siblings, and their fourth-generation children were Americans with all that means. Yet, all that was of value in the heritage of past Japanese indoctrination had also been learned and retained by these extended family members.

There was a gentleness of speaking. Though it was sometimes in danger of being lost in teenage boisterousness at school or business dealings, especially board meetings. There were strong and loyal family units within the clan, the descendants of the original Otas in Hawaii. From the first, they valued wisdom and learning, in that order. However the two virtues were interwoven, one fostering the other and blending into character.

They had benefited from schooling, through the Buddhist or Shinto temple, as well as the public schools. Their youth sought both scholarship and spiritual ties. They became inwardly strong, confident, and capable. They contributed to their respective communities. Proud they were, yet humble in their gratitude that the gods had placed them in a position to be able to contribute, rather than having to ask help from others.

When their own family members suffered infrequent misfortune, they got all they needed from within the expanding family circle. However, if a family member brought shame to himself, the family suffered the shame and disowned him.

"Sit down, Guy. Coffee? Tea?" Ross had heated water for his own tea.

"No thanks, Mr. Ota." It pleased Ross that in this era of familiarity, this employee always called him mister. It annoyed him that waitresses, telephone sales people, clerks, and his own employees called him, and everyone else, by a first name.

"May I call you 'Guy'?"

"Of course, sir." He always had, Guy thought.

"Fine. You may continue to call me Mr. Ota. I like that."

"Of course, sir." Is he toying with me, Guy wondered, then noticed a mischievous smile on his boss's face. He smiled also, and relaxed.

"I don't really know you, Guy. I know your work used to be favorable, and that it has recently become," he paused, "not acceptable." I have learned of your marital problems. I'm guessing that's the reason. It is not my policy to become involved in my employee's private lives. Not that I do not care, but it is simply impractical, and not helpful to employees either. I have very few questions to ask you. Please, don't think I am prying."

The questions were brief and elicited a clear picture once Guy had responded. His employer seemed to want to assure himself that Guy had family and friends to stand by him, to support him in his need, whatever that need or problem was. He thus learned about Guy's son Barry, his father, and a close friend, Noah Solomon, also working in this same office.

Ross Ota's tactful inquiry brought to light the Bensons' separation. His question as to how Guy intended to handle his pain and suffering, and whether he was learning to cope, puzzled Guy. If his employer's curiosity was due to impatience with Guy's failure to do his work, then that was a reasonable business concern. Guy was not sure he wanted to discuss marital problems with his boss. He momentarily feared he might be fired. But Ross Ota clarified his reasoning without seeming to lack sympathy for his employee, and without asking for details.

"I have listed some titles of books that may help you to adjust. What are you doing to help yourself?" Mr. Ota was not the kind to sympathize. He was a doer bent on guiding a sufferer to solutions available, then encouraging him to cure himself. He made Guy realize that his situation was indeed a health threat if he did not choose the right paths. Until then, Guy had not realized that his health was deteriorating. It was obvious to others. He had lost weight. His face and body showed weariness and distraction.

Guy blurted out the diversion he had chosen to escape marital anxiety. A failed marriage was unacceptable to him. His solution was escape. His dream of making the public schools effective became that escape. How would his boss react to such impertinence?

That concern did not stop him from telling Ross Ota about the organization he had formed to abolish the current school system and replace it with a revised system, so extreme that many people will deem it outrageous. "Careful," he warned himself as he found words tumbling out. He switched to a course to say just enough to . . . hopefully interest Ota, without arousing a suspicion that this employee was out of his mind.

Ota listened carefully, his mouth slightly open, seemingly astounded by this outburst. It was a brazen, bold venture he had not thought Benson capable of.

"Guy, as a businessman, I must ask why you are not committed to your job? You are obviously committed to your family. It is in the best interests for you to commit your time, effort, and talent to this job. Your workload is not excessive, yet you are lagging behind.

"Commitment is a jealous master. It demands all that you have to give it. The bulk of your time, energy, and imagination. You appear to have too many commitments. It's unrealistic that you can do justice to any of them unless you're a great organizer, and have an army of delegates. Your wife and child would not care to share you while receiving scraps of your time and attention. You will have to choose, decide your priorities in life. Your job can't wait. Consider carefully."

"Well, Mr. Ota. I won't take any more of your time. I appreciate your concern, but I am recovering very well. I will work extra hours to bring my work up to standard." As he was speaking he backed out of the door.

Back at his desk, he wanted to kick himself right in the rear, or more forward on his anatomy perhaps. How stupid to tell Ota so much. His only interest is in this business. How stupid to have shared his obsession of education with the boss. Now he feared he had given Ota an excuse to fire him. He forgot that his poor performance on the job was reason enough.

He rested his head on his hands, and stifled a desire to weep. Fatigue, he decided, and he dove into his work with a vengeance.

Chapter 8

Senior Citizens

Alf Benson dressed carefully. He always took care to be well groomed. His white hair, mustache, and black brows were trimmed. His clothes were not new, but always neatly pressed. He did not feel old. Only the calendar suggested he was a candidate for the local seniors group in the county. He was not a regular member. There were too many other things to do that would not confine him to any one age group. Today, though, he would attend their meeting and luncheon. He had a mission.

He knew that the elderly were critical of today's children. He also knew that, in spite of their impatience, they were interested in the younger generation. He expected to find people who cared about the future of education. Soon he would know whether they were withering away with only selfish interests, or if they could be counted on to add their votes and effort to a good cause.

He found a seat. He spoke to the two women seated on either side, as the chairman was calling the meeting to order. Ben's mind wandered, scarcely taking in the content of the meeting until he heard the question, "Is there any new business?" Well, that was a short meeting, his favorite kind.

He stood, grasping the back of the empty chair in front of him. "Mr. Chairman, I am Alf Benson. I am here to represent a new organization we call 'Apple A Day Inc', dedicated to improving the public school system. I would like a few minutes of your time to ask some questions regarding your membership's opinion of the effectiveness of our public schools. May I have your permission to do so?"

"You have the floor, Mr. Benson."

"Do any of you have an interest in public education?" Some hands were raised. "Do any of you have knowledge of the condition of our schools, and of the education our public schools are providing?" Heads were nodding. "If so, would you please share with us what you do know … favorable or unfavorable?"

One after another, a few people stood to make comments.

"I don't think the children are given a good education these days. I don't know why. In our business, we now have to train our employees in the basics. They don't know how to talk to the public. They catch on to the use of machines, but when our computers were down, why . . . they didn't even know how to make change."

"My granddaughter is a bright girl, but she has never learned to write decent sentences, and she is ready to graduate. Her grades have never shown that she had a problem, but she certainly has . . . and her spelling is atrocious."

"Schools don't teach manners anymore. I guess the parents don't teach them either. Children are rude. Teens don't even know that they lack social skills necessary in the working world."

"What they need is to repeat the Lord's Prayer every day, and memorize the Ten Commandments. Do you know that the schools don't even allow the children to celebrate Easter or Christmas in school anymore?"

That raised the hackles on the backs of some necks, thought Ben, who was noticing the frowning faces. Well, before the group got radical and spread any more misinformation or generalizations, he spoke up.

"Thank you. If you are interested in being a part of the solution rather than cursing the problems, there is an organization forming. The members are just getting started and have many ideas as to why our children are being graduated from a system that has short-changed them. One of our concerns is that many students are not doing their part to get an education. We are analyzing why that is so, and what can be done to change their attitudes.

"We feel that the country and our democratic system is at risk if this is allowed to continue. We are working toward change . . . toward an effective public school system. If you are interested, I have information here about our organization. It explains what we have done, and where we are going." Ben waved a flyer. "We would be pleased to have you attend to share your ideas and listen to ours."

"Thank you, everyone," the senior citizen officiating took charge. "Note the nature of the new business in the minutes, Sara," he told the secretary. "If there is no other business, let's have a motion to adjourn." Voices spoke up to move and second, and the meeting ended. "Let's eat!" said the chairman, already on his way to get a plate.

Ben had hoped to hurry out after some flyers were picked up. He expected a little interest, but the number of people stopping by surprised him.

"Oh, you were a school teacher?" Ben showed polite interest. Some were formerly aides, office help, even a principal, cafeteria worker, grand-parents, employers. All had good reasons to care that education was not measuring up.

Ben claimed an appointment to avoid sitting down to lunch. He smiled, recalling that Guy did not think old folks would respond to a call to arms. How many would attend the next meeting? Maybe they were all talk and no grit. Some of them were suffering from disabilities. Well, he would have to wait. Maybe he would say nothing to Guy about his efforts today to contact older citizens, that is, unless it increases their membership significantly.

Chapter 9

Noah, to the Rescue

The Thursday, before the Apple A Day Inc. Saturday night meeting, Guy was fighting a cold and a headache. Mr. Ota stopped at his desk and suggested that he go home as early as possible and not come in Friday. "We don't need your germs, and you do need some sleep to get rid of that." Guy followed the suggestion, and slept through from Friday afternoon until Saturday without waking. When the phone rang, he knocked it off the cradle, picked it up, and put the wrong end to his ear.

"Sorry to wake you, buddy, but the big meeting is coming up tonight, and from the flak I'm hearing we are going to have a big attendance. We arranged for a larger meeting place."

"What . . . what's that? Who are you calling?" Guy was sitting up in bed, completely disoriented.

"Oh, oh! Maybe I'd better not identify myself," the voice said. "You're really out of it. Remember you said to call you anytime after 8:30? Well, it's after 10."

"Noah, is that you? What time did you say? Holy shit, I'm glad you did call. I've got an 11:00 o'clock appointment. OK. I'm functioning now . . . I think . . . What did you say?"

"I'm hearing a lot of people discussing the Apple A Day meeting tonight. Seems that one of the local radio talk shows mentioned our interest in having a small independent radio station. They talked about our school concerns and intentions. It's stirred up a lot of interest. We'll have more people there than your apartment will handle. What do you say, buddy? Oh, and Igor Connifer's going to be our guest."

Guy emitted a slow whistle. "We haven't even discussed it with him yet. Noah, that Igor guy could make us or break us. Any ideas as to where we can meet? And how we can get word to current members about the change of meeting place?"

"Hey, partner! Need I start over? Not to worry, Buddy-O. Got a place. Sandy and a few others are calling people. Your Dad is helping."

Guy was only half listening. Too much for his foggy mind to deal with. "Well, we aren't tied in to that Connifer guy yet. Hey, I'll get back with you as soon as I can today to do my share. Right now I've got to run. Thanks, friend. This can profit us if we're prepared, or make damned fools of us if we are not. My thanks to all of you. I'll call you later. You're a pal."

"I know I'm great, my mother knows it, now you know it. Wow, I can't wait until the world discovers me. Take it easy, Guy. We'll talk later."

Noah and Sandy had arranged for a county room to meet in. The list of interested people had grown, and they had no idea how many people might be there. The room could be doubled if the adjoining room was not booked. Lucky to get a place on short notice.

Ben called the president of the seniors group and got names of people who had expressed interest. Sandy talked to a group of gifted senior high students, to test their ideas concerning a plan for a high school that would place more responsibility on students. They wanted to know more, so Sandy invited them.

Sandy called Ike, the custodian who had initially suggested that Igor Connifer might be able to set up an independently operated radio station. When that possibility was discussed briefly at the past meeting, the Apple A Day members had been noncommittal. Why concern themselves until the radio operator showed interest? They needed first to discuss the possibility, and potential problems, and then to meet Igor Connifer. It was a trick of fate that before they could meet, the idea would be aired on the local talk show. It had forced their hand. "Ike, we need your help." Sandy explained the sudden urgency and asked if Igor could bring a microphone and speaker equipment. "Hope Igor isn't shy because we may have a lot of people. Will this get him into any trouble?"

The answer was negative. He had cooperated with authorities when they closed him down, and any future broadcasting would be done within the law.

In spite of a late start, Guy made it to the appointment with Amy and her attorney on time. All thanks due to Noah's phone call.

The polished mahogany interior of the law office was formal and forbidding. Cold leather volumes lined the walls. Beige and brown. Files containing grim records of clients' lives filled crowded shelves. A secretary directed him to a room with the same dark decor. They were waiting for him at a round shiny table.

Bingington, a stocky proper sort, stood to shake hands. Amy was already seated so that they would be looking at one another. That was good. He had never gotten any information from her, except that she wasn't happy and wanted to be "on her own." Maybe today they could discuss it. Maybe she would open up. It made no sense at all to him.

"Sit down, please, Mr. Benson. We only need your signature on the divorce papers."

Guy's mouth dropped open. He had thought they were going to talk. Didn't a good attorney try to mend a marriage rather than to sever it?

"Whatever are you talking about? I am not signing anything. My wife and I need time to get back together, that's all. Amy, are you crazy? Don't let this coot con you into something we will always regret."

"I am not in the business of mending marriages, Mr. Benson, but neither would I pressure Mrs. Benson to end her marriage. Amy, you told me that your husband has been uncooperative, and did not want to save the marriage. His manner today appears otherwise. I would never encourage you to follow through with a divorce if there is a possibility of reconciling differences."

She turned to look out of the window.

"Mr. Benson, I suggest a good marriage counselor to unearth your problems. It appears to me that you two don't do much talking, at least not at the level necessary to get things done. Amy, I will put these papers on file, but I will not represent you until you both get counseling. It seems that you have not been honest with me."

Amy covered her mouth to stifle a sob, and dropped her head, cradled by her arms, onto the desktop. Still standing, Guy stared at her with uncontrolled fury.

"Where is my son?" he demanded. He had never used that tone, nor the possessive claim that the boy was his, not theirs. "This has gone far enough. You are deceiving me, and your lawyer. I'm beginning to see that you're not a fit mother to raise Barry. I suggest you see a psychiatrist to get yourself straightened out."

Her sobbing increased, her gasps for breath struggled to gain control over her anguish. Guy turned on his heel and strode out the same door the attorney had exited only seconds before. Guy was relieved to see Barry in the waiting room wiggling impatiently on a straight-backed chair. The babysitter thumbed through a magazine.

"Come along, son." He held out his hand. Barry grinned, and scooted off the chair before the sitter could react. She had never seen the child's father. Father and son moved quickly toward the elevator, stepped through open doors, and were gone.

Barry sensed the change in his father. They were always relaxed, cheerful, even exuberant when they were together. "Dad, you're hurting my hand. I can't walk that fast, Da-a-d!"

"Oh, Barry, I'm sorry." Guy sat on the marble wall at the entry to the building, pulled his son close, and hugged him tight. "I'm so sorry, so sorry" he repeated, fighting back the tears. They were tears of anger, fear, and despair. They were tears for himself and for Barry. Life was taking a terrible course. There were no tears for Amy. He was about to discover how thin a line there was between love and fury. He controlled the tears so as not to alarm Barry. How could he explain anything to his son when he himself did not understand?

The startled babysitter had jumped to her feet when Barry and his father hurried away. She looked pleadingly at the curious receptionist who was watching them stalk out. "Where is Mrs. Benson? Can you call her, please?"

When Amy was controlled enough to respond to the paging of the receptionist in the outer office, she saw Earlene staring at her in alarm. "He took Barry" she said. "Was it all right, Mrs. Benson?" One look at the distraught mother told her it was not, but Amy nodded yes."

"I'll take you home, Earlene."

Amy realized that this sitter was not bright. She had been caring for a neighbor's children. The neighbor seemed satisfied with her, so Amy considered that a reference. Earlene would have to do until there was time to find a sitter more to her liking. During the drive to her house, she was glad that the girl was uncommunicative. Uncommunicative? Hah! She was devoid of any trace of conversational skill.

The scene in the attorney's office had completely exhausted Amy. She had never intended that the separation from Guy would ever really result in a divorce. Instead, she had considered it a means to get her way in their marriage. This was the first time Guy had shown any real emotion, and it had terrified her. What she had expected was for him to listen to her, just listen. But listen to what? She was unable to put into words all that was troubling her. She would rehearse the words she wanted to say, but when she tried to tell him of her fears and anxieties, he took charge. Before she could get the words out, he willed it all away, solving nothing.

"Mrs. Benson, you passed my house."

"Oh! How far back is it? Will it be all right if I let you out here?"

"We-e-ell, I'll have to walk a few blocks, Mrs. Benson."

It was rush hour and she was on a one way road that ended on the freeway. "Why didn't you tell me sooner?" Amy's patience was at an end.

She pressed some dollar bills into the girl's hand.

"It will do you good to walk, Earlene. And I won't need you this weekend."... or ever, she promised herself. She would hate to trust her son to someone whose reactions and personality were almost nonexistent.

Earlene got out of the car without a thank you, goodbye, or fare-thee-well.

Chapter 10

One Step at a Time

Father and son busied themselves making peanut butter sand-wiches at the kitchen table. Guy settled Barry in front of the VCR to watch a tape. Meanwhile, he turned his thoughts to tonight's meeting of AAD. Thank God, Noah had taken over this morning. Nothing left to do now. With the cooperation of a few, they had handled all necessary preparations. He was grateful. The leak of information on the talk show had accelerated their plans. Maybe it's a false alarm, but if many people do show up . . . the best thing we can do is to field questions and answers.

This could get their plans off the ground, or it could be . . . think positive, he told himself. Their plans were not well formulated yet. The nucleus were in accord with the need for drastic changes in our public schools, and it should begin with students who are ready for it.

Guy was grateful for how much stress his friends had spared him today. They had anticipated and accomplished what had to be done. He picked up the phone. Noah answered on the first ring. "How's it going, partner?" Guy asked.

"Everything's under control. The radio station's phone is ringing off the wall, and I hear that a reporter from the local paper has been nosing around asking questions."

"Holy Smoke, Noah, are we ready for this? I'm getting cold feet."

"Ready or not, the condition of the schools, the lack of quality in education is ready. If the time is right, this will take on a life of its own. Don't worry. When a cause is right, the right people step forward to carry it through. Don't plan to say much tonight. The least, the better."

Guy was grateful to have someone to talk to. "So, Igor is bringing microphones and speakers. Our plan will be submitted to the people. I doubt that anyone outside of our group will agree or defend it . . . at first . . . so we'll throw them the ball. At least we'll know for sure whether people are willing to get behind new ideas."

"They will be expecting information. How much we can share in one evening is the question. Maybe what's being done in schools across the country?"

"I'll have that documentation on hand. We'll let them guide us to what they want to hear. We don't even know how many people are dissatisfied with our schools. If we aren't in accord that there are major problems and that they call for drastic changes in education, we may as well forget it."

"Noah, you should be leading this tonight. Would you? This couldn't be a worse time for me. Amy and I met in her attorney's office this morning. It was terrible.

"One good bit of news is that her lawyer refuses to touch the case until we get counseling. I'm so furious with her now that I don't know if I want to save the marriage. She has been acting like she is out of her mind."

"Of course, you want to save it. Barry's future is reason enough. Look, we've got everything under control with the Apple A Day activities now. Sandy, Ike, and a few others have been working very hard. We're all looking forward to this evening. Have you ever attended a New England town meeting?"

"No, why do you ask?"

"Because it is democracy in action. It has been their custom since the early colonies met in churches or halls to discuss major issues. It's still effective. We're going to see it happen tonight. You'll see, Buddy-O. Take care of that boy of yours and relax. One step at a time. It will all work out. And let's have a bit more optimism.

"There is one concern that everyone attending the meeting will have in common. Their attendance is proof that they have some strong feelings about our public education. Some will be there to support it. Some will be looking for easy answers. Some will be critical of our ideas. But I'm betting that most of them are tired of hearing the political garbage that offers the same old excuses and the same old promises for reform. They'll be looking for truth, reason, and action. But they may not recognize it when they hear it."

The obscure we will see eventually. The completely apparent takes longer.
—Edward R. Murrow

Chapter 11

Who are These People?

"Good evening, ladies and gentlemen. I am Noah Soloman, and you are here to discover what my companions and I, who represent Apple A Day Incorporated, have to say about the public school concerns on our island and in the state. We are here to answer your questions. I'm going to turn the mike over to Guy Benson, who with a small number of members formed this corporation. Guy?"

Noah stood tall, exuding confidence and appearing more than his five feet seven-inch stature. His deep brown eyes sparkled with excitement under the dark brows that dominated a friendly face. He, and the others, had dressed in their best.

Guy sprang to his feet, pretending a readiness he did not feel. He felt ill prepared to inform and impress this crowd of people. About two hundred faces were staring up at him. Many were standing or leaning against the walls in the large meeting room. They wore casual, comfortable clothes. That was the island way. He felt overdressed in shirt and tie. Would that detract from his image in their eyes?

He would soon know if some were foes with an axe to grind. Some would perhaps feel threatened by this newly formed organization. He took a deep breath, straightened up to at least appear self-assured. He tapped the microphone with his fingernail, and hoped his voice would sound strong.

"We'll not waste your time tonight. Rather, we will begin with your questions. We are pleased that you are here."

"What does Apple A Day mean?" a powerful voice demanded.

"Apple a Day may sound playful, but we are dead serious in our goals. Shakespeare asked, 'What's in a name?' Apples have been symbolic of many things. Some say the apple in the Garden of Eden symbolizes knowledge. It also was traditionally a gift for the teacher from a small child. It became a symbol for health to keep the doctor away. To us it's a symbol of education. And folks, our public education is not healthy. It has deteriorated. We want to rid it of decay."

"How do you propose to do that?" the same voice asked.

"To dispense with the continuing nonsense concerning what we are told is wrong with public education. By revising public education to make it effective in our new millennium. We are doing our homework to unearth the few places in the United States where their citizens have already taken creative, daring, and successful steps to prepare our children, and ultimately to save our country. We are dismayed that there are too few creditable schools in existence, and concerned that those that are good examples are not being copied and improved upon throughout the United States."

People who did not trust their voices to carry from their seats were lining up at the microphones that Igor Connifer had placed around the room. Two voices spoke at the same time canceling each other out. Guy pointed to one speaker, "You first, please, then we'll rotate this way around the room. Others, please feel free to speak without a mike if you can make yourself heard, but let's give people at the mike courtesy and priority."

"You didn't answer the man's question. Who are you people? What makes you experts?"

"Experts? We've made no such claim. We have attended public schools, or have been teachers, administrators, or staff workers in the system. Our children attend, or will attend public school. Some of us are tempted to place them in private schools because we have lost faith in the efficacy of the current public school system.

"The tinkering of Ph.D.s in the field of education has been ineffectual. For generations their new methods and devices have sold their books, and resulted in promotions, increased income, and stature among their peers. Meanwhile, the cost of operating our schools rose. Parents and students were confused by altered vocabulary without improvement. The attempts of experts have been esoteric, theoretical, and impractical. We don't need those kinds of experts."

Someone in the front row stood and waved an arm. "I agree. That's why I'm here. But I thought you'd have answers. Who do we trust?"

"Our members have researched, and studied the situation. We have laid some groundwork. We trust you, and ourselves. We are ready to trust teachers and administrators who have been on the front line, and who recognize that no one is addressing major weaknesses in schools. We are ready to listen to students, many of whom have given the public school system their all, yet find their education is inadequate. In the competition they face in the world of work, and in social and political acuity, they realize that they have been short-changed.

"A free country cannot afford to give up on our public school system. It is a major pillar supporting our strengths. We must educate the masses if we are to remain a powerful force. The faults in our educational system require drastic change if it is to be effective. The weaknesses reflect the rapid and extreme changes in our society."

The voice in the audience spoke again. Guy was surprised that the powerful voice exploded from a teenager. "You said that you wouldn't waste our time. What do you mean by 'drastic'? Are you ready to tell us some of the changes you have in mind?"

"I use the word 'drastic' to mean 'controversial.' Before I list some ideas we consider necessary, I am asking for your patience to listen with an open mind. You may not be ready to accept them. You may not even know how ineffective our public schools are. We hope you are ready to give our ideas consideration. We hope you will join us in our research, and support us in the many ways needed to succeed in this venture. We need help to investigate schools that are showing good results from changes they have made on the mainland and on our islands.

"Please, don't think I am evasive, but before we get specific it is time to introduce a new contributor in our midst. Igor Connifer. Mr. Connifer is a former radio pirate operator."

The word "pirate" certainly sparked an interest. Distaste more than likely. There was a sudden murmur of voices in the audience, then full attention.

"Mr. Connifer was ordered to shut down his 50-watt FM station. He wanted to serve his community with an alternative voice so he took the risk of operating out of his garage with music, political documentaries, and programs by and for homeless people. It was a form of 'electronic civil disobedience for a good cause,' as he told the officials, but he cooperated with the shutdown. I want him to tell you more about how he may now be of help to this community, and accomplish it legally. Igor Connifer is already at the other microphone." Guy nodded to the man as all heads turned. "Please welcome this gentleman whose intentions are to come to our aid." Some applauded. Others looked suspicious.

Igor had his hair combed neatly and tied in back. He appeared older than his 47 years. Tall and slim. He wore jeans and a plaid cotton shirt, his mustache and beard were trimmed. Nevertheless, some eyebrows were raised. Were they expressing disapproval? Guy hoped that Igor could win the censorious critics over. If not their whole group might be suspected of being subversives.

"Evening, folks. Didn't expect to be involved in anything like this when I moved here." His drawl fit the man's appearance. Country boy for sure, but, his words were a blend of many areas of the mainland. And good stage presence. Seemed reasonably well educated too, but not stuffy.

"A friend told this Apple A Day group about me. This meeting was intended for us to meet and discuss what we both are sharing with you tonight. This is the first time I've even talked to them about the possibility of working with them. I don't know yet if I care to do it. They don't know yet whether they want to be involved with me. Your input may help us both to decide.

"Fact is that some of you heard me when I was interviewed by a popular talk show host here. Somehow, the interview made many people curious. This group was suddenly in the public eye and they suspected they might have more people at this meeting than they'd expected. They asked me to set up the mikes." He smiled. "They're going to be surprised what they owe me for the service. I haven't been asked to say this, but they might appreciate some contributions from you tonight."

Guy was surprised, and interjected, "Hey, he's right. We did not ask him to announce that, but we are a new group with zero dollars in our coffers. We do want to pay Igor for being here, and for the use of his equipment, and his services. He spent a lot of time setting this up for us. That so many of you came tonight is a tribute to your sense of responsibility. What are your questions?"

"What do you think will make the schools better?" It was a young woman with Asian features, poised and attractive.

"Thank you, ma'm. My skills lie in communication. That's all. But in a democracy that's everything. I'd like to furnish the means for communication in your little community here."

"But you already said that it was illegal." Her tone indicated disapproval.

"No, ma'm. It's only illegal without a license. I shouldn't have been operating without one, but they're damned, excuse me, darned expensive, and the homeless people I was representing didn't have money for one.

"If we started a station here to represent citizens concerned about education, we'd get a license. I don't know who'd pay for it, but I trust God to find a way when somethin' is right and good."

A voice broke in, "How come you have so much faith in the Almighty now, when you didn't get enough money for a license while you helped the homeless?"

Igor grinned, folded his arms, then reached to scratch his head. Amused and deep in thought he continued. "Somehow the money for homeless people just wasn't out there. Guess most people with money never found themselves homeless. But public education, most American's lives have been somewhat, or greatly affected by it. I think many people are worried and confused about the effectiveness of our schools. There's a lot of interest, and it isn't being genuinely addressed by politicians. It's gonna be up to the people. An' the Almighty," he winked. "The Almighty depends on people, too . . . an' He . . . or She'll be talkin' to ya about it. Jus' refer to your conscience to get some answers."

"How do we know that you're reputable?" A middle-aged woman with an expression that looked like she had just sniffed a manure pile spoke up. She marched to her seat taking short, well-punctuated steps. She stretched her neck and pursed her lips in a 'so there' haughty expression, awaiting his answer.

Igor smiled, "Well, the fact Ma'm is that you don't know, and you'd be very wise to check that out. Meanwhile, I'll give you all some information that will be easy to verify:" and Igor continued, unruffled by what he considered a practical question concerning his reputation.

"What most people don't know is that there are hundreds of radio stations nationwide, on the mainland, operating without licenses. It's pretty hard for the government to control that, and it's got to be controlled because there are some dangers. Since 1997, the Federal Communication Commission has shut down more than 430 pirate stations, ranging in power from 1 watt to 800 watts. Most are run by average citizens wanting to serve their community."

"What about the subversive ones that are plotting against the government?"

"Yeah, there are those out there. But the government is able to tune into them to see what they're griping about. Government agencies can infiltrate, to find out what they're up to, hopefully before they do damage to themselves, or others.

"The subversives are tryin' to reach other gripers to join their cause. Yes, they get some converts, but the advantage we have in this country is that people who have a different view can call in to a talk show and be heard. They can dish out some common sense to balance the hate talk. We can't give freedom of speech to some groups, and deny others. Who is going to decide who has just cause? The people, that's who.

"If we educate our children to appreciate the advantages and responsibilities of our democratic heritage, they'll be capable of making right choices. We'll have leaders with the courage to make good long-term choices. Most decisions offer only short term solutions spawned by emotional, mindless gibberish to win votes." His voice rose in volume and intensity. Then he relaxed into the country boy image again.

"Sorry folks, I'm known to get carried away about things that endanger our country. This little experiment called 'democracy' is still young. It needs a lot of watching if it's to endure. The better educated our people are, the better able we are to separate the wheat from the chaff. That's my business. Just trying to figure out which is chaff so we can dispose of it."

A woman shouted, "I've heard that these stations are a hazard to airport radio towers, that they cause interference while a plane is landing. And you are called 'pirates', not a very savory name if you are responsible people."

"Well, about the first, you heard right. No radio operator should be in a location to interfere with the safety of airport travel. But, that 'pirate' title is disrespectful to the operators I prefer to call 'micro power broadcasters'. I want you to know that the people leading this group, Apple a Day, Inc., are decent people who care about our kids and education."

Guy stepped to the microphone. "We have time for one more question for Igor please, then we have a stack of packets available to you. We only need to cover our costs so a donation is appreciated. The packets contain some of the ideas we have put into writing: Our tentative "Cause for Alarm Statement; and A Student's Bill of Rights and Responsibilities, A Statement of Purpose." These regard public school education, and will answer some of your questions in more depth.

"Before turning the mike back to Igor Connifer, thank you all for coming, for your attention and interest. We need your input. If you feel that Mr. Connifer's service would be a favorable community endeavor we must find some 'angels' to finance it. We need more people, ideas and money for our cause. Igor they want to ask you more questions."

"Thank you kindly, Mr. Benson. I'll be here until they throw me out if need be."

"Mr. Connifer, did you have commercials on your station, and how many miles could your wattage cover?" The father of the teenage boy asked the questions.

"Well sir, I had a 50 watt station that reached listeners within a radius of about 22 miles. It depends on the antenna's height and the terrain. On a good day, I could reach a five-mile radius. I had no commercials, just services for the community. And I operated 24 hours a day."

"Sir, I can't see how such a small radius can be of help. How much wattage would be needed in a community like ours?" The question was from the teenage boy. He seemed sincerely interested, and had in fact jumped up to participate in his father's, and Igor's discussion. The father smiled at his son's eagerness.

"I'd have to know your community better to be able to estimate that. Like most places, it looks like clusters of communities. For $285 to $595, we could build a low power station.

"Technology makes it easier to set one up. It's very easy to build a transmitter, which is the key component. The government is looking at ways to open the airwaves to more new voices. In January '99 the Federal Communications Commission proposed to issue very low-power licenses. Their objective is to help churches, schools and other community groups to get legally on the air. We could be set up within hours." The boy raised his eyebrows in wonder, as if he could already envision it happening.

"Many groups, including the National Association of Broadcasters don't like this idea."

"Why not?" The boy persisted.

"Well, I guess you would have to ask them. I can only speak for myself. Some government control is necessary. Say, to provide cheap air-time for political candidates, and to regulate indecent material. But they should never deny our people communication over the airways. That's as ridiculous as expecting to license the use of telephones.

"If you ask me, the real pirates are the corporations that dominate the airwaves. A community talk show is a great way for citizens to air their educational frustrations and needs. Knowing what's needed is the first step. Then the sharing of ideas over the air would unify the citizens. In time, you can organize a work force to put the best ideas to use in the schools. Well folks, I'm gonna pack up. If anyone wants to lend a hand I'd be mighty grateful."

Kirk, the youth who had asked Igor many questions, turned to his father for approval then raced to help. The boy watched Igor a few moments then followed his lead to gather up and load the equipment.

Igor, in turn watched the boy. With his reddish hair, grin and freckles he looked like he'd just stepped out of a Norman Rockwell illustration. That voice though . . . that voice he had heard over the mike would be a boon to any radio station, Igor thought. It already showed an exultance rare in a boy so young. It emanated from a confidence, poise and an inordinate amount of maturity for his age.

Cliff, the boy's father had suggested they come tonight because Kirk was not scholastically oriented. When he told his dad that he hated school, Cliff was more than concerned. His oldest son, Clifton, junior dropped out of school and left home two years ago. They suspected he was caught up in drugs.

It was tempting to blame the schools, but it wasn't that easy. What if the schools were re-created? He suspected that major changes were necessary, as the man tonight had said. Cliff Collins knew that his boys were not stupid. To the contrary, they are bright and curious.

Kirk's father hurried over to the table where the packets were stacked, reached in his pocket, and pulled out three dollars. That was all he'd brought. Hell. He was about to put the packet back and return the bills to his pocket when the pretty woman they'd called Sandy, met his impatient glance.

"That's all right. You can pay another time, or just help us put this into practice." They smiled at each other in a more than casual way. Much more than friendly, it was a lasting, studied appraisal. He took the packet, walked away, and glanced back to smile at the pretty blonde.

Blankets lined the truck bed. A dozen men, boys, and a young lady made short work of dismantling and carrying the equipment to the truck, where Igor supervised the loading and covered it with a waterproof tarp.

Chapter 12

Chieko

Noah hurried outside as soon as the meeting ended. He tried to be inconspicuous while watching people and listening to their comments as they left the building. The expression on people's faces was revealing. Most seemed to be discussing what they had heard, and their impressions.

The woman with her lips pursed was one of the first to leave. She still seemed to be sensing a disgusting odor. Perhaps she was hurrying to report to her principal. A few others looked cross. Maybe the meeting hadn't justified missing a favorite television show.

It was a good sign that some people lingered in groups. Noah drew near enough to hear comments about the presenters at the meeting. The radio station interested them.

The girl who had posed some questions to Igor Connifer left hurriedly also. Pretty. Probably of Japanese heritage. She moved gracefully toward a car parked at the curb. Someone inside slid over to allow her to drive, and they were quickly on their way. "Uncle, thank you for picking me up. I saw you standing in the back of the room. What do you think?"

He ignored the question. "Did you get the packet of information?"

"Of course. I'll get copies made and drop one off at your office tomorrow. You seem more than a little interested in this group. Aren't you going to tell me what you know about them, and why you are going out of your way to learn more?"

"Not yet. I know almost nothing, except that I believe their intentions are honorable. We'll both read, the hand-out, then we'll talk Chieko." He said no more until they covered the few short blocks to her apartment house. "Drive underneath to park," he said. "My car's nearby. I'll watch until you are inside the door. Do you want me to go with you to your apartment?"

"No, my dear. I am getting much better. Soon I'll be able to go places by myself again. Thank you." She kissed his cheek, let the car door swing shut, then ran toward a door at the edge of the underground parking area. With the wave of her hand, she entered the building.

She was breathing with some difficulty by the time she had unlocked and entered her tastefully furnished apartment. Perhaps she wasn't yet ready to venture out on her own. Otherwise, why would she be holding her breath, listening for every sound, and tensing as the shadows toyed with her imagination? Once inside, she turned each of the locks, and felt safe. She leaned against the heavy white lacquered door until the beating of her heart slowed.

She undressed in the dark, pulled down the gold-fringed shades, and only then did she turn on the light, snuggle into her pillows and proceed to read the material she had picked up at the meeting.

Premise Concerning The Public School System of Education;
Its current effectiveness or lack thereof;
How we propose to alter, or replace sub-standard conditions,
and our reasons.

After considerable research into the history of education, here and abroad, and observing conditions in current schools, we the members of Apple a Day, Incorporated, have formed the following conclusions.

I. What Do Our Children Need?
Each child needs to belong to, and be accepted by family, friends, and community.

Each needs to acquire constructive, character building values, and to understand and respect oneself, and others.

They need to be discriminating in their choice of models to emulate.

They must learn to make and evaluate their own choices, and to accept the favorable, and unfavorable consequences for them.

They should achieve so as to gain self-confidence, and to persevere when they fail.

They should make short, and long term plans.

They need guidance and opportunity to gain and share knowledge and understanding.

They must broaden their knowledge to learn about the world at large, nature, and the universe.

They must develop analytical skills.

They must understand basic economics. Not to be educated in the above skills and knowledge, stunts their physical, mental, social and spiritual growth.

II. What Are Our Children's Strengths?

In the classroom, our children are likely to respond to hands on activities. They are skilled organizers, and have experienced working as a team. They are learning to be both leaders and followers.

In this information and technological era, our children are continually informed through television news, history, entertainment, talk shows and quiz shows.

Information is dispensed in quantity without guidelines to determine fact from fantasy, or how to apply critical thinking. It comes to them through osmosis, and they learn much with little, or no effort.

They do not shrink from high technology, instead they are open to its use. Some are capable computer operators. Others use it as a toy. We must teach to the strengths in today's children.

III. What We Expect of Our Schools.

Safety. Transportation, buildings, equipment and campus must be made as safe as possible.

Orderly, productive classes. Classes must be conducive to study. They must not be disruptive due to unnecessarily loud voices, or distracting confusion and behavior.

Authority. The principal is the school authority figure. The teacher has authority in the classroom, and elsewhere on school property. Students show respect for them, and toward other adults in the school, and those who are delegated authority on occasion.

Respect. Self-respect is demonstrated by courtesy, good behavior and treatment of classmates, faculty, administration and staff.

Rules and Regulations are to be accepted and obeyed.

Class time must be used wisely, never wasted.

Eating and drinking in the classroom is a distraction and adds to maintenance cost.

Clothing should be appropriate.

Education must be flexible to suit today's world, and to serve today's youth. Time and circumstances have created a society quite different from that of the past. We have different, and ever fluctuating needs as we enter the new millennium. Today's child is not like the children of the past.

It is human to stretch to measure up to high expectations. The reverse is also true, that if very little is expected of us we will likely sink to lower levels to meet those expectations.

IV. Society's Effect on Our Children

For generations literacy has been declining in America. Television and movies lead in influencing our children. Schools do not require as much reading. One rea-

son is that the reading assignments are disregarded by many students. They do not read enough to develop reading skill or to advance their education. Reading well is a requirement for continuing education. It is a necessary tool to acquire vocabulary. Vocabulary is of utmost importance to meet civic and family needs and responsibilities, as well as social, employment and medical requirements.

V. What Must We Do About It?

We must have different approaches to education to provide what is most effective for each child. Readiness is the most important prerequisite to learning.

An urgent step to begin with is to rescue the youth who need our guidance, but do not need enforcement. They are the ones with a hunger for learning. They receive gratification from the opportunity to read and study. They are self-motivated. We must cooperate with them to provide that opportunity.

With wise guidance, the opportunity to proceed at their own pace, in safety and without distractions, their education will expand, their pride and satisfaction will be rewarded. They will inspire other students. Our society will benefit by providing intelligent leaders and contributors.

This group of eager students must be given priority in a pilot school because their time and talents are hampered in today's public schools. We are losing our best youth to mediocrity by not fulfilling their potential.

VI. Outline of a Proposed Pilot School

We begin with a pilot school with as nearly ideal conditions as possible for those students capable and eager for scholastic achievement.

We must allow only those who are ready, and eager to learn, to enter phase I of revised schools. This is not to exclude anyone who is ready to behave like a student.

It does exclude those who have not yet acquired the basic skills of reading at grade level. It also excludes those with attitudes that may be a barrier to opportunity.

Registration must be limited to the number of students a school building will comfortably and safely provide for, and with a practical number of teachers and aides to guide and teach them.

VII Advantages of A Pilot School

The school will not have to deal with negative attitudes. Society with the aid of the media and technology should begin a campaign to improve attitudes of our youth. The use of a process akin to propaganda, but intended for positive, constructive rather than negative results is essential. The misuse of television has resulted in involuntary indoctrination of many children. Mimicking what they see on television has created an exaggerated contrariness in our youth that is in conflict with constructive growth. The pilot school welcomes those who have the desire to learn and are ready to take responsibility for their education.

Small groups are necessary when students are not dedicated to study, and do not want to be there.

Discipline is seldom if ever necessary in a group of committed students studying elective subjects. For the most part, they are self-directed.

Testing responsible students is not frequently needed as they seek help on their own when they don't understand. They take responsibility for their assignments, or study plan and arrive at school prepared.

Applying numbers to the ratio of teacher, aides and students, can only be done after these willing and able students are under way. It is a fact that teachers of eager and qualified students are quite comfortable with larger groups, if enough aides are available for individualized attention.

For the reasons given, it costs less money to educate the students targeted for the pilot school.

VIII. Selection of Students for Pilot School

Any students above C average should write an essay as to why they want an education; what they are ready to contribute in time, cooperation and personal effort; state their current and far-reaching goals; and interests. Adequate reading skill level is essential. Writing skill will improve according to how frequently it is put to use, aided by reading skills that are well established and put to constant use.

Applicants with below level reading skills, and essays that do not show the necessary communication skills for their grade level, should be given remedial classes in other schools. Reading activities and attention to any related problems must be addressed by the public school. They should be given the opportunity later to enter a pilot school after they have progressed enough to be qualified.

Students who are unwilling to follow rules and regulations should be barred from the school, until they are mature enough, and desirous of learning. Effective learning cannot take place where there is disorder. The pilot school is not intended to be punitive, nor to solve social problems. Students needing the latter should be directed to professionals who can help them. If qualified they may apply to enter after such problems are solved. They may also be placed in a remedial school if they need to learn basic skills.

It is not the nature of educators to give up on the uncooperative students, nor is it practical to do so. For that reason there are a few creative schools experimenting throughout the nation in an attempt to reach youth who have proven to be a problem to parents, educators and the judicial system. We read of Alternative Schools, Charter Schools, Correctional Schools, Pilot Schools, yet their characteristics differ too much to characterize them based on the above classifications. One commonality is that they are trial units, on a small scale, that serve for experimentation and testing.

IX. Evaluating and Record Keeping

Parents and their children will take responsibility for keeping records and for having them duplicated, and stored in a safe place. Backup records in different locations would be wise for if records are lost it will be necessary to take established tests of the subject matter, if available, or to write or give oral reports under supervision on each subject that will verify that studies were effectively completed.

Numerical and alphabetical symbols will not be used to measure the quality of a student's work. Records will not show progression of years of study as grade levels. They will only show credit for the reading done on any of the subjects in the school curriculum. They will also show the subjects a student has reported on, whether a report was a written, oral, or other presentation. The record will show the student's sources of acquired information, related thoughts and ideas.

In the absence of letter or number grades, a point system should be devised. A minimal credit would indicate that the student gave it cursory attention to learn related vocabulary, definitions and spelling, important people, places, dates and purpose of the study.

This permits a student to have a general knowledge of many subjects, yet not require an in-depth study unless it is a subject of more than average interest. If it does not arouse interest at the initial exposure the student will have other times to expand on any subject. This allows a student to gain a wide range of knowledge as he searches for information that captivates him or her. A study beyond the basic familiarity receives a higher point average.

Studying any subject to a degree of expertise would give the highest credit.

Quality of work should be improving with experience. Teachers, parents and students determine that quality by noting weaknesses and strengths in reports. Their observations focus on constructive comments. Expressing appreciation of what is done well, correcting and improving upon such things as errors in grammar, spelling, and sentence construction. The students take responsibility for seeking help, and correcting weaknesses observed.

X. The Curriculum

The list below is a guideline. The student must have variety in his or her choices. Other than that, each subject can be approached through its: history, biographies, culture, origin, location, philosophy, or other.

Required and elective subjects:

Psychology (human and animal behavior, feelings, mind and mental processes, etc)

Philosophy (principles for the conduct of life; principles that regulate the universe and underlie all reality)

Health (physical, mental, social and spiritual)

Mathematics (arithmetic, geometry, algebra, calculus, trigonometry, physics)

Science (systematized knowledge of nature, any branch as geology, oceanography)

Economics (production, distribution and consumption of wealth; related problems of labor, finance, taxation, etc.)

Government and Law (authority, rule, management, power and control)

Literature (the writings of a particular time, place or author)

Geography (surface of the earth, continents, countries, people, animals, natural resources, etc.)

English Language (Focus on review or study of needed grammar, punctuation, etc. as a student uses it in writing and speaking.)

Foreign Language

The Arts (music, painting, sculpture, gardening, culinary, construction, cabinet, metal, stonework, etc.)

When a student has covered the minimal material and also has a variety of subjects, which he/she has studied in depth, the student's records would contain certificates earned. The number of points will reflect the degree, depth or intensity the student has invested in each subject.

Secondary Schools and Community Centers

Centers of learning and sharing for all ages over fifteen years of age. Rooms in the building will be available for adult classes. Secondary students may attend some adult classes for credit. Responsible and capable younger students may also be approved to register for some adult classes.

Chapter 13

Gail A.K.A Sandy

Gail was on cloud nine on the drive home from the Apple A Day meeting. She had dedicated herself to teaching, twelve years ago. Her first classes had been so wonderful that each day she swept into the school building, flew effortlessly up the flight of stairs, surveyed her pleasant room, which was decorated with posters from exciting places in the Hispanic world. It was her home away from home. Her classroom faced east. The rising sun painted the sky every shade of rose and apricot. Miss Sanders was written in chalk at the top corner of a green chalkboard.

Soon the students would be coming in to pass the time, to get some help, or to get last night's homework assignments completed before the first bell rang.

She loved their youthful zest for life, their eagerness to learn. She shook her head in wonder, and smiled. Was she really being paid to do this? Learning and teaching were her passions.

She was known as Sandy to her friends and colleagues. The new name suited her appearance and bubbly personality. Her hair spilled in soft curls around her face in tones of gold and auburn. Her brown eyes were wide, eager to enjoy the beauty and excitement in her world.

What had happened to blight her perfect world of twelve years ago? Gradual change. The orderliness of her life turned upside down, and inside out. Well, no use to count her losses. The transfers to other schools and the need to teach subjects outside of her areas of expertise had not been problems. That had been a challenge. Often she kept just ahead of the students in the textbook. She read constantly, always alert to stimulating material to enlighten herself, and to share with students.

But about then a promising relationship with a very handsome and very demanding man in her life ended. He had given her an alternative. Him or her career. He complained that she didn't spend enough time with him. She was always correcting and grading papers. Always taking them with her on drives. Well, it would never have worked. He was too selfish. He couldn't accept her teaching career. And expecting her to give it up? What gall! Teaching was her life.

It was fortunate that she was so dedicated. She knew teachers who did not have to spend as many hours for preparation, and there were others who would not do it. A few had been teaching the same subject in the same way since their first assignment. Their notes, used for years, were now yellowed and dogeared. Even if she were not so driven to give her all, she could not have taught without updating her material and approach. Yes, it was challenging to teach new subjects, but it took more time and energy with every change.

But the most disturbing change during that time was a change in the attitude of students. They no longer had the interest in their studies. That varied with the age level, the neighborhood, the parental attitudes, the administration and faculty. Change was gradual but it was a distinct change in the whole society. An attitude that trickled down to the children. It began with only the high school students showing disinterest and disrespect. Then middle or junior high students mimicked the behavior of their older brothers and sisters. Until now, she was told by counselors, that even the elementary kids, as young as second and third grade, were violent, disrespectful, and disruptive.

It affected her morale. Her enthusiasm was waning. She was toying with the idea of a leave of absence, or some other escape. There was no longer joy and satisfaction in her work. She spent most of her energy, and much of her time on discipline in the classroom.

Tonight the meeting had stimulated her. She felt hopeful becoming a part of the solution. Many teachers and administrators would not share their frustrations outside of school. It seemed an admission that they could not do their job. Never would they admit that the students were doing less work, and learning less. Never would they want to give their principal the notion that they were unable to handle their classes.

The worst part was that many teachers were deceiving themselves about how much students were learning. To fail so many would result in parents and administrators blaming the teacher. So they altered grades. Oh yes, they had their justifications, nevertheless the grades they gave were lies. Lies they found ways to justify by watering down their expectations, and by rewarding behaviors that had once been requisites.

Sandy drove into her parking space under the building. She recalled the man at the meeting. Cliff, he'd said. The one who had a son who was so outgoing, and so curious about radio. She wondered if there was a wife and mother around. Sandy smiled wickedly. Not if the look Cliff had given her meant what she thought. Their eyes had met, and held position for several delicious seconds before they gave each other an appreciative, slow inspection, up, down, and sideways. She hoped she had understood that smile.

On the elevator, Sandy checked the time. Not too late to call Guy. One in the hand was worth two in the bush. She laughed at the analogy. She didn't know how to read him. Better to stay away from men who were in the divorce courts, or recently separated. What the heck? We have a mutual interest, and a lot to share now.

"Guy?"

A sleepy voice answered. "Who is it?"

"That depends. Did I wake you?"

"Yes and no. I was reading and dozed off for a moment. I haven't gone to bed yet. Is this Sandy?"

"In that case I'll admit it. I want to tell you how well it all went tonight. You and Igor Connifer did a great job answering questions. People were picking up the packets, and we have a basket of money. Donations I haven't counted yet. Are you okay?"

"Okay physically. Psychologically I'm a mess. Spent the afternoon in the lawyer's office. I don't even want to think about it."

That must mean, don't ask, she decided. "Divorce is always painful."

"It's not going to come to that. We're going to get counseling. Amy's really miffed, but I welcome it."

"Well, if you and I are both tired, guess this isn't the best time to discuss the meeting. Look, tomorrow is Sunday. Run over when you get up and we'll have some coffee and rolls. Might even make some pancakes, eggs and bacon . . . the works, then we can have brunch."

"Sounds great. Can I bring a friend?"

Sandy rolled her eyes.

"Amy is bringing Barry by about 8:30. Will that be okay?"

"Barry! Certainly." She sighed. "See you when you get here. G'night."

Why were all the men married, about to be married, breaking up, or trying to repair a marriage? Weren't there any single ones left? How about widowers? How about a rich, old widower?

Chapter 14

Miss Sanders to You

Dawn broke with an explosion of color that should have induced a symphony. Sandy reached to turn on music to get her in a mood to match. Six o'clock? Too early to get up on her day off, but not early enough to tidy up her apartment and be ready when Guy and his son Barry come for breakfast. Important to make it appear that this was her usual pattern, which it was not.

Her usual Sunday routine was to sleep late, roll out of bed prepared to lounge away the morning sipping coffee, munching toast and fruit while she read. Much of her life was spent in study, textbooks and classes, to further her teaching career. So important to prepare for whatever education was embracing at the moment. Now it was Special Education. From immigrants with second language difficulties to the physically and mentally handicapped. Now increasing numbers of kids were labeled as having "attention deficit disorder." Some were inclined toward violence. On and on it went.

Without a book to take her out of this time and space, she couldn't endure the present educational turmoil. Taking children out of classes to do remedial math, basic English grammar, vocabulary and spelling assured a future of continual catch-up.

Sandy gave the kitchen a hasty cleaning, and hid the living room clutter. She checked the groceries on hand. Lucky, she had what she needed. She prepared as much as she could in advance, ready to be cooked or heated for serving. She poured milk and juice and put the glasses in the refrigerator. She set the table.

She had a few seconds to run a brush through her naturally wavy hair, apply a pale color to her lips and cheekbones (no need to line her expressive eyes), and she was ready when the buzzer sounded.

"Come on up, you two," she called into the speaker, and pushed the button to release the lock on the lobby door. She estimated the time it would take the elevator to reach the fifth floor, and was headed down the hall to meet them when she smelled smoke and heard the crackle. In her haste she had not noticed a pile of paper smoldering on the other side of her apartment door. The elevator door slid open. No one was inside. The paper was now aflame.

Sandy's screams of "Fire!" brought an elderly woman running from an apartment. Sandy ran toward a fire extinguisher. Her neighbor threw the robe she was wearing over the flames and the heavy fabric smothered the fire.

No one else had heard their shouts or come to their aid. Both were trembling. The two strangers hugged each other, grateful for their success in extinguishing the fire, and now filled with fear and curiosity about who had started it. Who could wish them or others in their apartment building any harm?

"We've got to call 911," the woman said. "Come in my apartment."

"What if there are other fires downstairs?" Sandy said. "You call. I'll check for smoke or damage on the other floors, or-or-or an intruder."

She raced down the stairs, looking down each hallway in turn. Her heart pounded in time with the sound of her steps on the treads. Nothing seemed amiss. On the first floor some paper in front of the elevator door might have been dropped by the person who set the fire, she thought. The sound of tapping at the glass door startled Sandy. The sight of Guy and Barry peering in at her with big smiles filled her with relief. She raced to open the door, covering her face with her hands and trying to control her trembling.

"Come in. Come in," she chattered. They stared. She had been on the verge of tears before realizing that she didn't want to frighten Barry any more than she already had. After all, it did appear that the immediate danger was over and done with.

She turned, beckoning to them to follow her up the stairs to the neighbor's apartment. She tried, though breathless, to tell them about the fire. The woman was standing in her doorway, peering down the hall, when they reached Sandy's floor.

"She's here." The woman spoke into the phone. "Was everything downstairs all right?" She whispered. "They want to talk to you. They're sending a police car, and a fire truck." She gave no heed to Guy or Barry.

Sandy took the phone and perched on a footstool. "Yes. Gail Sanders. Apartment 59, Quaker Apartments, 3206 Prince Street . . . 547-3624." The sound of sirens pierced the silence. Guy told Barry to stay where he was while he ran down the stairs to the lobby to let the policeman in, and to wait for the fire truck.

"They've just arrived, thank you." Sandy handed the phone to the gray-haired woman, and patted her on the shoulder. "He wants to talk to you, Miss Risley." Sandy paused a moment to give Barry a hug, and to assure him that all was well now.

Barry's eyes were sparkling as he watched the policemen. He was mesmerized by the excitement. He held Guy's hand firmly but noting no fear and alarm in those he trusted, the boy relaxed and enjoyed the activity, while thinking of all he would have to share with Mommy and Papa.

Barry listened carefully to the interrogation while Sandy relayed what had happened. The police officer took notes, the firemen searched the area and examined the elevator, the unburned and charred pieces of paper, but found nothing.

Later, they indicated they would check for fingerprints in obvious places. A follow-up would include checking for any history of arson on the part of residents, and examining the owner's and manager's books.

The officers took Guy's name and noted that he had arrived shortly after the fire was discovered. Neither he nor his son had seen anyone in or near the building. The officers thanked him, and they returned to Gail and Miss Risley. "Had she received threats from anyone? Is there anyone she knows who might do this?" They asked.

All questions were answered in the negative. No clues . . . unless . . . the note Barry had seen pushed under Guy's door. Is Sandy also being targeted? Guy didn't want to alarm her, so he walked out with the police officer to tell him of the threats in that note. He explained that he and Sandy were members of Apple A Day. If there was a link connecting the two, it seemed wise to record it.

When they finally closed Sandy's apartment door behind them, they sighed. Guy was distressed to see his friend as a possible victim. He felt responsible, somehow, but he didn't say anything about the mysterious letter. Sandy slumped against the wall. Guy gave her a comforting hug.

The embrace was of great interest to Barry. He could not remember his mother and father showing affection. He sat quietly. Sandy was crying as Guy held her; he kissed away her tears and tried to reassure her that some nut had by chance rung her buzzer. Yes, of course arson was a serious offense. Maybe she should move away until the police caught the offender.

Guy and Sandy both noticed Barry's attentive observation. At that same moment they stepped away from each other. "Well, partner, I'll bet you could stand a hug right now, too. Pretty confusing, right? What do you make of it?"

"I'm hungry!" Barry said, showing a child's ability to adjust as soon as everyone around him seemed to be in control.

"Oh, of course you are. It must be very late. Here's a doughnut for you until I get breakfast on the table. Is there anything you don't like to eat?"

"Nothing we don't like, right, boy? Just give me a pan, and between us we'll have this show on the road in half the time."

His words were prophetic. The pancake batter was ready in an instant. Guy turned out beautifully browned hotcakes. Meanwhile Sandy had eggs and sausages done to order. Barry carried the tray of milk and juice glasses to the table without a spill. The already brewed coffee was poured. They all ate as if breakfast was the most important event of the morning.

"A feast fit for a king, wouldn't you say, your majesty?" Guy asked the boy, who was showing signs of being very satisfied. He looked very small enthroned in a chair that wrapped him in its mahogany arms.

Barry grinned. "Can I watch TV Sandy?"

"Miss Sanders to you, Barry," advised his father.

"He can call me Sandy, Guy. We're good friends. Aren't we Barry? Only my students call me Miss Sanders. You're a special friend."

"Tell Sandy thank you. She paid you a compliment because of your friendship, but we don't usually call adults by their first name." Guy shrugged. The old courtly ways were disappearing. What could he do?

Barry nodded knowingly. "Thank you, Miss Sanders." He grinned. "I dub you Sandy, queen of the court." He touched his spoon to the top of her head.

"That better not be the jelly spoon you're using, your Royal Highness."

They quickly stashed the dirty dishes in that magical twentieth-century implement, the electric dishwasher. Time to relax. Fortunately, Barry could entertain himself. He was seated at a table with old magazines, scissors, colored paper, and glue.

The two friends and associates were at a dead end in the discussion concerning the morning's puzzling happenings. So they shared their observations of last night's meeting. Sandy had done an excellent job of providing written information defining their criticisms and solutions to problems in the public schools. The subject was too involved, and complicated, to cover in one meeting.

"Guy, it was a wonderful meeting. Of course, the star last night was Igor Connifer. Wasn't he great? We were nervous about the impression he might make. I don't mean to sound snobbish, but if he hadn't come through with his speaking ability and information, well, any negative impression the audience had of him could have damaged our group in their eyes."

"You mean his rough as a cob personality and appearance?" Guy said. She nodded. "You're right. He didn't actually represent us, but it could have appeared so. He made that clear when he spoke. He left it open for us to make that decision whether to . . . hire him? . . . or ask him to donate his effort and equipment? He didn't sound like he was ready to do it for free, did he? What did you think about a radio station, his station, to get the word out?"

"Publicity is the only way we're going to be able to carry this off. Most of the media would tear us to shreds and set us up as weirdos then refuse to cover us. We'll have to have consistent information and ongoing discussion. The kind of radio station he described could do that. I'll bet he's great on the air. Some good music. Some selections to appeal to the people we're trying to reach."

"Whoa, girl! Now you do have me scared." He smiled.

"There's a great assignment right there. Just to decide which music will be acceptable to everybody. Igor played rock and roll before. A lot of people would turn him off with that music, and the message would be lost." He was overcome by her enthusiasm. He had seen her as efficient, but now her vigor excited him.

He paced, lost in thought. Then paused to stare at her. The thoughts he was about to share suddenly evaporated. He had never noticed how glowing her skin was. The spaghetti strap on her dress had slipped off her shoulder revealing a cleavage between slightly tanned breasts. Her legs tucked under her, limber as a teenager. He caught his breath, swallowed uncomfortably, and knew that she had felt the same . . . Well, he would be certain this didn't happen again.

He looked at his watch, pretending that it was running. It wasn't. He wore it out of habit intending to have it fixed. "Well, we've got to go. Have a million things to do."

The spell was broken. Thank God. That was all he needed, to complicate his life now.

"Guy, we must meet with the others and discuss this. I know it is hard now for you to give your whole thought to our group and our goals. If you want, I'll get on the phone and set a time and place ASAP. We have to get going with this while people are wound up, don't you agree?"

"I'd appreciate that." He got Barry's equipment in order and put it in his backpack. The boy looked about ready for a nap. "Give your new friend a hug, and tell her goodbye. Gotta go, boy."

His hustle and bustle activity did not fool Sandy. She held her arms out to embrace Barry, who dutifully and sleepily thanked her for breakfast. Guy moved quickly toward the door and thanked her for her hospitality.

He seemed to have forgotten the fire, and was already trying to forget much of what followed.

She closed the door behind them, stared at the empty apartment, and sighed.

Chapter 15

Memories

After she watched Guy and Barry drive away, flashbacks bouncing around in her memory refused to be shut out. She couldn't stand the silence and the nagging replay of the morning's events. Sandy picked up a sun hat, dark glasses, and a book, and drove to the park. It was the same park Ben often took Barry to.

Alf Benson and Gail Sanders lived at opposite ends of the park. Their paths had never crossed there in spite of the fact that Sandy went often to enjoy the nature walks, the lake, and the children on the playgrounds. Sometimes she felt lonely as she watched happy families, sweethearts, and elderly couples strolling hand in hand beneath the sturdy branches of old acacia and banyan trees.

Today she would not walk. She would read. It was her favorite way to escape thoughts she didn't want to deal with. Sandy hurried toward an empty bench in the shade. Out of the corner of her eye she noticed a young couple also headed that way. They paused and turned, recognizing that she would reach it first. Sandy arranged herself comfortably and opened the book where it was marked, but she couldn't concentrate.

She rummaged through her bag, looking for the notebook she always carried to jot down impressions, reminders and such. It helped her to retain ideas and pleasant memories. She would have preferred to share companionship with a close friend, but she had left friends behind in Montana, Wyoming, Colorado and San Diego. Therefore, she recorded her memories. There had been little time to make new friends, since this most recent move. Apple A Day, and the people involved were beginning to fill that emptiness.

As she wrote to put the AAD plans in motion, she also listed ideas she could use with junior and senior high school students. She wrote rapidly, preparing for the opening of a new school year. Then, memories of so many past schools and classes, sidetracked her current preparation. She continued to write anyhow, feeling a need to record the memories, whether good or unpleasant.

Sandy had once turned to substitute teaching when she was between class assignments. She gained insight into what was happening in many classrooms. Reading could not be assigned. Not enough books. Even if there were books, few students did assignments at home. They expected to be given class time. Sandy felt that time should be used to talk about important issues of the day.

Time, and the way it was spent, was of crucial importance in class. Time wasted at the beginning or end of each class could grow to an exorbitant loss during a semester. Consistent disruptive behavior was usually attributed to a small number of students. Besides being a distraction, half of the class then egged on the "entertainers" through laughter, then joined in with their own contributions to waste more time.

Teachers could at one time have controlled students with a raised eyebrow. That would have made students aware that it was time to settle down. But misbehavior was now so usual that many teachers had accepted it as the norm and they surrendered their position of authority to become their students' "pal".

The list of parents to be called grew longer as the semester progressed. Besides the disruptive students, there were the frequent absentees, and those who did not turn in assignments. Parents had to be notified when grades were going down. Teachers were criticized for not being able to deal with so many required conferences.

The business world sent trained counselors to schools to instruct teachers how to conduct their classes without missing a beat when students were out of order. How to deal with troublemakers. What to do, and especially what not to do when a student became violent.

Sandy would have preferred calling to congratulate the parents of the few in class who were always prepared, attentive, and mannerly.

Teachers' meetings addressed the problem. The conscientious teachers wanted to be able to send students out to administrators for discipline, because it was becoming a full-time job, eroding time and energy needed for teaching. Counselors were overloaded with students who wanted attention for negative behavior. There was no time left to help the well-behaved achievers solve problems they might have, or to give them praise and encouragement.

Her frustrating memories were spilling out. Recorded in her notebook. Too much negativity. Sandy regretted getting into the frustrations of the past. She wanted to do her best, to bring about the best in her students. This was not the way to go about it.

Sandy had wanted to work on constructive things for this new semester. She wanted to have the same excitement that used to delight her at the beginning of each school year. She, like so many teachers, felt that they were damned if they did and damned if they did not. They were getting burned out; some were just hanging in there until retirement. She would not let it happen to her.

Newly graduated education majors after a short time, sometimes even while completing their student teaching, redirected their acquired skills into the business or industrial world. Who could blame them?

Teachers experimented with all ways to reward, or bribe students for their work. Some permitted partying in class. That escalated as students lobbied for every imaginable reason to celebrate. Students learned the art of conning teachers, that is to say, bargaining. They offered to behave in exchange for party time. Class time was then used to socialize, eat snack foods, drink soda pop, and escape from studying. If the teacher held to the deal by canceling a "party" due to misbehavior it was bedlam in the class.

Some teachers became "screamers." They tried to shout the kids down. Sandy would not become a screamer, nor would she squander time and disregard her teaching responsibilities.

There were those teachers who showed videos almost every day, justifying it by choosing videos based on good literature. They allowed food and soft drinks in the class so the students would be lulled into feeling as if they were at a movie. Pizza was sometimes ordered and delivered, or a student was sent to pick one up.

Sandy watched the lazy clouds drifting overhead, she remembered a bookkeeping class she had substituted for. About half a dozen hefty young men were seated at computers. The other students followed their teacher's instructions to study a chapter and write answers to questions. Then Sandy noticed that those at computers were playing games, but not educational games. When she confronted them, they and their classmates assured her that it was a daily-acceptable behavior. Unbelievable! Sandy wrote, "I always wondered what grade each game player received for the class. Did they receive credit for honoring an agreement with the teacher to not disturb him, or the class?"

It was a student who told Sandy that his best classes involved two teachers combining their classes to watch the World Series on television. They learned all about baseball, an important cultural symbol, he told her.

Many times Sandy had substituted for one of the most respected teachers in the school. The teacher was known to be conscientious, hardworking, and resourceful. She was given hard-core eighth-grade students for remedial English. Class activities ranged from everybody taking a daily walk around the baseball field to a project of painting their own chairs. Their attention span apparently did not allow for much work in the exercise book.

Sandy felt sorry for the few students who were put in the class because English was their second language. They had not learned enough to function in a regular English class. They shook their heads in disbelief at the behavior of their American classmates.

And the painted chairs? The chairs were shabby, but serviceable to begin with. The students used primary colors to paint designs, initials, shapes, words and a kind of graffiti. They were not painted with care. It was busy work assigned by a teacher and an administrator at their wits' end.

She sighed and shook her head. Who would believe all of this if she told parents, or protested? Every teacher should begin a teaching career as a substitute. If that didn't discourage them nothing else would. Well, she had lasted through it all.

Now she was in the best place to bring about changes in public education. The purpose of Apple A Day, Inc. was to find solutions, not to blame any group, be it teachers, administrators, parents or children. Those four groups should be working together to get at the real problems. In fact they were all victims of the educational system.

Physically drained, Sandy sighed, stretched, and looked lazily around the territory she had claimed in the park today. She had not taken time to relax or rest. The couple that had been interested in this bench was stretched out on the grass, eyes closed, embracing, talking and occasionally laughing. Another group was singing to the strumming of a guitar.

Near the bushes, an untidy looking man was sleeping. Homeless? Probably. Sandy's jubilant mood, inspired by the tranquility of the park, changed suddenly. She was uncomfortable about returning to her apartment, but felt she should before darkness fell.

She looked around as she approached her car, keys ready. A runner was coming toward her. A man? She hesitated. She watched the runner out of the corner of her eye until she was sure his path was not in line with her blue coupe. Quickly, she moved to unlock it and slipped in behind the wheel.

In a matter of minutes, she was parked in the garage under the apartments. She didn't move from behind the wheel until she gave her attention to every shadow, each dark corner. All of her senses were alert.

"Please let the elevator be there waiting." It was. Her footsteps beat a lively staccato as she ran down the hall and slipped the ready key in the lock. In one motion she was on the other side of the door, panting.

The red alert on her answering machine caught her attention.

"Sandy, please call me as soon as you arrive home. I am concerned for you."

She was so grateful to hear Guy's voice at that moment, and pushed numbers she had memorized. Guy answered.

"Sandy, I should have asked if you had some place to go to tonight."

"Why, no. I'm home now. I won't answer the buzzer from the entry door. I'll be all right. How nice of you to be concerned."

"It isn't that simple. We don't know who set the fire, or why. They could do it again. If this is an arsonist, there's the possibility of a bigger fire, or one that will smoke before it flames. That's even more dangerous. Who do you know that you can stay with for a while? Maybe it would be wise to move." He hesitated, then blurted . . . "in case this was someone who was directing anger toward the AAD people."

Sandy sank down to kneel on the carpet and put her head on the chair seat. "Guy, I don't know a soul here that I could approach to take me in. My family and friends are all out of state. You really feel that it is dangerous to stay? I'll admit that today I was scared as hell to go out, and then to return."

"Well, if you can't think of anyone else you are welcome to stay here as long as it's necessary. I'll take the couch to sleep on while you are here."

"Are you crazy? You're a good friend to suggest it, but can you imagine how this could screw up your reconciliation with your wife?"

"Yeah. It occurred to me, but people, including Amy, will just have to understand. You and I have never given anyone the slightest reason to gossip about us. We'll make it clear to everyone why you are here so it won't appear we are hiding anything."

"What about Barry?"

"Honesty is the best policy. Barry is the least likely of anyone to think anything is unusual. Get some things packed. I'll be right over. Stay in your apartment until I get there. I'll get you to your car, then I'll follow you to my place. No argument. We're leaving as soon as I hang up."

"You're wonderful. I really am very ill at ease about staying here alone." She hung up the phone, on the verge of tears.

Chapter 16

Sandy's Notebook

Barry was full of questions. "Why is Sandy living here?" He listened, full attention, to anything about the fire. The word fear was never spoken, but he saw it in their eyes. He sensed the intensity when they talked, and the way they moved. He was curious. Experience had taught him to be quiet and observe. When he asked questions, grownups sometimes hushed one another.

Barry picked up the receiver on the first ring. "Hello." the child shouted, happy for the diversion. "Papa guess what . . . Sandy moved into our apartment." A long pause followed while Guy shaking his head, took long, hurried strides across the room, and took the phone from him.

"Da-a-ddy. I'm talking to Papa. He was asking me a question," the boy protested.

Guy covered the mouthpiece. "Yes, Barry, I'm sure he was. You're going to have to learn some telephone manners."

"Dad. How's it goin'?" Guy tried to sound casual . . . Silence. "Dad, are you there?" Guy pulled the long cord into the bedroom, and closed the door for what promised to be a long explanation.

"Are you going to be my mother?" Barry directed his question to Sandy. He knew that he had to get answers while his Daddy was out of the room.

Sandy motioned to him "Barry, come here." The boy hesitated, and then moved to where Sandy sat. She felt uncomfortable. Leaning over she took both of his hands in hers. "You have a mother, Barry. You don't need more than one mother," she hesitated. "Did you want me to be?"

"No", he said, shaking his head briskly. "I just want my mommy. I wish she'd come here to stay."

"Well, you and I, we're friends, remember? I'll only be staying a little while."

"Are you scared to go home?"

"Yes, a little bit, but I'll be okay, Barry. I'll get over it, and very soon I'll move back there."

"Good."

Guy returned to the room. "Well, I don't know how Dad really feels about all this, but he tries to stay out of my affairs, uh . . . my life," he corrected his Freudian slip. "He'll be fine with it."

Guy had put clean sheets on the bed, and had a folded set for him on the couch so it was to no avail that Sandy resisted taking his room. "Barry can sleep on the sofa cushions, on the floor. He goes back to his Mother tomorrow."

"We'll have a little talk before you leave, son." Guy had no idea what he would say to Barry. He couldn't say, "Don't talk about it". He would be bubbling over to spill it all.

Late afternoon and evening, the plan was dinner and board games at Ben's apartment. Sandy, refused the invitation to join them, and stayed at Guy's place. She curled up in Guy's armchair to finish her planning.

She always spoke courteously to children. Never talked down to them, not even to elementary level kids, as some adults do. She considered what she would say about their responsibility. She dated the page and wrote. "Subjects of discussion" as a heading.

It seemed that growing up too soon is a problem in today's world. But they are not growing in constructive ways that make them more capable. Instead, many children are experimenting with drugs, cosmetics, with wearing revealing clothing, body piercing and sex. Many indulge in one of the most damaging and disruptive behaviors in our youth, the power struggles with all authority figures in our society.

Sandy's muscles ached from intense concentration. She stretched shoulders, neck, legs, and fingers. Then relaxed with a few deep breaths, and wrote:

We are allowing our youth freedom to choose many things they are not ready for. Why would anyone be reluctant to have them make choices about their reading and study material?

Their future is swooping in so fast and clashing with yesterday's patterns of life. Predictions are almost impossible in the midst of such complexity. We must make intelligent guesses. The pit of unpreparedness is dark and deep.

Our students will need creative minds capable of problem solving to cope with, alter, prevent, or improve, thereby to avoid potential problems. We cannot rely on technology to provide wisdom.

The public would argue that youth will take the easy path, not the industrious way, if given responsibility for their education. She disagreed. They would be guided by what interests them.

Sandy was scribbling her notes so eagerly that she took no notice of the time. She looked up when she heard the key in the lock.

"Hello roommate. Get a lot done?" Guy smiled at her across the room. Barry was asleep on his shoulder, making groggy, unintelligible sounds as Guy put him on the cushions beside the couch.

"Yes, and no." Sandy replied. "Nothing is specific. Much of the night has been spent unraveling ideas spinning around in my head. Some are original. It's the way I've always taught my students. Much of it I've taken from our meetings, of the way we hope to change the schools."

"You mean, the way we *intend* to change the schools, don't you? Mind if I read it tonight? I'm not going to be able to sleep for a while anyhow."

"Not at all, Guy. I'm ready for sleep. I'm setting up plans for an Apple A Day meeting as soon as we can do so. Will you be able to work it in, say . . . mid week?"

"You are all taking so much of the responsibility, and doing a great job. I'll be back with you as soon as I can work it in. Thanks, Sandy." He was reminded of the work he had stuffed into a desk drawer when Ota entered. The work was still there waiting for him.

Chapter 17

The Next Week

It was awkward the first night in Guy's apartment, and for a few days following, but he and his guest both tried to be considerate of the other. Their waking hours differed enough to ease the morning rush. Guy worked many nights at the office, so most days their paths did not even cross. They communicated by notes if necessary.

Because their organization was now in the news, the tail, the media that is, was now wagging the dog. They had intended to enlarge the group gradually, as each pitched in to do what was needed. However, the publicity brought interested people out of the woodwork. They had lists of those ready to join them. When the pot is boiling, interest is high. It must be done now. Meanwhile, the founders had to make major decisions so that the organization was already in motion, with established leadership, rather than having the whole plan bog down with confusion, and misinformation at the first major meeting.

The week following was productive. Sandy had arranged a meeting on short notice to discuss whether to go forward with a radio station backing them, with Igor broadcasting. Guy could not make it. Noah offered his apartment for the few members who had initiated the Apple A Day plan and who had written mission statements.

It was a lively meeting. "What if" became the most repeated interrogative in their discussion. No one seemed to question Igor's ability, once Ike told them what he knew about the man. Igor had been somewhat of a loner, but he directed his efforts to help others. He had just fallen into the laps of their AAD group. He had been an undercover police officer in California. His long hair, beard, and "tacky clothes" had been an asset in undercover work.

A major problem was the license. They would look into that. Igor had his own equipment, but might need additional equipment or replacements. Someone was assigned that responsibility. There was still the question of a monetary source to support it, and what about income for Igor?

Wednesday the Fourth

When they met with Igor the following evening, his beard was trimmed. His hair was still long and tied back. He had replaced his jeans and flannel shirt with shorts and a colorful cotton shirt purchased at the local thrift store. His white legs marked him as a tourist.

He provided a tape of some of his radio programs broadcast to help the homeless. The listeners appreciated how he handled the callers and guests during his talk show. He was firm, but never rude or crude. He was witty, without sacrificing the seriousness of the situation.

He was too young to be a retiree, so, yes, he would need some income. He had a small disability pension from former employment. He could hold down a part-time job or start a small "fix-it" business out of his living quarters, he said.

They didn't think it would be appropriate for him to be living as he was now, among the many homeless here. Maybe he could stay at the YMCA for awhile. His equipment was en route to the islands by ship. It would give them time to work out details, to find a place for him to live, and to set up the radio equipment. They shook hands all around. Igor was on board. Now, they needed an angel to supply the money to get started. They needed a business manager. The time had come to vote for officers and establish committees.

They would draw on the lists of names from the meeting they had opened to the public. Hard to believe they had moved so far and fast with so few of them to start out, but by necessity AAD was expanding. A meeting must be arranged to vote for leaders, and hopefully some of the original members would be voted in. It was unacceptable that the ideas they had already agreed upon might be tossed out. Their creative, and probably controversial, ideas must be presented, and yes, they must sell them to the public. They had no illusions that it would be easy to alter the timeworn patterns of education.

Thursday the Fifth

"For too long we have been hearing educators and politicians expound on problems without solving them. This is a new era with unique problems. Our children differ from those of past generations. We must teach to their strengths. They will measure up to our expectations, and respond favorably to wise and effective guidance."

Sandy took notes on the discussion. She highlighted parts to include in her speech to students on the first day of the school year. Principals in other schools had staggered assembly times to allow her to speak to their students. She promised to give them an invigorating, inspiring talk to instill pride and promise into their studies. She would call it "The Latitude of Attitude."

Later in Guy's apartment Sandy typed out the minutes of the meeting and the handout Guy had suggested would be informative. The bulk of the notes she had taken were to keep the group oriented in their mission.

Statement of Intent To Improve Public Education.
In Regard to Students' Responsibilities

Latitude: *Shows the extent, scope, or range of applicability. Freedom from narrow restrictions.*
(Well, that certainly applies to what Apple A Day wants to accomplish. There is no limit to what students can accomplish if they are put in charge of their education.)

Attitude: *A feeling, a tendency or orientation, especially of the mind.*
(Which is so often a negative force, but if students can be made to understand the importance of being positive, it could empower them toward enrichment and achievement. The attitude of most of our youth needed a lot of attention, she agreed.)

Orientation: psychology *the ability to locate oneself in one's environment with reference to time, place, and people.*
(A very clear goal to guide students in educational needs.)

Tendency: *An inclination to proceed in some direction, or to some point, end, or result.*

(Unfortunately, most youth are given so little guidance and discipline that they have a tendency to drift rather than to proceed in any direction toward established goals.)

Considering its depth of meaning, "The Latitude of Attitude" applied.

A positive, constructive attitude is productive in the search for paths through which we must travel to broaden our education. We want to be free to reach out where our interests and curiosity now lead us because that will be the most joyful journey available. We most certainly do not want to be restricted by time tables, or schedules. Our success is assured if we are permitted to go at our own pace, which is likely to be faster within a well-planned curriculum.

Each century has made it increasingly imperative that we understand our world, our community, our nation, and ourselves. The environment we must learn about is the world at large, and its people.

"Yuck," Sandy groaned. "Sounds like I'm talking to the School Board, and they wouldn't get it either."

She wadded that up and pitched it into the wastebasket.

Sandy summed up what she hoped to convey to the students if their discussion showed they were in accord with the organization's plans. Everything depended on their attitude. She counted on the better students to feel favorable toward it. If they did not, then AAD Inc. might as well fold up its tents (or tenets) and return to the past. Business as usual . . . or complete and eventual decay.

Another false start. Another paper in the basket. Then she chose her words carefully. Would they listen?

"Today you are here because you are about to start on a new path. Have you chosen this path, or are you here because someone, parents probably, have placed you here as we might place a token on a game board? Are you here because someday you will have a piece of paper called a diploma if you attend each day until then? Do you have a goal beyond that time? Do you have a goal other than a grade for this semester? It is never too soon to have goals, or dreams for your future.

"Today decide where you are going this school year. How will this year prepare you for your future? The vehicle that carries you along that path is education, or learning. What makes education move along the path is 'attitude'. Attitude empowers the vehicle of education. Just as a car is powered by good gas, education needs attitude, a good attitude to get you where you are going. Good gas and good attitude move you toward goals. Bad gas and bad attitude leaves you at the side of the road, going nowhere. Who would put bad, or watered down, gas in a car? Who would begin a new semester without the enthusiasm and expectation that are products of a good attitude?

"This school year start training your attitude to be positive. Positive, the opposite of negative, means looking for the best. The best you can give, and the best you can gain. Train that attitude to be wise. Wise is better than smart. Smart means that you have a good brain. Wise means that you are using your brain, making decisions the best you know how. What good is a brain that is fueled by a bad attitude?"

Better! At least it's a start.

Chapter 18

Miss Sanderson's Lecture

"Welcome back, Surfers." Sandy went right into the introduction. The stage lights blinded her. She wished she could watch the students' faces. The analogy comparing education and a vehicle to an attitude and gas as the power that moves both forward held their interest.

"You each received a poem written by Charles Osgood. We're going to read it together. As we read, think about it very seriously. If we pay attention to Mr. Osgood's message and heed his concerns, this may be better than a pretty good year. It may be the best you have ever experienced.

"Stand up, please. This is worth your best effort. Read along in a natural voice. Don't shout. Don't mumble." There was a rustle of sounds and shuffling. She waited in silence. "And the title is . . .

A PRETTY GOOD EDUCATION

There once was a pretty good student,
Who sat in a pretty good class
And was taught by a pretty good teacher,
Who always let pretty good pass.

He wasn't terrific at reading,
He wasn't a whiz-bang at math.
But for him, education was leading
Straight down a pretty good path.

He didn't find school too exciting,
But he wanted to do pretty well,
And he did have some trouble with writing,
And nobody had taught him to spell.

When doing arithmetic problems,
Pretty good was regarded as fine.
Five plus 5 needn't always add up to be 10,
A pretty good answer was 9.

The pretty good class that he sat in
Was part of a pretty good school.
And the student was not an exception,
On the contrary, he was the rule.

The pretty good school that he went to
Was there in a pretty good town.
And nobody there seemed to notice
He could not tell a verb from a noun.

The pretty good student in fact was
Part of a pretty good mob.
And the first time he knew what he lacked was
When he looked for a pretty good job.

It was then, when he sought a position,
He discovered that life could be tough.
And he soon had a sneaky suspicion
Pretty good might not be good enough.

The pretty good town in our story
Was part of a pretty good state,
Which had pretty good aspirations,
And prayed for a pretty good fate.

There once was a pretty good nation,
Pretty proud of the greatness it had,
Which learned much too late,
If you want to be great,
Pretty good is, in fact, pretty bad.

by Charles Osgood
"The Osgood File", copyright 1986, CBS Inc.

Speaking the words into the microphone, Sandy controlled the pace
and gave emphasis to the meaning by reading slowly, and pausing at the

end of each line to let the meaning sink in. It spoofed the sing-song tempo of the light-hearted limericks that Osgood had imitated, but she wanted the students to recognize the serious intent of the writer.

She paused a bit longer at the commas, and changed her tone of voice for the last five lines. She intended to make it sound ominous. She intended to make it sound menacing. She intended to make them realize that this was a warning, a prediction of the future, unless they responded by altering their attitudes.

The improvement of public education did not stand a chance without the youth being included in the project. Yes, it would be an immense project, and the immensity of it was due to the need to gain the confidence of students, to instill confidence in themselves as well as confidence in the adult world.

The auditorium was silent when they finished reading. A few giggles came from a few of the youngest students. The rest were hushed. They stared at Miss Sanders. "Sit down, please.

"Very well done. Welcome back. What we just read together is an introduction to a project that is going to involve our community of adults who are greatly concerned for your future. For your future determines the future of our country, which then has great effect on the future of our planet. Do you see how very important you are?

"All projects begin with the germ of an idea, like a tiny seed. The results of that idea grow outward, and upward without limits. It requires faith and persistence to nourish an idea, so that it grows and blossoms like a flower. Your community, your parents, and your teachers have faith in you. We have enough faith in you to include you as coworkers in the project ahead.

"And the best prepared will have positive attitudes. Those who expect the best of the future will be systematically, directing themselves toward all that will be constructive.

"Thank you all for your attention and participation today. Someday, after we see results from our increased effort in education, we will rewrite the poem we read. It will then read . . .

> There once was a <u>very good</u> student,
> Who sat in a <u>very good</u> class,
> And was taught by a <u>very good</u> teacher,
> Who would not let "pretty good" pass.

"Congratulations on a very good start today. You are excused to go to your class."

Chapter 19

On the Air

"Good morning, Hawaii. Welcome to the birth of KABC, your station. Handling the equipment today is Kirk Collins. This is Igor Connifer, your host. You are the first listeners to KABC, a station dedicated to revising public education on our island. We have a long way to go. We are not intimidated by that fact. Success begins with the first steps. This is your station to express your ideas, approval, or disagreement with those you hear on our programs."

Noah had come with Guy to witness the first broadcast. He was happy to be in the background after some frantic weeks getting the equipment set up. Igor's equipment arrived, but getting the permits and ordering other equipment from the mainland kept them all up in the air until everything came together. By following Igor's instructions, Noah, Ike, Kirk, and his father furnished the manpower necessary. Besides the radio equipment, they constructed a roof for shelter and a shed with shelves for tapes and other storage. What was just an idea Ike had voiced weeks ago was now a reality. They were "on the air" with the magic of radio.

Igor's voice interrupted Noah's thoughts about the preparation that led to this moment.

"We will intersperse talk with music to lighten your steps. Try a twirl and a fox trot across your kitchen floor. Enjoy as you go about your daily tasks. Call in. Tell us your favorite musical selections. We want to know the music you like to live by. We will narrow them down. The selection getting the most votes will be our theme."

Igor grinned, and turned toward the young man at his side, who had just started a musical tape. It was a peppy tune the youth did not recognize.

"This is our debut, Kirk. How does it feel?" The youth smiled back and nodded. He had been coached by Igor on the dos and don'ts of radio broadcasting, and was overly cautious now, in fear of making any wrong moves.

"Hey, you're not going to freeze up on me, son. I'm depending on you to take over the afternoon through early evening shows as soon as we get going. Don't worry, I won't put you on the spot until we go through many shows together. You'll get used to the equipment, and feel comfortable with it before you take over."

"Just can't believe this is really happening. I'm ready whenever you think I am."

The man smiled, and congratulated himself for recognizing the potential of this seventeen-year-old. They were going to get along fine. Just fine. The music ended.

Igor's voice created an image in the listener's mind. To women he would sound like Tom Sellek. To men, he sounded like a cross between Edward R. Murrow and John Wayne. None of those images fitted Igor.

"The time is 9:00 A.M. Listen in, everyone out there. KABC isn't just to lift your spirits with upbeat tunes. We are here to dedicate ourselves to a cause, that of public education. I want to introduce you to a local citizen in your community who is determined to turn this island's educational system upside down and backwards, if necessary, to educate our youngsters. Guy Benson. Morning, Mr. Benson. Just who do you represent?"

"Good morning, Mr. Connifer. Congratulations on your first day of broadcasting, and thanks for giving me and Apple A Day Incorporated a chance to make our cause better known."

"Forgive me, Mr. Benson, but the name Apple A Day sounds frivolous. The 'Incorporated' on the other hand gives it some dignity."

"We hope it gets a lot of attention. We kept it simple intentionally. We are concerned citizens who are ready to do whatever it takes to provide the best education for our children. Today I am not going to speak about what is wrong with our attempts to educate. Nor, am I going to blame, point fingers, or accuse anyone or any group for the condition of our schools. We are determined not to concentrate on the ineffectiveness of our educational system. We are working toward what is right for children of the twenty-first century."

"Are you referring only to the schools on this island?"

"No. Our research shows that we have inherited the same problems endemic in all of our states. Our group has put all the problems and inadequacies aside as realities that exist, and we will not be deterred by political ploys, unrealistic fears, and by blame. Nor will we be held back by the traditionalists who insist on spinning their wheels in the ruts of worlds long past. They provide no intelligent solutions to carry us into the future."

"Sounds like you have taken on a massive task if you intend to improve schools all over the USA."

"Change, for us, starts right here on the island of Hawaii. We are taking one step at a time."

"And that is . . .?"

"We will start with the students who want to learn. They have been ignored while all attempts to improve, have focused on the many students classified as needing 'Special Education'."

"Excuse me. Do you resent the Special Ed programs?"

"Not if they are doing their best to mainstream students whenever possible. There is a need for many specialized kinds of education."

"Explain 'mainstream'."

"Some kinds of special education should be temporary. Then, when students are able to function, they should return to regular classes. That's called 'mainstreaming'."

"How do you propose to bring about improvement in education?"

"Briefly, we will choose students with the following characteristics:

A. Curiosity, and the drive to move forward.

B. Reading skill adequate for the grade they are entering.

C. An adequate to good vocabulary for the grade they are entering.

D. A positive, respectful attitude toward self and others.

E. A blend of self-confidence and trust in their mentors."

"That's all, sir? That doesn't seem like you are asking too much of students.

"Mull that over a bit, folks, while we take a musical break." Igor switched off the mike, and turned to Guy. "Okay, partner. We don't have a script. Where are we going with this? We can hope that people call in with questions, or I can throw you some."

"Both. Let's see if we can get some listeners calling in. They don't even know you are out here until you get established, so if we get no calls, it's up to you to keep the ball rolling. Ask me anything, and we'll both keep our fingers crossed."

As if on cue, the phone rang. "Station KABC." Igor said proudly.

"What is this nonsense? And what is that idiot talking about? I'm an educator starting my sixteenth year of teaching. Where does he think I am going to find this ideal group of students he is talking about?"

"Hang on there, partner. I want you to ask Mr. Benson on the air." Igor signaled Kirk to end the music. "Okay, folks. This is Igor Connifer. We are back, and we have an educator with fifteen years of teaching experience. He has a question for Mr. Guy Benson. (Kirk, give them the phone number over your mike.)" Igor switched the caller on. "Go ahead, sir. Repeat your question."

Guy waited eagerly while the educator fumed.

"That's a good question, caller. There must be a lot of burned out teachers starting the school year who agree with you. We are asking for what is necessary. It is only a guess. We expect to find these qualities in less than fifty percent of our public school students, but with those assets and with dedicated people to guide them, there is no limit to how far their education will escalate."

"Thank you for your call, sir. I can understand your frustration, because you will not find such a class facing you each day. Would you say though that half of your students have some of the qualities I mentioned . . . say, adequate reading ability and vocabulary?"

"Yes, but they are so strong-willed and overconfident, and intent on showing their disregard for learning that I doubt they are curious . . . at least they try hard to convince us they are not. Trust? I don't think they trust anyone anymore. But you didn't answer me."

"My answer is that you are right, caller. We must have a reshuffling to separate the students who want to learn, who are ready to learn, from influences that reduce them to the level of classmates who do not have those qualities. We must allow the cream to rise to the top. They provide the ingredient we need to transform education into a productive force. We are cheating the cream of our youth. We are wasting our most precious commodity. We are destroying ourselves by allowing the schools to continue as they are now."

Igor was dancing a little jig of joy. This is why he loved this work. Especially when it aroused this much passion.

"There is another caller on line. Go ahead, Beth." It was Kirk's voice. Igor was helping to field the calls, and directed his young helper to cut the chaff when one caller became repetitious, and to bring in new blood.

"This sounds like a very heartless and undemocratic way to educate. What about the children who need help with their reading, and those who need help for many other reasons?"

"I did not say that we are in favor of abandoning them. We feel that they also will progress more favorably in other ways. They are being helped more than in any other society, at any other time in history. And many of them are turning their backs to opportunity, for reasons I won't go into now. The top students should spend part of their time to help teach the slower children. Teaching is another way of learning."

"What about the 'gifted and talented' program?" Beth asked.

"It is better than nothing. With the right guidance, it could be good.

We are not convinced that they are as challenged as they should be. Perhaps there are many who are gifted or talented who are not included in that class. Perhaps there are some included for reasons other than their capability. Let's say that they have 'connections'. I don't believe we can generalize about them, but if they really are exceptional, then they will welcome our program, because it is challenging."

"Well, you haven't told us very much. What are you going to require of administrators and teachers?"

"Ah! Thank you, Beth, for that question," interrupted Igor. "Thank you, Guy Benson. I'm pleased to tell our radio audience that this will be an ongoing subject on station KABC. Tune in tomorrow. Tell your friends and neighbors. If you are interested in joining Apple A Day, Inc., this is a community endeavor to improve our public educational system. KABC is dedicated to this purpose. Igor Connifer signing off."

The three broadcasters stared at each other and smiled, pleased with their first broadcast to the community. Noah joined them, and they shook hands all around.

"Let's work up a rough plan for tomorrow. We had callers hanging on the line today just waiting for a chance to get at you." Igor rubbed his hands together. He grabbed the stub of a pencil and a grocery sack to write on. "Okay. Teachers next? What kind of teachers do we need for this program?" He wrote as Guy spoke:

1. "We need teachers who can inspire, be alert to the best qualities of each student, and willing to listen and draw students out, until the young people intuit their own questions, when possible, or the teacher directs the student to materials where questions and answers can be found.

2. "We need teachers who will lecture less, and who will require their students to read, speak, write, and listen more."

Chapter 20

KABC

"Good morning neighbors. Igor speaking to you from KABC. Our guest Guy Benson is here to continue sharing with you the philosophy of Apple A Day, Incorporated, and to expand on plans to revise our way of thinking about public education. My right-hand man, Kirk Collins, will give you the phone number while I put on 'Teach Me Tonight'. We'll be right back."

Guy and Kirk were discussing a copy of 'A Pretty Good Education'. Guy had found it taped to the door. A note from Sandy said that she was going to use it, and that he might want to read it on the air.

"Kirk, this poem looks good. Want to read it to our community?" Igor wanted the boy to get all the exposure possible.

After a hasty reading to himself, Kirk nodded, smiling. Guy instructed him to pause between lines, since it was a lot for the listener to digest if he read too fast. When the musical break ended, Kirk read it beautifully.

It was a good lead into the subject Guy was to discuss today. "Teachers in our public schools." After the final two lines, Kirk paused for effect.

Guy waited just the right amount of time to let it sink in, but not enough to allow listeners to change the station. "Good morning. That was Kirk Collins, who volunteers his time on KABC before and after school." Igor was answering phone calls that were beginning to come in. Guy indicated he would take the first call.

"Hello. It's my first year teaching school. Are you using Mr. Osgood's poem to say that the teachers are to blame for the children being unable to do good work? I'm teaching second grade. It's demoralizing to hear this when I'm just getting started."

"I told the listeners yesterday that I am not here to blame. There is no one factor responsible, and it's too late to spend time and thought on it. What I do want is for all of us to work together to make our public schools the best they can be. Mr. Osgood points out that we are a long way from that.

"I'm glad you called this morning. From our observations, the teachers who are getting the best results are the ones in the early grades. Children are being taught to read and to do basic arithmetic. We have seen some very creative procedures in elementary school. Up to a certain level, the children seem to progress very well. Then something happens to many of them. At some point their attitudes change, their efforts diminish, and the results are defeating. They turn negative, disinterested. Is it that they are discouraged? Is it that they are lazy? Are they reflecting problems at home?" Guy paused.

"I don't know, but you're right. The reasons vary with each child. I do hear that the upper elementary grades have more problems with the children's attitudes and behavior than we have. That's why I chose elementary grade levels to teach. So far, I like it, but we are beginning to have wayward, disruptive kids as early as third and fourth grades. You are right in your appraisal. Do you have the solutions to the problems?"

"We are working on them. We can use your help and want to wish you a successful first year. Thank you for calling."

Guy continues. "I have known many teachers, and we are fortunate that they are so dedicated. If teachers were paid only the minimum wage, based on the excessive hours they devote to their career, they would earn more than the salaries they now receive. We owe the dedicated teachers our thanks and a salary commensurate with that of other professionals."

(Kirk announces Jess on the line.)

"You criticize the schools, praise the teachers, and I just don't get it. What do you want teachers to do?"

"Thank you for calling, Jess. We want teachers to give students experience using all of the communication skills they are learning. Many people in the past had very little actual schooling, but by using the skills they learned, they educated themselves.

"Teachers need to do less of the work. Students need to do more. Our students are not self-impelled, but they will be if learning becomes a joy to them. Teachers, parents, and the community need to be there to guide and inspire our students. They are needed to read and listen to student reports on research, ideas, and feelings. As early as possible, students should be allowed to select subjects they wish to pursue."

Igor signaled that it was time. "Thank you, Mr. Benson, and thanks for calling, Jess. A caller is on the other line. Ask your question, Grace."

"I'm a mother of three children. I was so shocked at your last statement that I forgot what I wanted to say. You really think that children are capable of choosing their own subjects?"

"Yes, of course. It would have to fit into the curriculum. There still has to be a base. But they should be allowed to choose their own reading material related to what they are studying. Say the subject is American History. Wouldn't you prefer to choose the period you want to read about? Then everyone can share their research with classmates, and they will have learned about several time periods. They practice reading and listening, plus writing and speaking."

"But they might miss out on some things if they choose at random like that," Grace protested.

"A school can't teach all information available anyhow. How do we prioritize?"

Igor intervened. "Thank you, Grace. Ray is on line. Go ahead, Ray."

"What do you think about the long lists of vocabulary and spelling words some teachers assign? My tenth-grade son comes home with long lists to study, write, and rewrite. He has words on that list that I've never seen or heard in my whole life."

"I don't really want to judge the value of those assignments, only to say that a student who reads and writes extensively has an advanced vocabulary. Misspellings can be caught in the writing of reports. A teacher, or the student himself, can make a list of spelling words that are a problem to him."

"Folks, this is Igor interrupting. Avery is asking some very good questions about reading. Ask your question, sir."

"I wish you would tell me how to get a kid to read. I could tie mine in a chair with a book in his hand, and stand over him, and he still won't read. What's more, neither of them can write legibly or grammatically. What magic are you going to use to boost them to the level of skill you're requiring to enter your pilot school? He's a dumb (bleep). He's in fifth grade, and I have one in tenth grade, who's just like him, that I don't even bother with anymore."

Guy scowled. "Well, I'm sorry you feel that way about your son, because I'm sure he has some good qualities you can focus on.

"I could ask if you or your wife have ever read to them. If they are around people who read, it is never too late for them to develop an interest in it. So, do you and your wife read a lot?"

"I think you're trying to be insulting, so I won't bother to answer that. I think you and your apples all have a screw loose."

"One question I do want to answer. There's no magic, my friend, just heavy doses of high expectations, constant exposure to interesting materials, and continuous involvement. Liberally sprinkle on praise and love for their achievements and you will see them reap the resultant feelings of confidence and self-respect. You will notice an ever-increasing acquisition of knowledge and wisdom."

Igor gave the signal to Guy to sum up, because the end of program was approaching.

"The amount of reading should be endless. Allow them to skip over the material that bores them, material they may not understand. If that information is crucial, a teacher or mentor can explain it.

"Don't try to make them experts on everything they read. An awareness of its existence is often enough. It can be expanded upon at some future time if need be. The students' notes need not be excessive, rather a record of what was understood, and considered interesting.

"There are many reasons that some children have not learned to read, write, and speak well. Find out what is keeping your children from learning the skills they need.

"There are many reasons why a child's attitude may be negative toward schooling. Too many to discuss it in brief. You deserve an answer even though this is not a part of our organization's concerns at this time. Love your children, and make it clear to them that you do. Get help if you do not understand their behavior, and attitudes."

"This is Igor Connifer signing off. Let us know if you like our programs and how we can serve you on KABC. Today's speaker, Guy Benson, Kirk Collins, and I bid you good day."

Chapter 21

Friday the 13th

It was crowded living together in Guy's apartment. It had worked out well, thanks to his and Sandy's sense of humor, and patience. Meals were shared. The cook was whoever got hungry first. The other cleaned up afterwards. Each washed his or her own clothes. Guy didn't even complain about his backaches from sleeping on the couch.

Sandy knew that she must make the move back to her own apartment, or find another place. She had occasionally phoned her neighbor, Miss Risley, and picked up her mail.

No, Miss Risley said that nothing more had occurred. She and other tenants seemed to have no fear of staying there. What if there was another occurrence? Miss Risley might be in danger. But the neighbor insisted that she was awake so often at night that she would probably see someone sneaking around outside.

The time she had stayed with Guy was productive for Sandy. The Apple A Day founders had arranged for a meeting to include new and prospective members. There had been an election of officers. Everyone had been surprised when Guy was unwilling to accept the presidency. He had worked so hard to get the organization started.

"How can you bow out?" Sandy asked him. "You've lived it since the birth of ideas we are now nurturing and will fulfill."

"Sandy, you and my other friends have borne the weight for me. If I persist I'll be digging my own grave. Yeah, I know that some people are super-beings. They are able to handle several commitments, to delegate authority, and not lose touch. I'm not one of those people." Ross Ota's cautions had struck a chord.

"I took on marriage and parenting as a commitment. That requires that I be committed to my job. My sense of honor requires those commitments come first. You are all carrying on valiantly. You would be a very good president for AAD, Sandy."

"No, I'm a good partner, but I back Noah, as president."

The voting turned out according to Sandy's wishes. Noah received a large majority of votes and stepped into leadership of AAD Inc.

Friday the Thirteenth

She was awake before the alarm sounded. Sandy peered at the calendar. Thirteen. Not the most auspicious number but it did not dim her enthusiasm. There would be time this morning to launder the sheets. The apartment would be neat and clean for Guy when he arrived home to read the note she placed on top of them.

The note read; "Dear friend, you are wonderful to have provided this respite. It allowed me to gather courage to return to my apartment. Today is the day. You will be busy with the broadcast, then later the appointment with your marriage counselor. I have had a sense of safety, peace, and quiet during my stay. May we both have a lucky day, and I will be seeing you through AAD. With sincere gratitude, Sandy."

Guy and Amy had finally found a marriage counselor they could agree upon. Yasu Sunn was a Buddhist, and a psychologist specializing in marital counseling. His strength was that he listened to each, and he spoke seldom. It was marvelous the way he set the scene for them to listen to their own voices, as their minds met with the wisdom to see their own faults in the marriage. It was a better way to learn than to have it pointed out to them.

Yasu would not allow them to accuse or blame. It disturbed the peace of understanding self. The sessions had been proceeding well. Then, this afternoon as Guy entered Yasu's sitting room, Amy's posture and her grim expression flashed a warning as clear as a red flare. She said nothing in answer to his greeting. That in itself was a threat, considering how far they had come with their counseling.

"Amy is very upset tonight, Guy. She has asked me to speak for her. She has discovered that you are living with a young woman. Do you care to explain? She considers this a break in the trust you two have been building these past sessions."

"Oh, God," Guy sighed. "I should have come out with it, but it was to be so temporary that I thought it was better not to mention it, unless the subject came up. The fact is . . . ." Guy explained it as well as he could, which was clumsily and awkwardly, because of his stress. "Yes," and he was pleading, "it must be hard to believe that a woman would have no one else to turn to for refuge, but it's true. We are living together platonically. We are both rather tired of the arrangement, and she will be moving back to her own place soon."

"Barry saw you hug her," Amy said.

"Now look here, Amy." Guy exploded, springing to his feet, and wagging the index finger he used to intimidate her. Instead, it incensed her. She glared. Guy continued, his voice rising several decibels, "Don't you put Barry in the middle of this. He's a child. He doesn't know what he saw, or the meaning of it. The lady was unnerved from putting out a fire purposely set by an intruder. She was shaking like a leaf. I tried to calm her. And that is all I am going to say about this, because it is too ridiculous to even speak of."

He turned to the counselor. "I've had all I can take tonight, Yasu." He was shaking. "I'm sorry this happened, but if not this, there would be something else. She expects perfection, and has a complete lack of trust in people . . . especially in me. Her own unreasonable fears bring on the turmoil in our life."

Yasu Sunn, stood. "Will you both stand while we pray for guidance? We should still our anger and confusion before we leave. This is not the way to improve patience and understanding."

Guy looked toward Amy to look for any sign of response. Nothing. "I'm sorry, Yasu. It takes two to tango, and my partner is crippled. Goodnight." He stalked out, resisting with great effort an urge to slam the door.

"Daddy, see the picture I drew for you. It's a fire."

Guy managed to close the door quietly. He hesitated, inhaling deeply to get his bearings. He had almost forgotten that Barry was waiting in the outside office. Good. It was agreed that his son was to spend weekends with him.

"Come, Barry," he said, ignoring the secretary who had been entertaining the boy during the counseling session.

"Look, Daddy, look at my picture." It fell to the floor as his father seized his hand and pulled him into the hallway outside. Barry glanced at his father. He tried to make his short legs and little steps match Guy's angry stride. There was no conversation all the way home, nor into the evening. The small boy had learned the value, and the pain of silence. He had wondered many times what he had done wrong to make his parents so angry at him, and at each other.

Chapter 22

Another Perfect Morning

Ben Benson enjoyed the morning hours the most. He had been a frail child, and his mother had not been sure he would survive to become an adult. Yet here he was, enjoying more than eighty years. The exact number was so unimportant to him that when it became necessary to give his age, he just shook his head. Smiling, he would figure it from the date he was born.

Ben welcomed Saturdays, when he could be with his grandson. He inhaled the brisk morning air, and squinted at the sun's rays dancing on the ponds. Guy had been a bit withdrawn when he turned Barry over to him. But he has a lot on his mind, Ben decided, and gave the matter no more thought. Memories took him backward in time.

His life had been interesting, and showered with love from his mother and his dear wife, Ella. His mother, Hilda had encouraged him to be persistent in following his hopes and dreams. Ella had given birth to their two sons, one of whom had died at an early age, nearly breaking Ben's heart. Guy and Amy had presented him with Barry, a handsome grandchild. Smart as a whip, the boy was. His pride and joy.

Ben was delighted to have the child visit him. They would spend the day together. One of Ben's favorite places to go was a neighborhood park. Even before Barry was born the park was Ben's retreat.

As he aged, he had wondered what it might be like to grow old in an Asian country. The elderly were esteemed, even honored by their families. Quite different than in America, where, as soon as the young left the nest, they were so involved with survival, followed by a driving need to succeed financially, that they seemed unaware of how much the elderly and the very young needed them. It was a blessing for the two generations, the old and the young, to have each other. In Asia, they would likely live under the same roof. In America, not so.

When Amy and Guy separated, much to the old man's despair, Barry was shuffled back and forth between the apartments of his mother and father. Ben rented a small apartment near the building where his son lived, in order to be available when needed, and to fully enjoy his grandson.

Oh, he knew that he was loved by his son, but he felt adored by Barry. Ben worked at planting images in the boy's mind that might live on after he was gone. Ben accepted the fact that at his age there were just a few years left to make a difference in Barry's life. Only through this grandson did the old man expect to live on. Every hour with the child was valued beyond measure.

Monuments or gravestones served no purpose. They offered nothing of permanence to the passage of time. There was nothing permanent in this world, but the most lasting are the memories, and the ideas we share with the young. Each generation shares the jewels of wisdom, as they see it, with the following generations.

It was that awareness that guided Ben, or Alf Benson as he had been christened, into the field of education, before he came to America. The trust that he could make a difference had impelled him toward a dedication to knowledge, truth and wisdom. Ben truly believed that passing on memories and truths to our children would guide them through life's trials, and help them to make wise decisions. The boy's birth had brought meaning to his life.

The morning air was brisk. The sun's rays sparkled and darted through the gently swaying fronds of the palm tree, promising to warm the cool earth beneath their feet. Hand in hand, grandfather and grandson set out to explore and share this God-given day.

"Papa, what is that on the leaf?" Barry's sharp eyes didn't miss a thing on their walks.

"Well, glory be, my boy. I think you have discovered a rare kind of dinosaur," Ben said, teasing the youngster as he reached for the delicate, almost transparent form and placed it on the back of the boy's hand.

Barry inhaled slowly, open-mouthed as always in the face of discovery. "Really, Papa?" His dark eyes widened, examining every detail of this magnificent creature. A praying mantis stared back at him as though it was every bit as curious about him. It nodded its head. Its shiny black eyes watched, unfrightened.

"Well, no, not really a dinosaur," Ben chuckled. "I am just imagining . . . pretending. Long, long ago before people were on this earth the dinosaurs were here."

"Here, on our island, Papa?"

"Well, no, not on this island." Ben returned to the subject at hand. "This is a praying mantis. Why do you think it was named that?"

"Because he prays. See, look, Papa, he really does. Look at the way he holds his hands." He inhaled again as a new idea struck him. "Could I keep him?" His eyes danced with anticipation.

"Well, you are much bigger than he is, so I suppose you could, but let's think about it a bit. Where would you keep him?"

"In my room."

"Oh, is he going to sleep with you at night, under your covers?"

"In my room, next to my bed. No-o-o, I wouldn't want him IN my bed, under the covers. I might roll over on him. I'd get a jar to keep him in."

"What do you think he eats? What would you feed him?"

"I don't know . . . ice cream, maybe?"

"If you were that little insect, would you rather live in a jar in your room or out here in the bushes and trees?"

Barry pursed his lips. "He might have a mommy who would miss him if I take him away from here."

"Good, boy. That's very thoughtful of you. Why don't you look at him, the way he is looking at you, then close your eyes and try to see him in your mind. What shape is his head? What do his eyes look like?"

Barry squinted through partially closed eyes to remind himself. "His eyes are very, very big. His head is shaped like this." He held his fingers to indicate an upside-down triangle. "And he's a beautiful green color."

"Which of his legs are longer?" his grandfather asked.

"He only has two legs, Papa, and they're both the same. And he has two short arms and hands, and I think he likes me. I'd better leave him here. I can come back to see him, can't I?"

"We will certainly try. I'm sure he likes you and that he is glad you are not going to carry him away from his friends and family. Wild things might die if you take them from the places they're used to. I think you made a wise decision. Tell you what . . .we'll go to the library and find a picture of him. If we take a piece of paper maybe we can draw our own picture to remember him by."

Ben guided his hand to place the beautiful, fragile form back on the leaf. It was the subject of conversation until the next discovery, a dove cooing and wooing its lady dove. Each new wonder was worthy of several minutes of discussion and examination, before the two pressed on toward the park.

By the time they arrived at Ben's favorite park bench, the aches in the old fellow's legs and back were begging him to sit. Barry, on the other hand, was like a bouncing ball, with unlimited energy to expend.

"Papa, may I ride on the merry-go-round?" He jumped up and down with excitement, his short legs like two springs as he waited for permission to go to the playground.

"Wait a bit while Papa rests, then I'll take you there."

Continuing to jump up and down, Barry could not contain his eagerness. "Papa, it's just over there past those bushes. I can see you from there. You can wave if you want me to come back, and I'll come right away."

Ben turned his head about forty degrees toward where Barry was pointing. Many times, he had taken the child there first, but today he was so tired, and yes, he would be able to watch him from here.

"All right, my boy. Stay right there where I can see you. I'll come get you in a few minutes." The small playground with the merry-go-round, swings, rings, and ladder to swing across was visible, even to his old eyes. He would follow the boy over there after a short rest.

"Thank you, Papa." Barry darted off waving a small hand over his shoulder as he ran.

"Ah-h-h." A contented sigh, a smile, and the old man settled his bony rump on the welcoming seat of the wooden bench. The sun still provided comfortable warmth on his weathered face, and did not yet require shade. He closed his eyes to its brightness.

Ben's head nodded forward. "Oh, my. I almost fell asleep," he thought. Someone was seated beside him on the bench. How was it that he had not heard the man, or the crinkling sound of the newspaper the man held? His head turned to focus his sleepy eyes on the playground. Then immediately he was on his feet, hurrying with small uneven steps, driven by panic.

He saw no children in the playground. He heard no childish voices. He almost walked through the end of the hedge that concealed the rest of the play equipment from his view. The branches of the bush scraped his hands, as he short cut the turn, rather than taking a few seconds to go around it.

"Barry!" he called, as loudly as his weak voice could project, for he was breathing hard from the effort and his fright.

Chapter 23

Missing!

"What is the old fellow doing? He's obviously distressed," observed a casually dressed woman leading her dog on a leash. They had just rounded a curve in the path to see him shuffling across the gravel-covered playground, his head cradled in his hands, and breathing heavily. She hurried to his side.

A few others nearby had also noticed that something was disturbing the man. Ben was unaware of any of them. When he had reached the playground where Barry had gone to play, there was not a soul in sight. Fear erased reality. Disturbing thoughts crowded out reason. First, anger that the boy might have wandered off. Then, anxiety that someone had taken him away by force. Guilt fell in somber folds of grief. He had not been there when he was needed to come to Barry's aid. Surrealistic images passed through the recesses of his mind. He had failed his treasure, the dear grandchild entrusted to him.

Ben's emotions sapped the little strength left to him. His knees buckled, and he fell, as if in slow motion, to the sandy surface beneath him. Someone was shaking an arm trying to communicate with him.

"What is it? Are you ill? How can we help you?"

A well-dressed man reached his side, checked Ben's pulse, took a cellular phone from his briefcase, and dialed 911. Ben was not responding to any one of the several folks now trying to get information. He had rolled over onto his side. His eyes stared without comprehension. His breathing continued to be labored.

A siren, then an emergency vehicle approached. It left the park road to drive across the lawn to where the anxious circle of people surrounded Ben, some holding his hands and others speaking encouraging words. The two attendants soon had him in the ambulance and were on their way without anyone understanding what had occurred, or who he was. By this time Ben's eyes were darting from one person to the other. He wanted to get up. He wanted to speak to them, and only unintelligible noises came from his efforts to communicate.

The sharp intensity of the siren was muffled inside the ambulance. The attendant was persistent in his efforts to follow emergency procedure, all the while speaking gently and asking an occasional question. Ben only stared back, his mouth gaping. The attendant took a billfold from his patient's pocket, reached for the phone, and gave his report to the desk in the emergency room, where they were headed.

"The patient is Alf Benson." He proceeded to give all the information found on Ben's identification cards. He found Guy's phone number and address. Before the ambulance reached the hospital, the person who had filled out the necessary forms there was phoning relatives. Mercifully, Guy was working at home.

"He's my father," Guy said. "And the boy is my son. What happened? Is my son all right? What is my father's condition?"

A pause as he listened. "What do you mean, there is no boy with him? Then where is my son? Yes, of course, I'll be right there. Kona Hospital, emergency room."

The paramedic started to put the contents of Ben's pockets in an envelope, but he hesitated to look at the picture of a young boy about the age of his own child. He held the picture up for the old man to see, but he regretted having done it. Ben squinted to look more closely. Recognition triggered moans and gibberish.

"Okay, old-timer. We'll get you taken care of, then you can tell us all about it." The intravenous injections, the EKG report, a blood pressure reading, temperature, and a nitroglycerin tablet were given before Ben was rolled out of the ambulance and into the emergency room. Moments later he was placed in an intensive care unit where he was hooked up to equipment that monitored his heartbeat and blood pressure.

Guy hurried into the hospital, through the emergency entrance, and was led into the room where his father lay pale and helpless. He was grateful that Ben was conscious. A nurse had assured him that a doctor would be there shortly to give him as much information as they had, most of which was on the paramedics' report, which indicated where he was found, his condition, and the fact that he could not communicate. They were watching him carefully. His symptoms had indicated the possibility of a stroke or a heart attack.

"Dad. Where is Barry? Did you leave him in someone's care?"

Tears filled the old man's eyes, and sobs shook his body. He was trying to say something, but, could not.

Initially, Guy was certain that some kind bystander had taken charge of Barry's care so that the grandfather could be treated.

Guy was sorry that he had upset his father with questions. Best to take care of this situation now. Someone would no doubt be calling him soon so that he could pick up his son. Maybe the police took him to their station, or a kind neighbor took him home. He wouldn't bother his father with it now.

"Good afternoon. You're Mr. Benson's son?" the doctor asked as he entered the room. Guy nodded and shook the doctor's hand. It took very little time for the doctor to read the complete report to Guy, since the 911 call had resulted in the brief report the paramedic phoned in. He could get the name of the gentleman who had called for the ambulance, and the doctor pointed out the names of the two paramedics, if Guy Benson wanted to talk to them. There was no mention of a child having been with him, but it would be easy to find out who is caring for him. Someone no doubt was trying to reach him by phone right now.

The doctor confirmed that it would be best that he not bother his father tonight. Guy looked toward the bed and saw that Ben was sleeping from the sedative he'd been given. The monitor was beeping as the steady, then irregular squiggly green lines alternately moved across the screen. At last the heartbeat was controlled and being watched by the nurses at the desk across the hall.

Best that he head for home and wait for a call. Maybe someone had called Amy, or she might already have picked up Barry somewhere. Guy was worried about his father's condition. All else would fall into place.

Chapter 24

Waiting

At home, Guy sank down on the sofa to wait. There was nothing on the answering machine messages. That was strange in itself. Barry would be trying to call no matter where he was, however careless or unfeeling the person caring for him might be. It was almost noon. The ambulance had picked up his father at the park about nine o'clock.

Waiting was too difficult. Guy called the police station to ask if they had a record of the 911 call, and his father's affliction. The switchboard operator listened to his explanation. As soon as he mentioned that he was looking for his son, the operator transferred him to a Missing Juveniles Department.

"He isn't really missing," Guy explained. "It's just that in the confusion of my father's emergency, someone decided to take care of Barry, and I don't know who yet."

A clerk asked him the routine questions, which he answered as well as he could. Then he gave her the description she asked for. "Look," he said to her, "this isn't necessary. If he was taken to one of your stations, he can identify himself. I have to hang up so my son can reach me on the phone." He slammed down the receiver. The clerk shook her head side to side. That sounded like many a call she had taken involving missing children. The parent's stage of denial. She typed her notes onto the appropriate form. The man thought that his son might be in one of the police stations. She referred to her list of numbers and called them. Answers all negative. No boy had been picked up or brought to any station today. She called the hospitals and got the same answer. No boy of that age had been admitted today.

She phoned Guy's number. He answered the phone before the end of the first ring. "Mr. Benson, this is the Department of Missing Juveniles. Have you called everyone you know yet? Friends? Family? Neighbors?"

"Ma'am, I don't consider my son to be missing. Someone is just thoughtless, or inconsiderate. I'm a bit impatient, but I'm sure that they are just trying to entertain Barry to get his mind off of what happened to his grandfather today."

As Guy spoke he reassessed the circumstances of his father's attack. Barry wasn't there when the ambulance arrived, nor was he there when the first person had happened by to help his father. Maybe Barry had witnessed his grandfather's strange behavior and had then run for help. If he had found someone to help, he would have returned with them, or with police. Things were not adding up.

Maybe Barry recalled some of the phone numbers of his father's or mother's friends. Guy had often let him push the buttons when he was calling a friend. No. If he had phoned any of them they would have gone to the hospital where his grandfather was taken, and they would most certainly have called Guy by now.

Guy had a sick feeling in the pit of his stomach as he realized that it was time to call Amy. He had no idea what he could tell her now, but he must. And she would be as frightened as he was. His hand was ready to pick up the receiver when it rang.

It was the nurse at the hospital. "Mr. Benson, your father is awake. The sedative should have kept him sleeping for hours, but he woke up shouting. He is trying so hard to make us understand something, and he is so determined that we thought it best to call you. It is dangerous to have him raving like this. Can I tell him that you are on your way to talk to him? When we suggested that, it seemed to quiet him down."

Guy assured her that he was on his way. "Oh, God, let Amy be home," he thought as he dialed the familiar number. He could pick her up on the way to the hospital. She should be there. "Busy! Damn." He slammed down the receiver and raced out of the apartment to his car. On the way to Amy's house he repeated every prayer he had ever learned, and made up a few new ones.

Screeching his tires, he came to a sudden stop. He was calling her name frantically before he reached her porch. The door flew open, and his words tumbled out. Just enough, at first, to make her willing to go with him to the hospital. Just enough to inform her of Ben's stroke, and possible heart attack.

Amy was in the car before he tried to tell her the whole story, as he knew it. "And who did you leave Barry with?" she asked. Since their son was not with him, and in the midst of the confusion at hand she had assumed that Guy had chosen not to bring him. The hospital was no place for a child, after all.

The tires squealed again as he pulled into a parking place. They were out of the car, and almost running, till they entered an empty elevator.

"Amy, we're here to get some answers from my father, if we can. I've told you all that I know. Thank you for coming with me. I need you so. We have to get information from Dad without getting him unnecessarily excited. I don't know where Barry is. He wasn't with his granddad when the ambulance was called."

Amy's hands rose to cover her mouth. The elevator door opened. She stared at Guy, trying to comprehend what she had heard. He held the elevator door, reached for her hand, and pulled her gently through it. He put his arms around her, wanting so much to protect her, but her eyes reflected the fear in his. She let him hold her for the first time in many months. Neither spoke.

Doctor Levy was approaching them. His concern was evident as he guided them into the intensive care room. A nurse was sitting at the bedside just stroking Ben's forehead, his arms, his hands, to calm him. She beckoned to Guy to take her place. Ben's eyes were closed. Guy glanced at the monitor. Did it only seem to be producing a more irregular pattern than when he was here earlier?

"Your son is here, Mr. Benson." The bleary eyes popped open, but the doctor had determined they could not risk another outburst like the earlier one. He spoke in haste to caution his patient. "Guy is going to ask you questions, Mr. Benson. You are not to speak. We can't understand your speech yet. Perhaps tomorrow you will be able to speak clearly again."

Ben waved his hand, irritated that they were delaying him. He had to tell them everything, and there was no time to waste. The doctor was well aware of his state of mind and that he must be controlled at all cost. "Do you understand, Mr. Benson? If you do not stay calm, we will have to stop and wait until morning." Ben was listening carefully.

"Your son and his wife will do the talking, by asking you questions. To say 'yes' press your son's hand one time. For 'no' press twice. You understand?" Ben pressed Guy's hand once.

The doctor was emphatic. "Ask only questions he can answer yes or no. Stay cool!"

"Amy is here, Dad." The old man smiled and nodded his head to express his pleasure, then reached out to her with his left hand to draw her closer. With one of them seated on each side of Ben, Guy kissed Ben's cheek and began.

"Dad, has the doctor explained what happened to you in the park, and why you are here?" The hand Amy held raised one finger. "Pwehwee?" Ben's face was twisted into a frown, his mouth drooped on the right side. The eyes were pleading, questioning.

"No, Dad, we don't have Barry, but answer my questions like Dr. Levy says, and we'll find him. Did Barry see that you were needing a doctor when you were in the park?" Two fingers.

"No? Was Barry with you in the park?" One finger. Then Ben waved his left hand as if to erase that, and raised two fingers. Guy hesitated and then rephrased his question. "Barry was not with you in the park?" One finger, then two fingers again.

"Yes and No you are telling us. Was Barry with you part of the time?" Ben's head nodded ever so slightly. He raised one finger of his left hand. "When you entered the park were you and Barry together?"

"Yes." Now the nurse, doctor, Guy, and Amy were eagerly interpreting the finger signs.

"Did Barry leave because you needed help?" No.

"Did you see Barry leave you?" Yes.

"Did he go far away from you?" No.

"The paramedics found you collapsed at the edge of the playground. Did you both go to the playground?" Ben hesitated a moment. Yes. Then No.

"Did he go to the playground by himself?" The old eyes filled with tears, one sob, and he raised a finger.

"Did someone threaten him, or attack him there, or . . . carry him away?" Ben shrugged his left shoulder and pointed to his eye.

"You don't know? You didn't see any thing happen?" No. Ben was using his head instead of the finger signals. Guy looked at the doctor, who nodded for him to continue with the questioning.

"Did you see anything happen after he got to the playground?" The tears were pouring as Ben moved his head from side to side. He could not look into their eyes for the shame he was feeling.

"Did you follow him right away to the playground?" No.

"Did you stop to talk to someone for awhile before you followed him there? No, you didn't. Did some time pass before you arrived at the playground?" Fear clutched his heart.

"How much time, Dad? Five or ten minutes? . . . a half hour? . . ." Ben shrugged. The sobs were gasps now. The doctor looked worried.

"You know we love you. We know you love Barry. Be patient with me. I'm going to do some guessing. We know that you would never do anything that would hurt Barry, so something happened that you could not help."

"Let's see. Something delayed you, it doesn't matter what it was, and when you got to the playground where Barry went, was Barry playing there?"

"Nou-wou-u." Ben sounded like an animal in great pain.

"He was not there? Was anyone there? Was he anywhere in sight?" Again the groan.

Guy was exhausted. Amy had an expression of tension and fright on her face. She wanted to know more, but did not know if she could bear it. The nurse's eyes were tearing. The doctor recognized that Ben had to get this information out for his own good. There was no time to waste. There was much to do. He allowed the questions to continue.

"Do you know where Barry went?" The groan again.

"Did he tell you he was going somewhere away from the playground?"

"Nou-wou-u."

The doctor stepped closer. "Alf," using the name on record, "was it after you saw that Barry was gone that your symptoms of paralysis, speech dysfunction, and numbness began?" The nodding indicated it had triggered an attack already on the verge of happening. "Did you feel very, very tired when you got to the park?" A nod. "Did you have to sit down somewhere because you were too tired to walk further?" An emphatic sound accompanied by the nods confirmed that.

"And you sat down somewhere, Dad. Were you near the playground? And Barry begged to go there while you rested." Nods. "Could you see him from where you sat?" One finger, then two fingers. Yes and No.

"When you couldn't see him anymore, did you see him after that?"

"Nou-wou-u-u-u-u." Ben sobbed, but seemed relieved that they knew. He looked at them pleadingly. Now they could find him . . . couldn't they? He seemed to beg for the answer to his unspoken question.

"We'll find him. You just do what the doctors and nurses tell you so you'll be well when we bring him to see you. Promise us."

Ben managed a look of relief . . . almost a smile, with his eyes at least, then his frail body seemed to dissolve into the bleached white sheets, exhausted. His face pale as the bed linens. The nurse watched the doctor for an order to sedate him, and quietly turned to do so. Amy and Guy kissed him on the cheek, stroked his hand and left the room to the monotonous sound of the monitor overhead.

In the corridor outside, they gave in to their grief. Holding each other closely, they wept, each assuring the other that they would find Barry. He was all right, just waiting for them to find him. They could think no further than this, but must soon formulate a plan, and seek help.

Chapter 25

The Search

Kirk Collins was in charge at the community radio station while Igor took a break to do errands. "Good afternoon, listeners. This is KABC, Kirk Collins here to make your day more pleasant with musical favorites. This is Mel Torme 'The Velvet Fog' to mellow your mood."

Someone had just driven up to the station. The messenger handed a note and the flyer with Barry's picture on it to the young announcer. Kirk stopped the music without hesitation.

"I have an important announcement. We just received notice that the son of an AAD member is missing. Last seen in Makai Park, Barry Benson, six years old, wandered away, or was taken away from the park playground early yesterday morning. Barry has dark hair, brown eyes, and fair skin.

"Please make an effort, folks, to talk about this to others, neighbors, friends, and passers by. We need your help to get information that will lead us to Barry. Time is of the essence. We need you to ask questions of others, and to relay even the smallest bit of information you uncover to the authorities, or this station. We will keep you informed."

KABC had scooped the newspapers, the television, and the other radio stations. It constantly updated telling listeners about the missing boy. It broadcast messages in case Barry might be near a radio. Friends kept reporters at bay by repeating over and over that the police had all of the information, and the parents had nothing to add to it.

Volunteers were placing notices in every public institution: schools, libraries, bus stops, and airports. The police had put out an all-points bulletin. Restaurants and stores, taxi and bus drivers all had posters. Amy and Guy had no idea how many people were out there working to find Barry. They were humbly grateful.

It was a shame that so many hours had elapsed before the search was begun. It had given an abductor time to get on a highway leaving town.

Now reporters considered the story big news. It was on page one of the daily papers.

Following a recent Apple A Day Meeting, Igor Connifer was introduced as a potential contributor to the community. After all of the hurdles were accomplished to obtain an FCC license, good things began to happen.

A sizeable grant was made available from a local community organization that had a neighborhood grants program made possible through Utilities Industries. Eligible were any groups that "sponsored projects to build communities by increasing cooperation and collaboration, develop self-sufficiency, improve and enhance the use of physical resources, and promote longevity." The grants could be used for many causes including youth. The intended purpose of Igor's station KABC was to review, revise, renew, or replace current public education. A well-written request for the grant fell on sympathetic ears . . . or the desk of a sympathizer at least.

Kirk had caught on so fast to station responsibilities that recently Igor was giving him almost free reign to broadcast and play listener-requested musical selections. His voice and manner of speaking were those of a grown man. He took care to lower the pitch, as Igor had coached him to do.

Chapter 26

Anxiety

The emotional toll was tearing Guy and Amy apart. Information had seemed to come to Guy in a dream early this morning or perhaps an angel had put the idea into his mind. In the dream, it was important to order Hawaiian pizza. That was Barry's favorite kind. Now Guy was going crazy. The Pizza Pan would be open by this time, and they were on their way there to get more information. Information that they hoped would lead them to Barry.

They arrived at a busy time, and waited for a lull to talk to the first clerk they could find who had been working last night. A kid who looked like he wasn't old enough to be working listened to their story. He recalled the uproar and the reaction of an older kid who was upset with a delivery he had to make the other night. He was called "Scooter," because he moved so fast. He was taking a few days off and he'd be back next Wednesday.

No, they couldn't give out his phone number. If they should see him before he returned to work, they would tell him to call the Bensons. The young kid was putting Barry's picture with their phone number on a bulletin board so overloaded that business cards overlapped. Business was building up for another rush. Everyone was busy and they might as well leave, they decided. The clerks couldn't see what this all had to do with the missing kid.

Back at the apartment, Amy fell to the couch. Her energy had drained away. Where were they in their search? What were the police accomplishing? Guy sat down next to her and took her hand. As though he had read her mind, he reached for the phone and dialed the office of the detective assigned to their case.

Reilly answered.

Guy Benson went straight to the point. "We haven't heard anything from you."

A brief silence. "Mr. Benson, no one has seen your son since he disappeared. I'm sorry. We are waiting for some information to act on. Do you have anything else to add?"

"Well, we have been making every effort to put our imaginations to work. We have canvassed the neighborhood at the park's edge and left flyers. Have you done anything to question the people living there?" Guy waited for a reply. "Well, we have! We spoke to some of the neighbors. I think there is every possibility that someone there saw something."

Guy was not going to reveal his suspicions about the pizza orders. It was too remote a chance, yet he clung to it as a drowning victim clings to an empty floating container.

"Mr. Benson, our officers are continually on the alert. We can only hope for a call from someone to give us some direction. The news media, especially radio and television, is continuing to seek information."

Guy's nerves were so frayed that he wanted to slam down the phone. Stories like this always showed the law out there interviewing everyone, searching, sometimes finding the missing person, and sometimes . . . not finding them, but that thought entered his mind for only a moment. He hung up. No heart for the courtesy of saying goodbye.

"He says that he'll have someone patrol the park neighborhood," Guy told Amy, who was listening intently to his side of the conversation.

The detective stood there just staring at the phone after the circuit was broken. He well understood the pain of parents whose child was missing. He had a dozen recent cases on his desk that seemed to have reached a dead end.

Guy slid to the floor beside his wife, reached again for her hand, and gently kissed each fingertip. "Barry would be very happy to know that we are together again."

"He will be happy," Amy corrected. The fear of losing their son had forced them to reexamine what is important and what is not. But at a terrible cost, if they didn't find Barry. That painful thought hung in the air, unspoken. They both stared into space.

The phone rang. "I'm Scooter Serensky," a young man's voice announced. "One of my buddies at work called. Said you want to talk to me. Something about that woman who acts so weird."

Guy had been on the verge of exhaustion, in a state between consciousness and sleep, when the phone rang. He shook his head, trying to comprehend the caller's words. "Oh, yes. The Pizza Pan employee and the woman who doesn't tip."

"Well, it's a little bit more than that. She's a nut. Gives me the creeps. And she doesn't want anyone to see her, I guess."

"Can you be more explicit? Where does she live? Is it true that she changed her usual order to the pineapple and sausage recently?"

"Mister, people change their orders all the time. I can't tell you where she lives or I'd be fired. There's some kind of a law against that, but I've seen the flyer about your little boy, and I know that he disappeared from a park."

"Is that all you have to tell me?"

"Yeah, except that she lives near the park, and the house is spooky. The other night someone upstairs was tapping on the window. I couldn't see anyone in the dark, but I heard a tap-tap, tap-tap, that just went on and on. I got out of there fast."

"What's she look like?"

"I dunno. She keeps it dark. Slips money through a crack in the door. Doesn't come out 'till I've gone."

"Thanks, Scooter. I may be in touch with you. And your phone number is . . .?"

Guy was surprised when the boy gave it to him. He wrote it down with a big exclamation mark beside the number.

Amy was listening to the one side of their conversation.

"Come on, Baby. We're better off when we keep busy, and we're going to drop in on Detective Reilly at the station house."

Guy told her what Scooter had said. Somehow, it had seemed more eventful hearing it from the kid than it did when he repeated it to his wife. Was he losing it, to be so impulsive? There are plenty of weird people in the world. From what they had seen earlier, the whole neighborhood was composed of strange, antisocial people.

Chapter 27

KABC: Baldrige[1]

"This is KABC, Igor Connifer wishing you a peaceful good morning in Paradise. If you're listening, Barry, we're with you boy in thought, and spirit. We are doing everything we can to have you home again. Chin up, son. It is 7:10 A.M. Get moving, you late sleepers, and let us tell about the progress of AAD, also known as Apple A Day. You, in turn must call us to share your experiences and feelings concerning the public schools.

"This morning's news commentary is by David S. Broder of the *Washington Post*, in the city of Washington. He tells us about the late Malcolm Baldrige, the secretary of commerce in the Reagan administration, whom he calls 'a visionary'.

"Baldrige started a competition, . . . *Its first goal was to restructure American business firms, with the intention of creating a relentless drive in management and workers, to strive for quality and customer satisfaction. The award was named for him after his untimely death in a horseback riding accident. Winning the Baldrige became a prestigious honor in American business. It was a systematic effort to set goals and to measure progress. It was significantly responsible for the economic dominance the United States now enjoys.*"

"The reason I am calling your attention to this, folks, is that with the support of Congress, the Baldrige process has been applied to another threatened enterprise the public school system. David S. Broder says "According to the National Alliance for Business (NAB), the benefits in this area of education may be as great as the results in business."

The Baldrige model was introduced in seven school districts in North Carolina in 1992, and is now being used in 49 districts. The superintendent of education says that the system has helped his state and Texas school districts achieve great gains in standard test scores. It has also reduced school violence and boosted teacher standards and salaries.

Another participating area in Texas, the Brazosport school district, has proven that the system works for all children, not just for those from

111

the best homes. In the latter district about 40 percent of its 13,500 students are minorities and economically disadvantaged. In 1992, the school board of this district prodded Dow Chemical, the district's biggest employer and taxpayer. The superintendent of schools, Gerald Anderson, began training himself and his faculty in the 'total quality management' approach used by top-performing companies. His school board was committed to cooperate.

At the start of the 90's, tests showed the white students outperforming the African-American, Hispanic, and low income students on standard Texas reading, writing, and math exams, by 20 percent or more. Now, in all four categories, 92 to 98 percent of all students are passing the tests.

To top this record, Brenda Clark, principal of the Azalea Elementary School in St. Petersburg, Florida, reorganized her school on the Baldrige principles. Thirty percent of the students are African-American. Ms. Clark says that she indoctrinated both the faculty and the students with the ethic that 'achievement and improvement are everyone's responsibility.' Learning goals are clearly defined, and progress is measured, in notebooks, the children maintain themselves.

Thirty-two children in last year's kindergarten class might have been held back in former times, because they were so poor at word recognition, that they could not meet the Florida state and district standards for promotion. Ms. Clark and her teachers used what they had learned to bring the children up to standard. It took dedication and determination, special classes and assistants, and by May, all 32 were reading at grade level. The other sections of the class had 95 percent success rates.

The children in that school talk about their sense of pride and accomplishment. With backing from the major business organizations, the National Education Association, and many state officials, the Baldrige in Education initiative is almost ready for a national rollout. Our reporter ends this report with the words: 'Mack Baldrige would be proud."

"Well folks, what do you think of this report. Is this one of the best-kept secrets in education, or what? Have any of you educators out there heard of this? Maybe the teachers who have graduated from their colleges and universities within the past seven years know about it. Did your professors call this to your attention? Do the school board members, and administrators know about this?

"We don't know anymore than what I read to you this morning, but it sounds like good management that instills a positive attitude in everyone. We had some very poor management tactics in business thirty years ago, and afterward. But that statement about a readiness 'for a national rollout'? The date of the Washington Post report was 7-14-99. The NEA is obviously incapable of matching the success of the American business world."

One listener in a room darkened with shades against the early morning light, quickly turned off the radio when he heard footsteps approaching in the corridor.

[1] Broder, David S. of "The Washington Post" *Baldrige in Education model is ready for application in schools nationwide,* reprinted in West Hawaii Today, 7-14-99.

Chapter 28

The Plot Thickens

Guy and Amy were prepared to talk to Detective Reilly, and with him along they planned to go to the house they suspected was connected to Barry's disappearance. But Reilly was not there. He was on call though, and when they reached him by phone, their idea did not appeal to him in the least. Something about a search warrant being necessary; the court not being in session this late; the evidence being flimsy. They left the police building frustrated and frightened for their son.

They had no power to intercede. Notions of daring steps, such as going to the door and insisting on entry, ran through their minds. If only they could verify the address of the woman who had called in the order to Pizza Pan that night. They were only guessing that the shabby house on Parkway Drive was the one.

Guy drove back and forth. They studied the house. Barry needed them, and they had no power . . . yet. It would take at least another day to go through the lawful means of investigation. They parked a few feet up the street from the house, watching, waiting. They felt anchored to this place and could not bring themselves to leave it.

"Guy," Amy ventured, "I'm never going to leave you again."

Her sudden statement was just what he had been waiting so long to hear.

"But we must clear up some things if it's going to work. If it doesn't work, even if we stay together forever, it won't be a happy home for Barry unless we both change. He's very sensitive to our moods."

"I'll promise anything to make us a happy family." Guy spoke with conviction evidenced by the way his voice quavered. "At first I didn't see any reason for a marriage counselor, but I've changed my mind. I didn't like the first counselors we tried. Didn't know whether to get angry, tough, or to beg you to come back."

"You never seemed to understand why I felt so helpless and desperate as to leave you, and I couldn't put it into words. Every time I tried to explain my feelings, you got angry. I finally kept everything inside and gave up trying to talk to you."

"Yasu surprised me with things he said about both of us. I thought I was being a perfect husband. I had no idea that you felt bullied, or controlled by me. I never meant to do that to you. I still don't understand what I did or said to make you feel that way."

"We've been terrible at expressing what we felt, Guy. I was wrong to avoid issues. And you were wrong not to allow me to air my feelings I felt that the 'me' you had once mistakenly believed to be perfect, had fallen from the pedestal and there was nothing remaining.

"Your way was always 'THE' way. If I got a few words out, you would interrupt, thinking that you already knew what I was going to say, and usually you were wrong. I grew less and less confident." Amy had not realized that, as she spoke, she was reliving the past. As if in a dream, she was directing those words, not just to Guy, but to her parents. Fatigue and stress had taken its toll.

She paused. "My God, I just realized that I did this as a child, too." How many relationships had been weakened or destroyed by her victimized approach? So that was the part she had played to cause their marital problems. Like too many girls she had never learned how to speak politely, yet be assertive.

For Amy and Guy, this was a first move toward mending their marriage. They were really listening to each other. Listening with their ears, minds and hearts. They were able to see the part that each had played to weaken their bonds of love.

They had been facing the windshield, but glanced at one another intermittently. Now their concerns were so engrossing that they had squirmed to face each other, eye to eye. They held hands. Guy moved an arm around her shoulders.

"The strange thing is that our differences were always over small things." Amy continued. "They grew into major problems, because of the way we handled them. We must teach Barry ways to get along with others."

"You know, communication, and psychology are two of my favorite studies, yet I messed up. Knowledge is nothing without the wisdom to apply it. I lacked that wisdom."

"It's not surprising that so many marriages break up. The old rules have disappeared, and we are not teaching ways to cope with those changes, but we will learn."

They sat quietly. It was as if a cool, gentle breeze had taken much of their pain and sorrow away. It was as though the brisk night air was awakening a love stronger than they had ever felt for each other, even in their early years of marriage.

It was twilight, the time of day when a calm settles over all of nature and life pauses in retrospect. They could see a dim light behind the shutters in the upstairs window. There was another light in a shuttered downstairs window that appeared to be the kitchen.

Amy and Guy both needed sleep. They were powerless to do anything there so they left for the comfort of their apartment. Tomorrow they would get some action with Reilly's help. Their faith that Barry was safe sustained them.

Their manner toward one another was less self-conscious. They tenderly undressed each other, frequently embracing. Only the thoughts that they were not yet complete without Barry deterred their desire to make love. Guy leaned over her for a lingering, longing kiss that then traveled to touch every inch of her face, ears, throat, and each breast. Her arms encircled his neck. She stroked his forehead, touched his lips. Side by side, they fell asleep conscious of the sweetness of Kahili ginger blossoms drifting in from the gardens. Conscious of the miracle of their love.

They had left the Parkview Lane location shortly before the residents of the house arrived home from their vacation. If they had stayed, they would have seen lights going on all over the house. They might have heard the shouting and crying, and the bedlam inside.

In their state of mind, immersed in pain and frustration, their imaginations would have surely run wild. They had already conceived every plan possible to barge into the house to find Barry. If they had stayed, they would likely have been driven to desperation and would have tried to carry out those plans.

Listening to the radio somewhat helped relieve Barry of his fear and boredom. He wasn't being mistreated. She had promised he could go home someday. Not much comfort coming from someone he had learned to distrust. He was fed as often as he needed, considering his inactivity. It was simple food, probably from a can. Usually soup or stew, and one night the pizza. He had tried to get the pizza deliveryman to look up. There was a crack between the shutters where he could poke a ruler. He could not get it at an angle to hit the window hard, just little taps that the man didn't seem to hear.

Barry seldom knew whether it was morning, noon, or night. The room was dark with a small light. His favorite announcer, Kirk Collins, announced the time as 5:30 P.M. Usually it was talk, talk, talk. Sometimes they played music. He had heard his name on this station. Occasionally they spoke to him, told him to be brave and to be happy. They didn't know where he was, but they assured him that they were looking. So, he stayed tuned in and waited to be found. He hid the radio whenever he heard her coming.

Barry turned the volume down as low as he could, because he was afraid she would take the radio away from him. She had tried to get him to play card games. Said he could come downstairs if he "would be a good boy." But he felt safer in his little corner of the upstairs room.

Papa had told him that it was wrong to hate, but he did hate her. She had lied to him about all the things she had promised to show him in her house. None of it was true. When he came in, she had everything locked. Then she locked the door and wouldn't let him leave.

Sometimes he couldn't hold back the tears. He missed his Dad, Mom, and Papa so much. He wouldn't let her see him cry though. He was too mad at her, no matter how nice she tried to be to him, she should never have taken him away to her house and made him stay here. It was a mean thing to do.

Barry was getting hungry. He fell asleep often in the semi-darkness. He had been asleep for a while when he heard loud voices downstairs. One voice sounded very angry. Someone was shouting, cursing, and slamming things around. Another voice was crying and screaming, whining and pleading. Occasionally another voice, a man's voice, was trying to stop the others.

Barry jumped off the bed and put his ear to the door. He hadn't known anyone else was in the house. He couldn't understand what was being said. There were heavy footsteps on the stairs. Someone was coming toward this room. He leaped in the bed and pulled the covers up, almost covering his head, but leaving just a peephole.

The door opened. "Is he all right?" the voice growled. "Who is he? Why, oh why, did you do this? You little fool. We should never have left you alone. You don't have the brains of an idiot. Now what are we going to do? You are in trouble, little lady. You should be beaten within an inch of your life. Wait until the police get hold of you." The woman standing there silhouetted against the hall light was hurling a tirade of denunciation.

"Now, now Emma. Cool down. We have to think of what to do about this. It's true. We should have known better than to leave her here alone, but we must figure out what to do about it now."

Her husband's words made the woman more venomous. The shadowy figure stood in the doorway cursing like a mad woman. Barry hid under the covers, trembling and trying to make no sound.

"I'm going to bed. I'm worn out. Just knew something like this would happen." The sound of footsteps echoed in the corridor. He wondered what abuse someone had suffered, judging by the cries and screams he had heard earlier from downstairs.

Barry had spent long, lonely days in this dreary room. The past hour had been the worst. He lay there quivering from the explosion of anger. Sobs shook his small frame until he slept. At last, the house was quiet, and merciful sleep soothed the frightened child.

Chapter 29

Solutions

Both Amy and Guy were awake in the dark, in the silence, before sunrise. They each lay still, unmoving, unwilling to disturb the other. They listened to the birdcalls that gave credence to the arrival of a new day. Then sunlight formed patterns on the wall. Seeing that Amy was awake, Guy rolled out of bed. In moments, he was carrying two cups of coffee into the bedroom.

Yesterday, waiting and watching the house was the first time they had shared thoughts about their marriage and what they were willing, even eager to do, to remedy mistakes they had made. This morning their thoughts were so totally on Barry that words had to be chosen carefully to control their emotions. Talk became painful. Each tried to be brave and refused to consider the worst possibilities that came to mind.

"We'll get down to the police station as soon as it opens. Reilly will help us get a search warrant, . . . I think." He was afraid that the detective might be uncooperative. "Maybe I should call him first to tell him what we expect."

Silence interspersed by sounds from the cautious sipping of hot coffee. "Maybe we should get over early to see Dad before we go. My first thought was not to tell him until we are sure we are on the right track, but he told us off in no uncertain terms the other night for trying to spare him."

"He was mad as hell because we weren't sharing everything with him, Guy. Let's go for a short visit just to share as much positive information with him as we have, without exaggerating our hopes. He might think that we are keeping bad news from him. We'd better tell him that we are on to something that seems a good lead. Am I right, Guy?"

"Right on the button, Baby," he said, leaning over to kiss her on the tip of her nose.

On Parkview Lane, the birds in the trees that bordered the park were issuing forth so much noise to greet the new day that it could scarcely be called birdsong. It was more like a jungle of creatures defending their territories of nests and branches. A cacophony of scolding chirps, hoots, and trills.

An old woman with wispy gray hair awakened Barry. Deep grooves formed scowl lines between her black piercing eyes. The thin line of her lips turned down in disgust. The room had not been cleaned, or changed. It smelled stuffy and dusty. She poked her head into the bathroom and backed out bristling.

"Get up, boy. What's your name?" Barry was so frightened that he barely sounded his name. "Speak up! I can't hear you. Harry you say? Where are your clothes?" Barry was wearing his underpants, no shirt, no socks. He scurried about, gathering up his clothes, which were strewn all over the room, and she snatched them from his hand. "This is all you've got? I'll have to wash them. Can you give yourself a bath? God knows you must need one." Barry nodded his head vigorously. "Well then, get in there and bathe. I'm not going to wait on you."

In the kitchen, Emma laid out a plan to her husband to get rid of the boy without getting themselves in trouble. "If the authorities hear of this they'll put her away for good. That would probably be best for all of us. I'm worn out trying to cope with that girl. Now she's fixed us good, real good. We could all end up in jail. Now, here's my plan." She leaned over to speak confidentially to her husband.

"Oh, God. I don't know, Emma. I don't think we can get away with it. They'll find out who we are. Then we'll be in a heap of trouble. This is kidnapping. Do you realize what that means, woman?"

"Hush, old man. We have to do something, the sooner the better. You have a better plan? Turn back the clock maybe, like it never happened? Who do you think you are, the Wizard of Oz? Go tell that girl of yours to stay in bed until we get back, and not to move a hair. You hear?"

Early morning is the worst time to visit anyone in a hospital, but the Bensons had no trouble getting in to see Ben. He needed them. The staff knew that. His hopes were hanging on them. Above all, he needed to know that they forgave him for allowing Barry to be alone and out of his sight that day in the park. He was agonizing over it, and reliving what he could recall.

Guy stepped over a mop propped in the doorway. Amy followed behind him. Both chimed a cheery "Morning, Dad."

Ben waved, and pushed away his wheeled bed table with breakfast almost untouched. "Weh fa-you pin?"

"Dad, we were here to see you yesterday. We spent the rest of the day trying to learn more about Barry." The old man was all attention.

"Beh-weez aw-wite?"

"We feel sure he is, but we don't have him back yet. We're hopeful that today we'll find him. We'll call you as soon as we find out anything."

Ben was losing patience. Why were they here? Why were they not out doing all they could to bring his grandson home? But, in a sense he was relieved because they assured him the boy was all right. "Weh-ko-o den. Ko-o-o fine im," he said, making a shooing motion with his hand.

"We can't go now, Dad. We have to wait until the detective in charge is on duty. We want to take him with us to the place we think Barry is. And Dad, we're traveling on a wing and a prayer. We know nothing for sure, but we are confident anyhow. Add your prayers to ours. We'll need all the help we can get."

"Damn," thought Guy. "I have to give him some hope. It's hard enough for him to be here, unable to take part in getting Barry back, but how much can he take in his condition? If this doesn't work out . . . well, it just has to lead us closer." Guy could not bear to think of his father suffering further complications.

Amy was holding Ben's hand. "Dad, Guy and I are together again." She knew that Ben was as fond of her as she was of him, and that their separation had been hard on him. "We're never going to let anything threaten our marriage again." His smile was the first for a long, long time. His eyes were bleary as he patted her hand. "As soon as we find Barry we'll be moving back into the house. When they release you from the hospital, we want you to stay with us, at least until you get your strength back, and longer if you would like."

Amy looked at her husband. Whatever possessed her to say that, when they had not even had time to think or plan the future? There was a time she would never have said that without Guy's approval first. A look at his eyes and his grin assured her that they were in accord.

"We'll stay until you finish your breakfast, Dad. You've got to work to get stronger so you can get out of here."

It was the first time that Ben had believed he would be leaving the hospital alive. He had been sure his life was over. The depression had drained him of hope. His weakness was due more to his despair than to his physical condition. They had brought him hope today, and positive news about their marriage. He thought of Guy's mother, his wife of 56 years. She would be proud and pleased that their son and daughter-in-law were wise enough to treasure their love and honor their commitments. Ben's appetite returned, as they coaxed a few mouthfuls of food into him.

The three held hands while Amy and Guy alternated composing a prayer for Barry's safety and that he come home soon; for the return of Ben's strength and health, and that their family be blessed and strengthened throughout these trying times. "Amen," they said in unison, and squeezed their clasped hands.

Emma bustled about washing clothes, frying eggs and bacon, toasting and buttering bread. She grumbled about the condition of the kitchen. The unemptied trash, the dirty dishes left around. Ed ran up to his daughter's room to stay out from under his wife's feet.

A return to what was normal in this house did not fit what Barry had experienced here. Barry smelled the food cooking. Someone had taken his underpants away while he bathed. He had nothing to put on so he wrapped his body in a towel as he had seen his Dad do. He was experimenting with ways to keep it from falling off when a balding, round-shouldered old man with a kindly smile opened the door and beckoned to him to follow and get some breakfast.

It was the first time Barry had seen the other rooms of the house. The furniture looked old and battered, the walls drab. Cheap little knick-knacks cluttered tables and shelves. Barry followed Ed into the kitchen that Emma had made somewhat neater than the daughter had left it.

Emma and Barry stood staring at each other. Something made him unwilling to show his fear. His knees were trembling. She scowled. He scowled back.

"Come, sit down, boy." Ed said, pointing to a chair that needed paint.

Barry struggled with the towel to keep it from falling off, or opening up to embarrass him, and managed to scoot back on the chair seat.

"Hmmph" was all Emma could manage as she dished a greasy egg, toast, and bacon on the plate in front of him. He sat staring at it. "Well, go ahead. Eat. That's all you're going to get!" Emma moved her head side to side, with a sneer. "She gets worse and worse, all the time. Used to bring dirty, stray cats home. That was bad enough. Now you . . . the cats was better."

Ed took a plate of food upstairs to the girl in the back room. Apparently he ate his up there, too. The breakfast tasted better than it looked. Barry finished every bite. The crotchety woman ate without a word, removed the plates from the table, took the clothes from the dryer, and tossed them to the spirited little kid whose expression seemed to show that he would not be intimidated by her. "Hmmph," Emma said again.

"Now you skedaddle up those stairs, get your clothes on. Then you and I are going to have a long talk." Barry skedaddled fast, although he hadn't the slightest notion what that meant. He hoped it meant something to do with going back to Dad, Mom, and Papa. Halfway up, he stopped and retraced his steps, picked up his baseball cap, and raced back up the creaking stairway as fast as his legs would move.

Ed and Emma sat at the table in silence waiting for him to get dressed. "Come here, boy. Don't stand there like a suffering mouse. Now what did you say your name is? Harry?"

Barry scowled back at her. "Barry, not Harry."

"Well, Perry then, whatever," she grumbled. "Do you want to go home?"

The boy nodded eagerly.

"Do you know where you live?" Ed asked.

"No, you fool. We'll take him to a busy corner and let him out. Do you want witnesses to see you?" Emma drew a line on a piece of paper. "Here, we will let you out on a corner, like here." She pointed to two lines forming a ninety-degree angle. "You will walk down the street." She extended one line of the angle and drew an X. "There is the police station. We'll drive by it so you will know where it is. You walk into the station, go up to the nearest policeman, and tell him who you are and that you are lost. You understand?" Barry's heart was pounding with excitement. "Yes!"

Then Emma reached across the table, squinted her beady little black eyes, and grabbed him roughly by the shoulder. "You like the sound of this, don't you? Well, listen carefully, because unless you can do this right, you ain't goin' home . . . never." She said the final word in a menacing tone that made Barry's eyes open wide.

"Now, they's going to ask you a lot of questions. Just decide right now that you don't remember nothing.' Let's hear you say that." Barry was thinking this all over, puzzled. "Go on, let's hear you say it. 'I don't remember nothin'."

"I don't remember nothin'."

"Say it again!" she screamed, shaking his shoulder. His voice broke, tremulous from shock at her treatment, but he repeated it. "Now, ten times more, say it."

"I don' remember nothin'. I don' remember nothin'. Don' remember nothin'. Don' 'member nothin'," he repeated, his voice quavering until she was satisfied.

Ed sat, bent over, staring down at his hands folded. He let out a sigh and shook his head slowly.

Barry broke into heartrending sobs, digging his knuckles in his eyes.

"Now, they's gonna try ta get you to talk about where you been. Whatcha gonna say? Hurry up." She screamed in his ear. "Say, 'I dunno.'"

"I don' know." Barry sobbed.

"They'll ask you to tell them what we look like. You'll say . . ." she waited, and pinched his shoulder. Barry cried out in pain, managing to squeak out "I don' know-w-w. Ouch!"

"Tell them you couldn't see us, that you were in the dark. Now, here's what's gonna happen, boy, if you tell them anything about us." She spat out the words slowly, emphasizing each one. "The dev-il is gonna strike you DEAD. And then he'll kill yore folks, too. You don't want that to happen, do you?" Barry shook his head rapidly at the terrible threat she'd planted in his mind.

Ed was bending over with his face hidden in his hands. He straightened up, wringing his hands together. His eyes looked sad. The warnings, and threats continued until Emma was satisfied that her coaching had been effective. Barry was wavering between fear of her, and his delight at the prospect of seeing his family again. The woman reminded him of the stories of witches Dad had read to him. Mom didn't read him witch stories. Neither did Papa. Barry never wanted to hear another witch story, never again.

Chapter 30

It's Over!

An old woman begging on the corner watched a dilapidated 1970 model Buick slow down and come to a stop. She noticed the car because it was the same model that Cy had bought for them secondhand. Theirs had been such a shiny dark blue that she could see her reflection in it. It was maybe five or six years old at that time. The car she was now looking at was dirty and faded. The couple driving this one looked faded, too.

She had been about forty-five, Cy, about to turn fifty. She smiled. They had been a handsome couple. She saw her reflection in the showroom window of the store where she stood hoping to pick up a few quarters for the day ahead. Well, she thought, Cy wouldn't even recognize her now. Poor dear, struck down by a disease they'd never heard of, just as he was approaching retirement years. Her mind went blank so she returned to the present.

A little boy got out of the car holding on to his cap, and looking . . . all shook up . . . discombooberated, she decided. The man in the car reached over to pat his hand, and smiled. The cross woman made a gesture with her hand as if to shoo away a fly and glared at the child.

When Nettie noticed the nice lady who ran the art shop approaching, Nettie turned her attention to her and lost sight of the boy, and the car. Time to get busy greeting her public. Nettie felt that God had put her here, in this condition to humble her. She felt she was God's coworker who gave her public, as she referred to the pedestrians hurrying by, a chance to do the angels' work. The nice lady smiled this morning, and handed her a whole dollar. An angel indeed! Nettie's face lit up. The lady didn't need any more thanks than that smile, as she hurried along to her shop.

Detective Reilly had arrived at the precinct early. He was seated at his desk sorting through a stack of records of recently missing children. Where to start? Where were his priorities for today? His job was beginning to wear him down. If a child was missing, the first hope was that they had left of their own accord. Those children were usually picked up early and returned home.

The records on his desk were classified "dead-end" in regard to possible solutions . . . at least for the time being. They required imagination, creativity, much time, and a lot of luck. Some families were a lot of help. Sometimes they just turned to him as though he should bring about a miracle to find their missing child.

Reilly was staring at nothing in particular in the direction of the door opening into the street. A silhouette, framed by the glass door and backed by the sun's early rays, did not break his concentration. He recalled a parent wanted some help with his own investigation this morning. Which one was that? He had some far-fetched story . . . Reilly turned to read his notes from yesterday. On his calendar he had written the file number for the Benson case.

He was deep in thought, thumbing through the stack on his desk when he felt a gentle tug at his sleeve. He turned to stare into a pair of dark brown eyes in a child's face.

"Excuse me, sir. That man told me to tell you I'm Barry Benson."

The man he referred to was the officer who greeted everyone entering the main entrance. The same man who was standing there now with hands on hips, roaring with great guffaws at the surprise on Reilly's face.

"He just walked in and introduced himself, Red." Everyone was now turning to see Red Reilly's reaction. Some were searching for the candy and toys they kept in their desks, waiting for such an occasion when some kid would be brought in safe and sound.

"For crying out loud, Barry. Where you been, boy?" It wasn't often that one of his lost kids delivered himself to his desk. The grin on his face relaxed the lines of care and despair that seemed etched between his brows, and on his forehead from so many less joyful times he had faced in this job.

"I want to find my Mom and Dad, and Papa, please. Will you take me home, please?"

Reilly reached out to hug the boy, but the child leaped back, out of his reach. Whoa, Reilly reminded himself. We've got a way to go yet. This kid's not ready to trust anyone now.

"Here, Barry. Have a candy bar." Someone approached and offered it to him. Then other voices. "Are you hungry, Barry? Bet you'd like a hot dog, or a hamburger. What do you want partner? Some ice cream?" Everyone in the precinct was so happy, they wanted to please him.

He sat in the big stiff-backed chair they offered him next to Reilly's desk, and repeated, as though the dam was about to break in those eyes now swimming in tears, "I just want my Daddy, and my Mom, and Papa."

The secretary had immediately been alerted to call his family. No one answered. "Is there an answering machine? Well then, leave a message that we have their son." Damn, thought Reilly. Where can I reach them? "Where do they work? Did you call them there?"

"They haven't been working since the boy's been missing. What about the hospital? Maybe the old man's still there." Barry turned to look at the speaker.

"Well, get the number, for Christ's sake." Reilly bellowed. Then the phone on his desk rang. He grabbed it before the first ring was completed. "Reilly here." He was ready to tell the party he'd call them back. Instead, a relieved sigh issued forth from his lips as he heard a man say, "Mr. Reilly, this is Guy Benson. We are coming right down."

"How the hell did you know, Benson? We just found out."

"Know what? . . . Found out what?"

"That your son is here. He's okay. Here, I'll put him on."

"Barry's okay?" he almost whispered, disbelieving. All eyes in the room were on him. No one took a breath. The tension was at its highest when Guy yelled at the top of his lungs, out of control now, "Barry's okay. He's at the station house with Reilly. Barry, Barry, is that really you? Yes, Mom's here, and Papa, too."

Guy gave the phone to his wife. "Oh, Barry, sweetheart. You're all right." She managed to gasp out the words. "We'll be right there to get you, baby."

The nurse was weeping. The lady mopping the floor was frozen in her tracks. Like the statue game played by children, she held her position. Both parents were bawling. Unwilling to surrender the phone, they were both gripping it to hear the dear voice, but the sound at the other end was crying, too.

Ben was unable to cry until he had said a prayer of thanks. Then, he buried his face in the white bedcover, and let go with rejoicing from the depths of relief and gratitude. Amy held the phone for Ben, who said slowly, almost perfectly, "Hello, my boy. I love you."

There wasn't a dry eye at the station house either. Reilly got on another phone to tell the Bensons to stay just where they were. He would send Barry with one of the district patrol officers if they would tell the driver the room number. He made only one condition. He was not supposed to release Barry until he had a physical examination, and had answered some questions. "Arrange for a doctor at the hospital to examine him and I'll release him to you right now."

"Meanwhile, don't ask the boy questions. Let him offer what he wants to tell you, but you ask no questions. Get it? Write down everything he says, as soon as possible so you won't forget it, but don't write while he's talking. That might upset him. We haven't asked him any questions yet. I think it would be better if I go to your place to ask my questions. Is that agreeable?"

The answer was affirmative. Guy was appreciative of Reilly's sensitivity. He hung up the phone, weak from the emotion, spent from the effort to restrain himself, conscious of the toll this would take on his father, grateful beyond his ability to express himself for God's grace.

Breathless, the parents and the grandfather slowly regained control, still in awe of the boundless gift they had been given, the immensity of it. Amy and Guy stood across from each other on either side of Ben's bed. Once again they all closed their eyes, held hands, and spoke the beauteous Lord's Prayer slowly, and thoughtfully. Each word rang with a power they had never heard or felt before this moment.

Chapter 31

Drugs and Our Children

Barry had heard the detective refer to the hospital and something about "the old man." He was too frightened to even ask the officer why they were going to a hospital. The policeman's attempt at light patter even evoked a smile or two from Barry, but he was not the same child as before who scarcely ever stopped talking and questioning. During his ordeal he had been courageous and patient, but he was deeply affected, as his parents and grandfather were about to discover.

Amy was peering down the hall toward the elevator. She paced to the bed, and then returned to the door, until at last, there he was. She raced down the hall toward her son, arms outstretched.

The patrolman was looking at the directory to find Ben's room number. Barry caught a glimpse of his mother running to meet him, Guy was right behind her.

Barry pulled away from the startled patrolman, and took off, shouting "Mommy! Daddy!" All action in the halls was frozen. The couple reached him at the same time, and knelt to his level. His arms encircled their necks. Tears streamed. Guy and Amy clutched the child they feared they might never see again.

Words lacked power to express the joy. A crowd gathered. People touched their shoulders and patted the boy's head, unable to suppress the desire to be a part of this happy occasion, even if they weren't sure what was going on.

Ben, who had progressed to the point of being able to get up for daily exercise, was getting out of bed, refusing to be left out of the reunion occurring in the hall. The nurse fairly flew to help him to his feet and to put the walker in front of him. She stationed herself beside him and cautioned him to move slowly, but God seemed to lend him wings as he shuffled through the door.

His first view, hazy without his glasses, showed a crowd gathering.

His questions abated when the nurse assured him that his grandson was there, and all was well. Another nurse was coming up behind him with a wheel chair in case this spurt of adrenaline dissipated.

"Well, I don't think I need to ask for identification," chided the grinning officer. He helped the parents to their feet. Guy picked up his son. Amy clung to them both. An aide was handing out tissues to everyone.

Another aide turned to Barry and said, "It looks like you are the honored guest at this party, Barry. Would you like to ride in a wheelchair next to your grandpa's chair?" Barry hesitated, till Guy placed him in the chair. Amy held Barry's hand, walking alongside while Guy pushed. Papa, in the other chair now, took Barry's other hand while a nurse pushed him. The whole group proceeded down the hall to Ben's room, the room he would soon be well enough to vacate.

The crowd began to disperse, people were daubing at their eyes. Then, the family was alone in the room. Someone on the staff had draped a few paper decorations. Where the streamers had been found was a mystery. Obviously there are happy occasions in a hospital to balance the pain and sorrow, and this was one of them.

It would take a long time to catch up with all they had to say. Later, they would file charges against Ed, Emma, and their daughter, Earlene. Now, they could only concentrate on the good news, which would, of necessity, be interrupted by police business and decision-making.

Igor had hoped he would scoop other local media when Barry was found. He got his scoop. For now the family wanted as little publicity as possible until they had the story from Barry.

As Guy had promised the detective, the family listened to Barry, but did not pry except to be sure that their son had not been physically or mentally abused. The doctor made the physical examination of Barry as simple as possible. He noticed no marks on his body except some bruises on the shoulder where Emma had gripped the boy while intimidating him. Her attempt had been effective. Barry not only feared for his own welfare, but also for that of his father, mother and Papa. When he saw his grandfather in a wheelchair, and later in the hospital bed, he wondered if the old witch had carried out her threat.

For a long time Barry gave vague replies and answered, "I don't know" to Detective Reilly's every question. Barry also feared for the girl who had abducted him. He recalled her weeping and crying out in fear after the strange couple had returned home. At times, Barry referred to the younger woman as "she".

When Amy asked who "she" was, the story poured out. He reminded his mother of the babysitter who had cared for him weeks ago, the day Amy had driven her home. Things started coming together. Amy had never called the sitter again after the day she and Guy met at her lawyer's office. Amy had been right to doubt her. The girl was not normal.

Reilly traced the girl by phoning the mother who had given Amy her name. Yes, she had driven her home once. She lived on Parkview Drive. The Bensons' eyebrows rose in unison. The case was broken. A police car was dispatched to pick them all up for questioning. While they were at the station, a search warrant was obtained to allow the police officers to enter the house. A sketch in Reilly's hand revealed the floorplan as Barry had described it. The door leading to the kitchen, the stairway, the room upstairs where he had been kept. He explained all in detail, and drew some lines on a rectangle to show where everything was placed in the house. He described the room where he was kept in detail, the radio, and the shutters. They had the kidnappers in custody. Now to determine, why they did it.

"That girl will be the death of me," Emma said. "She's been a problem ever since I married her father. Why, you should see our bills for her medication. Disgusting what they charge. Look at this bill, and she's been on them for years. Never helps. This was all her doing. Doesn't have good sense, that's the problem."

In another room, Ed sat with his head in his hands and looked miserable. "Why didn't we take the boy to the police station, or call them? Well, the fact is, we was just plain scared when we got home and found him there. I knew it was wrong the way we did it, but you don't know Emma. That woman's insistent. She gets an idea and there is no talk about it. It's got to be her way. Fact is, I don't know what to do with the woman, but I'm scared of what would happen to my daughter and me if we didn't have her. Yeah, I know she seems mean, but she isn't really. She's just excitable . . . especially if she can't control everything and everyone."

It was no use trying to get anything out of the girl. They couldn't decide if she was stupid or drugged until the tests came in. "Doc Kepke," Reilly asked in a call to his own doctor, "I've got a list here of medications given to a girl we picked up." A pause. "Yeah, I can read them to you if I can pronounce them. Here goes."

After hearing the numerous medications and over-the-counter drugs, the doctor assured him that anyone mixing them or taking them in quantity would be in a bad way. Their investigation showed that they were being given to her without a doctor's advice, or supervision.

The couple admitted they shouldn't have left her alone, but a relative on another island needed their help. They took a chance that it would all work out, and they'd get a vacation of sorts. It probably would have worked out except that the girl was lonely. She intended no harm, just wanted someone around. Then she saw Barry alone. Told him things to entice him to go with her. Like claiming she had a bird and fish in her house to show him. When they got in the house and there was no bird, and no fish, Barry tried to leave. She was dumb, but smart enough to know that if she let him go she'd be in trouble just for having taken him there. Besides, she hoped that he would be a companion, and play games with her.

While her parents were gone she didn't take her medications, the stuff they usually gave her. They had been decreasing the dosage before they left, so the withdrawal was gradual. She began to feel better. She pretended that Barry was her little boy. In her mind she was taking care of him.

Reilly told Guy and Amy that it was up to them if they wanted to press charges. The girl had been put under a doctor's care and the police were waiting for a report from a psychiatrist.

"This is KABC, Igor Connifer bidding you good morning. The time is 10:00 A.M. I have great news to share with you listeners. The couple whose son has been missing have Barry back safe and sound. The parents, Guy and Amy Benson, and his grandfather, Alf Benson, who was the last one to see him before he was abducted, want to thank everyone for your help. Many of our listeners have been praying for all of them. Our prayers were answered. Welcome home, Barry."

"Our subject this morning is about a newspaper clipping from our local paper. It was sent to us by a listener. The author is Dr. Peter R. Breggin, a Bethesda, Maryland psychiatrist who has written this to make us aware of a hazard we are imposing on many children.[1]

"Dr. Breggin writes of the forced drugging of *about ten percent, or more school-age children who are given psychiatric drugs,* and how the practice is increasing. That's about *five or six million kids. It doesn't include the children in mental hospitals, foster care, special classes and in juvenile detention centers. Those rates are even higher.*

He says that *stimulants such as Ritalin and Adderall and antidepressants such as Prozac and Zoloft are among those drugs prescribed.* He reminds us that most adults these days are *steeped in the mythology of psychiatric drugs.* And that those adults are *tinkering with the children's brain chemistry.*

The reasons? . . . *Because their parents and their teachers haven't found a way to reach them with the necessary combination of rational discipline, unconditional love and engaging relationship. And because society has failed to address the whole range of problems that afflict our children—from the breakdown of the family and the educational system to child abuse, sexism, racism, poverty and inadequate health care.*

Dr. Breggin points out that the kids who get drugged are *literally any kids who do not put on a happy face and conform . . . children who are sad, anxious, angry and aggressive, as well as disobedient . . . even those who are shy or dreamy.*

They're given drugs, the doctor says, when we should be finding ways to *silence their signals of distress.* In recent years we are hearing educators echo the psychiatrist's labels. We hear about Attention-Deficit Hyperactivity Disorder, Oppositional Defiant Disorder and Clinical Depression. Dr. Breggin says that these labels *blame the children themselves and their presumably faulty brains.*

Folks Dr. Breggin is like a breath of fresh air. Listen to this, then we'll open our phone lines for your comments. The following is also from the doctor's article and we're talking about legal drugs, folks.

Drug companies and organized psychiatry have indoctrinated the average American to believe that personal suffering can be fixed by drugs. Now conflict in the family or the classroom is likely to lead to the drugging of the weakest link in the conflict, the child . . . We are forcing psychiatric drugs on children and teenagers to silence their signals of distress and to make them conform to our expectations.

Ninety percent of the world's Ritalin is used in the United States. The International Narcotics Control Board of the World Health Organization has warned us about the massive over prescription of stimulants to children in our country. We may be guaranteeing that future generations will be relatively devoid of people who think critically, raise painful questions, generate productive conflicts, or lead us to new spiritual and political insights.

This drug epidemic among our children comes increasingly from our prescription counters . . . It's time to stop . . . It requires a thorough reevaluation of personal and political priorities, and a determination to create a society that meets the needs of its children, for adult relationships, solid family life and inspiring education.

Instead of chemically restraining and gagging them, we need to do the hard work of reordering our private lives and our public policies to address the needs of our nation's children.

"Well, there you have it, folks. How do you like them apples? Call in to tell our other listeners what you think. This is the straight stuff from a reputable psychiatrist who has not been drawn into the over-medicating of our children, and is highly critical of it. This is KABC, Igor speaking. Anonymous is on the line."

"I am appalled by the news article you just read by Dr. Breggin. I'm a clerk in a school office, and I don't know how much I have been contributing to this. It's nuts. If we have verification from a doctor, we are told to give children their dosage. They have to come to the office to get it. I'm wondering if I would be fired if I refuse to do it."

"Well ma'am. Why don't you ask your principal and see what he says? Maybe you've hit on something to counter this sickness in our society. Thanks for calling."

"Bo on the line."

"What do you have to say, Bo?"

"I'm just calling to say, they never give up, do they? In the fifties, my pop turned me over to some egghead who said I needed shock treatments. Now those were a lot of fun. You've never been jolted till you've had a shock treatment. Hah! Before that was in fashion, it was lobotomy. Did you ever see the movie *Bless the Beasts and the Children*? Well, they need all the blessing they can get, 'cause our society is getting sicker, and sicker, and that's all I've got to say."

"Guess that said it all, Bo. Bless you too, man, and thanks for your call. The board is lighting up folks. Many people have something to say about this. Allen is next. You there, Allen?"

"One of the worst things we are doing now is the advertising by big drug companies on television, and in magazines and newspapers. We already know how effective the tobacco companies were at convincing people that nicotine was helpful, and legitimate. Well, here we go again to convince new generations. Now instead of only killing the body we are going to justify killing our kids' brains."

"I appreciate you bringing that up, Allen. You think such advertising is wrong, eh?"

"I don't just think it. I know it. The saddest thing about our culture is that we don't even know the difference between right and wrong any more."

"Yeah, you got that right. Thanks, Allen. I'd like to add another quote from Dr. Breggin, he says . . . '*Soaked in Prozac and Xanax, as well as alcohol and marijuana, the older generations now find it reasonable and expedient to force psychiatric medications on children*'. Yeah."

"Next caller is Bess. Go ahead, Bess."

"Am I on? I'm a nurse in a psychiatric office. I've read Dr. Breggin's article. He also said that children 6 to 10 years old are sometimes put on four or five psychiatric medications at once. It's inhumane."

"And that says a lot, Bess. We thank you. Go ahead. Melanie is on."

"I've had my son on Ritalin for six months now. I can't tell you how awful it was before we got this medication to help him. Now he is calm. He has lost the destructive ways that were driving the rest of the family crazy. We can't believe the change in him. So I want to say that your listeners should not be expressing opinions unless they've been there."

"Ouch! The lady slammed the phone down a bit hard. Well, she has a point, too. Many parents need help. We need to do a better job of supplying troubled families with answers. Wise answers, help, and education that will include a peek into what it means to get married and bring children into the world. We certainly need to be good models for our children, and that doesn't mean that we can abuse drugs and then expect them not to do it."

"Signing off now. Kirk will be on this afternoon at 3:30 P.M. This is Igor bidding you good day, and good future."

[1] Peter R. Breggin, "Today's children suffer from legal, prescribed drug abuse." Special to *Newsday* distributed by *Los Angeles Times-Washington Post* News Service, West *Hawaii Today*, Sept 27, 1999.

Chapter 32

Tutoring

"Sure, I know each of us is getting a hell of a lot of good out of the work we are doing. What I'm asking is, what are we really accomplishing with the kids we're tutoring? It seems to me that we are helping them to limp a little, but will they ever take off and fly?"

The other members of the group only stared at Rod Holcombe. He had been their most recent participant. Most of them were singles trying to put their lives back together, following crippling effects from the death of, or divorce from, someone they had loved. Tutoring kids afternoons and evenings had put some meaning back into their lives.

"What's the problem, Cap? Just because you haven't had any of our kids sign up for Harvard yet is no sign we're not helping them."

"Oh, we're helping them. I've seen a difference in their math ability . . . as long as we read a math problem to them, but give them the story problem in writing and they are lost. It's as if a gate blocks their reasoning."

"That's exactly it. They're frustrated because their vocabulary is so limited. Some of them can't read at all. Others can't read well enough, or fast enough, or their fear that someone will discover their reading problem simply closes the mind down. It's a no confidence reaction that results in fear, and we've lost them."

"Well, if all we are doing for them is getting them past each homework assignment with our help, then we have to do more." Rod Holcombe persisted. "We thought when we started this that these were kids who had learned to read. They haven't, so we need some specialists in how to teach reading. Who will follow this up by contacting some literacy resource teachers? They're in the phone book under Hawaii State Education." All eyes focused on him.

"Okay, done," he offered, since he had brought up the problem. That was the least he could do, he admitted. "But I want to know how many kids in our schools can't read and are able to keep it a secret. And how many learned to read but were never required to use the skill, thus never read enough to have progressed?"

"And here come the gremlins." Noah grinned, and nodded his head toward the library door. "Looks like a new one tonight."

"That's Keola's big brother," Sandy replied. "He usually dumps him out at the door when he is supposed to be taking care of him."

"Hey there, big guy," Noah called. "You joining us tonight? Where's Keola?"

"He's coming. And hell no . . . got more to do than sitting here."

"Yeah, what for instance? How are your grades?"

"Not to worry, I was suspended."

"No kidding." Noah persisted. "What do you do with your time when you're suspended, Brah?"

"Got lots to do, and don't call me 'brah'. I ain't got no haole brahs." Keoki said with a sneer. "See you later, kid," he said to his little brother as he swaggered out the door.

"Can't win them all," Noah reminded himself.

More of their regulars had entered and were taking their places. "Hi, guys. How's it going?" Noah Solomon tousled a few heads. "Put your homework out in front of you, and get started. If you don't understand something, raise your hands." All but two kids immediately began waving their arms for attention. The tutors moved in to help them get started.

Keoki strode down the street . . . turning his head first right, then left as he walked. About half way down the block, he took one last look around. As he opened the car door on the passenger side of the shiny black Datsun, there was a blast from the stereo. He slipped into the seat beside the driver. A dark film covered the windows and windshield. The car lurched forward, moved away from the curb. The tires squealed and they drove out of sight.

A nondescript Chevy pickup, too dirty and battered to recognize its color, followed at a somewhat slower speed, but kept the Datsun in sight.

Chapter 33

Apple A Day Meeting

It had been an exciting meeting, more positive than negative. Everyone was pleased with the radio broadcasts thus far. Many were disturbed that they lived out of the range of Igor's small station, but someone had gotten the idea of taping broadcasts to sell to members, who could then pass them along to others who also lived too far away to hear them. The cost would be minimal, just enough to cover expenses, and to put a small amount in their treasury for incidentals.

Igor was living in a coffee shack someone had offered him rent-free for a year. This still left Igor without income. Three restaurants offered him meal tickets until there were solutions to that problem. He found fruit and vegetables, coffee and rice dropped off at his door with no evidence of who was doing it. Igor found an early morning clean up job in a shopping center.

One morning he had returned to find an old truck with a note attached, and a card for gasoline credit at one of the stations. Most of his errands and his job were within walking distance, but it was nice to have transportation, he thought, if it runs that is. It did run, like a top. Igor felt like he'd "died and gone to heaven," as he told Kirk. What more could he ask for. Just the success of the people he had joined forces with, the community, and members of Apple A Day, Inc.

Igor was now a community celebrity. He, spoke at the meeting to thank those, known and unknown who were helping him, and the "cause", as he phrased it. Then he sat back to watch the people, and just listen.

They were as enthusiastic as though nothing could hinder them. They were going to change education, and make themselves into the most enviable community in the state . . . maybe they would set an example for the whole U.S.A. The general attitude of the participants was "Full speed ahead."

"Well, why not aim high?" he thought. That contest that the members had voted to post was to challenge all architects, or draftsmen, to submit a design for an educational center. It was to include a library large enough to be stocked with audio and computer centers, with books suitable for college, and high school level materials. A committee would be formed to determine the rules and requirements. The community needed meeting rooms, small, large, and expandable.

There was to be a contest for the landscaping, as well. A plan as maintenance free as possible yet useable, attractive and practical. That would have to wait until the best building plans were chosen.

Meanwhile, volunteers were beginning to write for government grants, under the guidance of people well versed in that art. Speaking of art, there would be competition among artists of all media to design art for gardens, walls, indoor and outdoor.

The people at that meeting were fairly dancing in the aisles with the enthusiasm engendered. Igor hoped that they wouldn't forget that the most important project was to change the emphasis on teaching skills and techniques.

How was the community going to accept the requirement that students must take responsibility for their own education? They would be assisted and guided by teachers, aides, citizens of the community, by business, manufacturing and technology mentors, toward receiving an expanded education to serve them well in the future. The students and their parents would take responsibility for keeping records of goals accomplished. It certainly would be a new way to look upon teaching in the twenty-first century.

Chapter 34

KABC on the Air

"Good afternoon, friends and neighbors, Kirk Collins with you wherever you are. Igor has some time off. Gail Sanderson, guest teacher, and a dozen students are here to share their thoughts and experiences in public education. We honor their wish to be anonymous. I'll use first names only, or names they provided me for this program. Who is our spokesperson?"

"I'll start." Sandy offered. "We are discussing ideas that are new to us. We may embrace or reject them, or just listen and discuss to get different perspectives. Apple A Day, Incorporated has some plans."

"Ms. Sanderson, would you give us a broad idea of subjects we'll cover today?"

"Thanks, Kirk, for this opportunity. We want more people to know about us. People may think that our ideas are extreme. The other day I picked up a current magazine and realized that one of our ideas has worked elsewhere."

"Can you say what this is?"

"It's not such a new idea after all, according to this magazine article by Doctor Andrew Weil. I'll quote: *"In his second year at Harvard Medical School in the mid '60s, Weil led a revolt against what he called its 'deadening curriculum'. His group petitioned to be excused from all classes, saying they could teach themselves better and would take the comprehensive exam at year's end to prove it . . . Harvard officials complied, but unannounced, they changed the exam's usual format to assure the tests would be valid. Weil's group passed anyway. It was his first attempt to change the way doctors are educated . . . He is currently designing curricula for a program he is developing at the University of Arizona College, called Integrative Medicine.*

"We are hoping to use a similar self-directed study program for above-average students. We are concentrating on students who already know how to study. We, of course, must provide sources, inspiration, and guidance. This is not for students doing average or below average work. We believe that if our young people are encouraged to read and are allowed to choose according to their interests, those interests will broaden until the students will want to educate themselves."

Kirk jumped in to involve more of the students. "Do you all agree that you would like to be excused from classes and be allowed to study on your own?"

"At first I was shocked at the idea; then I considered how frustrated I get when so much study time is wasted by well-meaning teachers who are helping other students. It is usually help I don't need. I try to just get started on the assignment while in the classroom, but the class activity is distracting at the least, and often completely disruptive."

"I agree. I don't need time in class to read my assignment. Sometimes I need the library, or my computer to complete other assignments, but I'm sitting there waiting for class to be dismissed. Sometimes they're reading aloud. That bugs me."

"Well, I always have something with me to do or I can read when that happens. Sometimes the teacher is repeating what I got the first time. The assignment is to read the textbook before class, which I do, but most kids don't. It isn't right that teachers pamper those who don't study by spending class time going over what they should have done before class. We could use that time to discuss the assignment, or to introduce related material to broaden our knowledge."

"That's true. They know she'll nurse them through it. She has to do that because we are in the same classroom with some who don't read well, or they just don't have confidence, so . . . yeah, there's a lot of time wasted every day. There are sometimes kids in class who don't even know English yet. I could get a lot more done at school and wouldn't have to study as long at night, if I had more freedom during the day."

"I've had a couple of teachers who just dismiss the 'A' students to the library. We don't need to go over all of the question-and-answer exercises she reviews with the other students. We know how to proceed on our own to do reports or do research. It makes me feel good to be trusted like that."

Kirk spoke up to summarize what the students had been saying. "So, you all seem to agree that you could do the assignments without attending entire classes, and that for your needs, much of class time is wasted. But you also seem to be saying that what you call 'wasted time' may be necessary for most other students?"

The students looked at one another and shrugged. They seemed uncomfortable.

Kirk jumped in to fill the silence. "Our listening audience can't hear shoulders shrugging, but you seem to be saying that you don't know how many students would be capable of going off on their own to study."

"For most of the students it isn't a matter of being unable to work on their own. If they can read, they could do the work, too. Many guys in the class just don't have any interest in school. I'm one of the 'dorks'. I don't mind what they call me. We get along with each other even if we're different. I like school. I like to learn. I've always been interested in everything."

"Ms. Sanderson, I understand that Apple A Day does not think highly of text books. Why is that?"

"The ever-rising cost, plus the degree of educational value to students make textbooks prohibitive. Teachers spend hours checking them in and out so that several classes can use one set. Parents must be called to find books left at home. Records are kept by teachers to record fines owed for lost or damaged books. Many students don't value books, and they deface them. Many never read them. They may fail the test, but still pass the course. Books used to be replaced every seven years. Now the information in them is obsolete in much less time, so the books need to be replaced. Textbooks contain limited, often dull facts, while contemporary books go more into depth by expanding on interesting material that relates to the subject."

"Are you saying we should do away with textbooks?"

"No, keep a few in the library for reference the same way encyclopedias are used for reference, instead of issuing one textbook to each student, or trying to have three or more classes sharing one set. Students could then get the gist of a subject, list necessary vocabulary, and then look for books or magazines about what interests them. This would assure that their information is up to date in this era of information overload."

"Can someone explain how a student can pass a course without reading the book?" Kirk asked.

"Some students get a high school diploma, yet they cannot read well enough to function in the world. For the past half-century or more some students have received high school diplomas without being able to read. They suffer terribly trying to hide their secret, but they learn to compensate, usually by having someone else do their necessary reading.

"There are students in almost every teacher's class who lack the necessary reading and writing skills. The teacher tries to compensate by spending limitless class time to help them understand the subject matter.

"That's why we're here today. It is why these students say that their time is wasted in classes, and they could use that time to read, and learn by themselves."

"There are varying degrees of illiteracy. Many cases could be improved just by requiring students to read more, a lot more. It is important to start where a student is now. Then gradually require more advanced material. It is important that reading material appeals to their curiosity and their interest."

"Your group also suggests that students choose their own reading material. How can that be done? Let me direct this question to our student guests: Would you like to do that to get a grade for reading anything you want to?"

"Speak up. No head nodding, please. Rod."

"Sure, I read textbooks, but I'd rather not be tested on them. I'd rather expand on a subject by reading more human-interest things related to the subject. I learn a lot about places, history, and even historic figures by reading a good novel, a biography, or a current history book. I'd like that. I don't mind being tested on vocabulary, or related names of people or places in a textbook, but it's easier to remember things that interest me."

Kai interrupted. "Anything that gets students to read more is a good thing, especially if, some students are graduating without even knowing how to read well."

"Well, everyone hang in there. Igor is back to help with phone calls. We'll need the help of our student guests to answer our callers. Esther is on the line. Go ahead, Esther."

"I'm glad you're talking about reading. I know my son learned how to read, because I used to listen to him when he was in the first or second grade. Now he's in high school, and I never see him reading anything. Says he doesn't like to, yet the school keeps sending home . . . passing grades. He never brings a book home to read. Could someone tell me how this happens?"

"Lottie?"

"We never have very much reading assigned in classes. I love to read so I read on my own. If you read a lot, your vocabulary increases, which makes reading easier, and more fun. If you don't read you lose the skill you had in early grades when you learned only basic words. There are always new things, and then we have new and more advanced vocabulary. If some kids don't read they aren't learning as much vocabulary as the other kids are. They'll be shut out of what's going on in the world.

"Reading skill is just like basketball, or football. You get better when you practice, and you get worse when you don't. Secondary school students don't read first-grade stories anymore, but that's the level their vocabulary is stuck in."

"Cal?"

"Not only that, but it gets to be a game. The non-readers are trying to hide their inability from everyone. Teachers want to help the poor readers by having people read aloud in class, and they lecture to cover main points. In fact they will even give grades for "Mickey Mouse" projects so the nonreaders can pass. They give grades for effort, or good citizenship so that overrides the low grades they got in their work."

"Whoa! If they can't read how can they be asked to read aloud in class?"

"Easy. Reading aloud doesn't mean you understand it. When I read aloud I am concentrating on pronunciation, not on meaning. They are two different skills, but it sure fools some teachers. Heck, I can read Spanish aloud because I know how to pronounce it, but I don't have enough Spanish vocabulary to understand what I'm reading. That's their trouble, too."

"Eddie, you want to add to that?"

"Not really, except to say that even people who are dyslexic can be taught to read by specialists. Some teach themselves. There's no cure for people who don't read well, except to read more and more, starting at the level they're at."

"Etta's on the line. What's your question, Etta? Does this all make sense to you?"

"No. This Apple group . . . or whatever, believes that letter grades should be eliminated. That's just crazy. How do students apply to colleges if they have no grades to submit? My question is for the teacher you've got there."

"Guess that means me." Sandy smiled. "Anyone who thinks that letter grades show what students have learned should read a study that proves otherwise. Ten teachers took part in an experiment. Each teacher was given a report from each of ten students. The teachers, without any discussion, recorded a confidential grade for each. The grades showed disagreements that differed as much as from failing to 'A'. Most grading is based on the teacher's subjective standards. Percentage grades may be more objective, but there is a degree of subjectivity in any evaluation.

"Furthermore, as Cal said, teachers will substitute other assignments rather than fail students who can't do the required work. Each teacher has his or her own set of standards. The terms "excellent, good, average, below average, and failed" seem to be clear, but each one can mean different things for different people.

Students know when they receive inflated grades. Receiving unrealistic grades is the worst preparation for the world of work, where bosses will someday hand out evaluations that do not coddle their employees."

"Then how can parents know whether the work their children are doing is sufficient, and well done?"

"Exactly! That's the key question! Thank you. Do you ever have your children show you the work they've done, the achievements that their grades are based on?"

"Well, I don't know if I see all of their work. They probably only show me if they got a good grade. Sometimes I think the grade is too high for the quality of their work."

"Exactly. The only way we can tell if our children are accomplishing is to see their work. Save and compare one year's work to that of the previous years. A grade point average only shows consistency, cooperation, or conformity. It doesn't show how students are progressing. In the upper grades our students are required to read and write much less than is expected of students in other countries.

"Pass or fail is enough appraisal for the work of each quarter. Failing should mean no credit, which translates to 'not enough effort to have made progress.' It is determined by how much a student has read. The student has been able to write or say what was learned through each study. The teacher's role is to just read or listen to the students' reports and to help them do better and better work."

"And Gilbert is on the line. Yes, sir, your question?"

"My son came home with a failing grade last year. He was at school every day. I can't see how he could be failed. He must have gotten something from the class if he was there every day."

"Who wants this one? Pat? Go ahead, Pat."

"Some students are in school every day, but do almost nothing. Some parents think they are there every day, but they're not. Be glad that a teacher had the guts to fail him. Were his grades good in his other classes? (Is that a 'no' I hear?) Well, something is going on with him. From my experience as a student, it is hard to fail. He just doesn't care. Or he wants you to notice, and care. He must feel like . . . well, I almost said a naughty word. He must have low self-esteem. I sure hope you, or the counselors, will listen to him."

"We have time for one more caller. Lydia. Hello, your question is . . .?"

"I still don't see what teachers are going to grade on."

"Briefly, please, Ms. Sanderson."

"Students can choose from an established curriculum that prepares them for their future, for survival and fulfillment. That future may be higher education, technology, art studies, construction, medicine, law, sports, etc. The students may explore the world at large until they have preferences.

"Study means first to read and understand the basic vocabulary of each subject, and the basic knowledge related to it. Then the student can watch related videos or read books, or listen to what other students have read or written. After a subject is covered to the minimal degree, students can decide whether to continue studying that subject in depth, as long as they're interested, or move on to another required subject.

"Report, means to share with others; teacher, parent, friend, or the children of lower grades. Reports may be written, read, spoken, or presented through visual arts such as photography or drawings. The reports must be of value to others and show that the student making the report has learned something.

"Students are constantly reading, studying, and reporting. There is no limit to how much they can accomplish. If subjects required for each grade level are covered, students may move on to higher levels of study for the topics they choose. Students must master the basic requirements in a predetermined number of subjects. After that, they can explore the basics of new subjects or go for in-depth knowledge of something they've already studied. Furthermore, students can work at their own pace.

"Points may be determined to measure and record how much students accomplish. Those points are the guides to awarding of credits, and the accumulation of sufficient credits leads eventually to a diploma. Teachers and parents will make sure that the required curriculum is being studied."

"And that brings us to the end of our broadcast for today. Thank you, teacher and students, for your participation. Thank you, callers. This is Kirk Collins, here with Igor, as we sign off with a promise to be here tomorrow. You be here, too!"

Kevin turned in his chair to see Igor giving him a thumbs-up sign. They smiled in mutual appreciation.

Chapter 35

Chickadee

Chieko sighed with contentment. She had finished her courses at the New England Architectural School. She had graduated, not with honors, but she had given it all she had. Her professors praised her creativity. It was good to be back on the island of her birth.

She rolled over, stretched luxuriously, and then snuggled back down under the covers. The breezes were cool, even chilly this time of the year. She sniffed the air wafting through her room, trying to identify the wonderful aroma.

So good to be here, but was it the place to begin her career? So much more opportunity in a large city. This Kona village was remote. It would be up to her to make connections and to sell herself. She would probably have to travel.

Meanwhile, she would take a while to just enjoy. Maybe join Apple A Day organization, and do some tutoring. Maybe flirt a little. She had had her nose to the grindstone for the past six years. She had been wary of any romantic entanglements that might be a threat to reaching her goals. Well, she hadn't actually reached the most important goal. She needed a job.

Some of her high school friends might still be around, though so far, she had struck out. The few she had called were on the mainland or on one of the other islands. It appeared that she needed to make new friends.

The phone ringing brought her to sudden wakefulness, just as she was about to drift back into a sleepy oblivion.

"Yes, good morning," she answered brightly on the first ring.

"Good morning, Chickadee. Are you up?"

"Of course, Uncle," she fibbed, knowing that he had been awake for hours.

"Good. Can we have lunch?"

"I would be delighted."

"I'll meet you at the Inn at 1:00 o'clock prompt. All right?"

"Perfect. Bye till then."

Chieko loved her Uncle dearly. She loved to have him call her by the nickname he had given her. Maybe this was just a friendly invitation, yet somehow she sensed that there was something on his mind. She suspected that this was more important than just a lunch treat.

She put her apartment in order and laid out clothes he would like to see her wear. When his brother, her father, had deserted his wife and daughter, Uncle Ross had taken over the responsibility of caring for Chieko and her mother. They had never wanted for anything. They never had to ask. He had anticipated their every need, and more.

After her mother's death, she and Uncle Ross became even closer. He was her confidante, her hero, and her mentor. He had guided her into the career of her choice, had chosen the college she would attend, and had paid the tuition. She had worked for expense money. All else, he took care of.

She sat brushing her raven black hair. Her flawless complexion was almost wax-like in the early morning light. A light touch of rouge, and the tinted lip gloss. Her dark eyes sparkled under arched brows. She took her beauty for granted, which made her even more lovely.

The morning passed rapidly with minor chores and reading the community newspaper. She had just enough time to slip into the black and white silk tank dress, put on white sandals, and minimal jewelry. She fastened her long hair back on one side with a silver clip. She had planned to be there waiting, to surprise Uncle Ross when he arrived. He would expect her to be late, which would not please him. Instead, by the time she entered the restaurant, early, Uncle Ross was already seated and looking out at the sparkling Pacific waters.

"Ah, you are on time my dear. Commendable."

"I am not on time, Uncle, I am early so that I could greet you when you arrived. Thank you for calling me. I am a bit at loose ends. It is not easy to adjust to so much spare time, and relaxation. This is the first time in many years that I can enjoy this luxury. It is wonderful, but it is also bewildering."

"Well enjoy it, Chickadee, because I suspect you will soon be quite busy."

The waiter arrived. Ross Ota ordered for both of them. "And two glasses of your best Cabernet," he said.

"Aha, the plot thickens, Uncle. I've read too many mystery stories not to recognize the clues. What is going on?"

He smiled his most gentle, whimsical grin at his niece. "You are right, Sherlock. You missed the Apple meeting the other night. I couldn't wait to tell you." It was unlike him to get so excited.

"People were quite worked up with the anticipation of altering public education. They even got into a discussion of determining what an ideal learning center should be like. They threw out a few ideas, and before we knew it, there was a motion made to choose people to set up requirements for a contest. The contest would be open to architects or draft persons, the objective being for the community to award the project to the one submitting the best plan. It is still up in the air. The rules committee for the contest will find that it is very complicated. They will need legal advice. In addition, the plan must be detailed, and flawless. And . . . you are not on the same wavelength with me yet, Chickadee."

Chieko stared wide-eyed at her Uncle. "You're not thinking that I could be considered for this contest?"

"Why not? You are a certified architect. You have paid your dues. Why not you?"

"I'm just out of school. The ink on my diploma isn't even dry yet. I have no background, no experience."

"You have everything you need, and you have the feel of this community, having grown up with your feet in the Pacific and your head in the clouds that move over Pele's volcanoes. You've picked coffee and planted pineapples. You've swum with the dolphins, and communed with the whales." He smiled and placed his hand on her shoulder.

His excitement was contagious. "Of course, Uncle. It is a wonderful opportunity to begin my career with such a project."

"That's my girl!" They clicked their wine glasses together and struck a deal. The opportunity was incalculable. Ross Ota picked up her dainty hand, and kissed it. She was his joy, his reason for living.

Chapter 36

Purpose, Direction, and Goals

Chieko walked briskly through the village toward the post office. What a difference, she thought, to have a purpose. She had been a dedicated student for so many years that she was not able to lounge for long. She had been searching for a direction, now that she had her credentials, to put her architectural talents to work. In a major city, she could have joined an established group of architects, and perhaps she would do that someday. But she loved her island and being here with Uncle Ross. She knew that he was pleased to have her here, too. The contest would be an exciting challenge.

At the post office a line of people were waiting to mail packages for the holiday. She stepped to the end of the line. Everyone indulged in people-watching while biding their time. She enjoyed observing the collection of townsfolk waiting patiently. Most were dressed in casual shorts. There was a large, brown-skinned, regal Hawaiian woman in a colorful muumuu and a man dressed in smelly clothes who appeared to be homeless. The people were keeping their distance from him.

One man allowed his glances in her direction to linger, then looked away when their eyes met. The line moved rapidly. She dispatched her envelope and turned toward the exit. In the courtyard seated on a bench was the same man relaxing, as though he had nothing else to do. As she approached, he moved to a position where she must pass by. She was accustomed to men's stares and was prepared to ignore him.

"Hello, didn't we meet at one of the Apple A Day meetings recently?" His voice was deep and friendly.

"I did attend one. I'm sorry. I don't recall meeting you, but I do remember now that you were one of the speakers."

"Noah Solomon," he interjected, considering her comment to be a reasonable opening for introduction.

"I beg your pardon?" She didn't offer to introduce herself, which made him feel awkward.

"Solomon," he said, getting no response. "With three 'o's," he added. She raised an eyebrow, not understanding. "Oh, your name."

"Right." He already felt like a fool, so he continued. "SO-LO-MON. Noah as in Ark."

Chieko hid her grin behind a dainty hand. She was rather enjoying his discomfort.

"Are you by chance a member of our group?" he asked. "We are in need of tutors, organizers, and speakers."

"As a matter of fact, I am planning to join the tutors if I can help."

"Are you by any chance familiar with teaching children to read? That's a specialty that we all lack."

"I've taught with the Literacy Council."

"Fantastic. We have a meeting tonight. I could pick you up and take you there."

"No, thank you. I am quite familiar with the street names." She pulled a scrap of paper and a pen from her purse. "Just write the address and the time and place. I'll find it."

Noah did so. It was obvious that his approach had been too abrupt, and not appreciated, even if she did welcome the information. She thanked him politely, without enthusiasm, and backed away leaving him feeling as if he had overstepped propriety by speaking to her. Now he would be late getting back to the office. "Damn, she didn't even tell me her name."

Noah had not been able to take his eyes off her while they had waited in line at the post office. Her dark Asian beauty, cameo complexion, and petite figure fascinated him. If she showed up tonight, he looked forward to getting to know her, if he hadn't already ruined his chances by playing the buffoon. He was not good at this dating game. He had noticed that she didn't wear a wedding ring. That was a plus. Seemed every woman he met was either married, spoken for, divorced with several children, under whelmed by his short stature, or just not attracted to him.

That evening, when she entered, he was standing by the front desk, arranging with the librarian to use another part of the library. Tonight they would need to separate the pupils who were working effectively with workbooks from those who needed help with reading. He had arrived early, eager to welcome her, and hoped that he could smooth over the boldness he must have displayed when he spoke to her that afternoon.

The librarian led them to the children's area, where there was a small table and chairs, a reading corner with beanbag chairs, and pillows to stretch out on. Noah was about to say that this would not do, that they would need a standard-sized table and chairs.

"This is perfect," Chieko said.

The other tutors were gathering with some of their pupils in the adult section. Chieko introduced herself without waiting for Noah to introduce them. Then she turned to Noah, and said, "I'm so sorry. I have forgotten your name and you didn't write it down for me."

"Great!" he thought. What does it take to make an impression on this woman? He was getting annoyed. "N-O-A-H." he spelled with a sardonic smile.

"Oh, yes. S-O-L-O-M-O-N," she spelled matching his pace.

Keoki entered, leading his little brother Keola by the hand. Big brother looked her up and down, raised his eyebrows in appreciation, and mumbled that maybe he ought to stay for tutoring. Noah gave him a dark look. Keoki returned it with a "drop dead sneer" and headed for the door.

Chieko took Keola's small hand and they went into the reading corner. When Noah checked on them later in the evening, they were curled up on pillows enjoying a book. Chieko was reading. She was curled up like one of the children. A disheveled-looking little girl had joined them. Apparently this was one of the kids whose parents dropped them off at the library regularly, so the parents could escape their responsibilities for the evening.

The evening passed by quickly, as usual. Chieko waved a goodbye to all, and disappeared through the door. The pupils and their tutors were soon gone, or waiting for a ride. As Noah was leaving, he heard the librarian's voice.

"Aretha, where are you? I'm locking up. Come on. You can't stay in there." The little girl who had joined Chieko and Keola, dragged her feet across the threshold. She hung her head and would not look at the librarian.

Noah watched from his car. When he realized that the child would have to wait alone on the lanai till someone picked her up, he was reluctant to pull away.

"Hurry up, child. Where is your mother? Or your father? Did they tell you to stay here? Did they say they would come to get you?"

No response from the little girl. She appeared to be about seven or eight. Maybe the family was homeless, Noah thought. Good grief, he didn't want to get involved in this, but the librarian was leaving.

"Ma'am, you're not going to leave that child here, are you?"

"Well, what am I supposed to do? Take her home with me?"

"If you'll take her in your car, and follow me," Noah pleaded, "we'll drive to the police station. I'll take her into the station, and you can be on your way."

"Why don't you take her? I don't want any part of this."

Noah was toying with the idea because the old witch was so unco-operative, but he knew that men were sometimes falsely accused of molesting a child. No thanks. Not a good idea. While he hesitated, the librarian got into her car, and drove away.

Noah wished he had invested in a cell phone. He had no idea where there was a public phone. Mercifully, headlights blinded him as a car turned into the lot. Time to get out of there, he decided. He doubled back and watched from the opposite side of the street to be sure the vehicle belonged to the kid's parents. The child ran to the old truck. The driver spun his tires and sped away almost before the car door had closed.

Noah stopped at the nearest store. He made a point of engaging the clerk in friendly conversation, bought a magazine, and asked the time. "Are you sure that's the right time?" he asked. "My watch must have stopped."

"It's correct," she said as she handed him the change.

Weird that we live in a world in which we must think of protecting ourselves with an alibi. Those must have been the parents of the little girl. What an existence for a child, Noah thought.

Chapter 37

Our Saving Grace

Chieko arranged a corner of her condominium for working. A window above her desk framed a Shower tree. The creamy blossoms with blended shades of pink and apricot spilled earthward from delicate stems supported by sturdy branches, each blossom a collection of small, perfect flowerets. The most beautiful tree in Hawaii, Chieko believed. That is, until the next season when the Royal Poinciana trees would put out dramatic scarlet flowers. After that, spring, when the Jacarandas burst into a cloud of lavender that hide bare branches until the leaves reappear. Tiny lavender petals fall to earth, carpeting the whole base of the tree. No need for calendars in Hawaii. The trees mark the seasons.

Her workbench was comfortable, with good lighting, and her tools within reach. A radio on a small shelf was tuned to restful music. She was ready to get to work. Many sketches. Brainstorming, that was what she needed to find direction. A great deal of architectural planning was dependent on the arts. The greatest architects had reached out, unbound by tradition. They had dared to dream, and to act on those dreams. They had discovered, or created, new scientific and engineering means to make their dreams possible.

The people in charge of the contest had only begun their planning. There were neither guides nor restrictions yet. But Chieko did not want to wait until those were written and made public. Dreams came first. All she knew was that the architect or draftsman who submitted the best plan for an educational center would win.

Chieko had received her early years of education in Kona. She knew its strengths, and its weaknesses. Later, she had made it through her years of higher education with considerable effort, buoyed by persistence. Many of her peers had been from private schools. They were better equipped for the university and the professional world than she had been.

"This is your community station KABC. Igor here to greet you this wonderful morning in paradise. This is your only station totally dedicated to improving our children's education, and how to accomplish the best education. If you are with us daily, you know that we believe our youth must be challenged, and given guidance and support from our community, to bring about constructive change.

"Today's subject is the efficacy of Merit Marks, intended to reward top teachers and to rid the schools of ineffective teachers. We have with us today Cliff Collins, who is related to our very own Kirk Collins, one of our favorite people here at KABC, who shares with me the broadcasting and technical responsibilities."

"It's a pleasure to be here, Igor. A friend of mine wrote a clear and concise article about Merit Marks. I am going to quote him. I shared his experiences in the university, and we are in agreement with what he has to say about this subject.

"Paul Trout wrote about how they are used in public schools and at college level.[1] 'The results of merit mark ratings determine: (1) whether a teacher is given a share of the allotment available for raises; or (2) whether a teacher is retained or dismissed, receives tenure or promotions.'"

"That presents an image of working with an axe hanging over your head," Igor commented.

"That's an interesting analogy, Igor. Teaching had always been a joy to me. I was a principal when merit pay first started. The whole idea seemed implausible to me. I left secondary education to work toward teaching in a university. Then, as an administrator, I was faced with making grave decisions that affected the lives of dedicated teachers, that determined their future. It had drastic, destructive effects on our faculty. Merit pay is a disaster.

"Before I enumerate my reasons for that statement, I must add that I believe giving grades to students has caused many of the same problems. Each has played a part in watering down education in this country."

"That's a very harsh condemnation, Mr. Collins. After all, we evaluate other skilled workers. Give us your reasons for that remark, please."

"First, a question: How would you like to have students evaluating you if you were a professor? In industry, the employees do not evaluate the management in a company. Employees in the workplace and students in high school and college, include a number of disgruntled, frustrated people who are likely to relish being in a position of power. We call their condition 'an attitude.' It is an unfounded, negative attitude born of innumerable frustrations. The frustrations often stem from the student's, or the employee's lack of self-esteem. But to continue professor Trout's report...'Procedures may differ from department to department and from campus to campus, but evaluation scores are usually the primary way to assess teaching. This is what happened when our university put merit evaluations into practice:

"'Numerical forms are intended as a way to reward and punish instructors, and are supposed to improve teaching. In reality it is dumbing it down.' Say I am a college level instructor: A committee of colleagues meet to evaluate the quality of my work in three areas: service, scholarship, and teaching. If I meet expectations, no bonus money. If I exceed expectations in one, two, or all three, I get a share of the money allotted. To succeed in teaching, I have to receive high scores, at least 3.6 on a scale of 4. To get scores that high, I have to make many students happy. What makes students happy? Understanding and friendly instructors, comfortable courses, and good grades.

"'To rephrase those qualifications: They want teachers who do not demand work loads that challenge their students, and they want high grades for low expectations. This is what students themselves say that they want. They give lower ratings to instructors who have high standards and requirements, and realistic grading scales.

"'A researcher's study on students stated that (quote) for every ten percent increase in the amount of material that a student learned in class, the professor's rating decreased by a half-point (unquote). That bears repeating, or rephrasing, in case you didn't get it the first time. I'll just quote the researcher after the results of his study were analyzed. He advised professors seeking a perfect rating to teach nothing and give at least 66 percent of the class A's.'"

"This may be a shock to the listeners, Igor, but I would venture that it is no surprise to the teachers in public schools, who have been forced to demand less of their students, while giving them higher grades than they have earned. Look at the number of names on honor rolls these days. Ask your principals for the percentages of students who are given honor roll status. Is it a realistic percentage of the class?

"Look around. Consider how many people in any group excel in any category. Not many. Whether they are professionals, jobholders, or social acquaintances, they may do a good job. But excel? I don't think so.

"Then look at the numbers of students who receive A's. Ask for statistics on the numbers who fail. What were the teachers' principle assignments, and standards? How many of those assignments were not turned in? How many were given a C grade just because they made an effort? How many A's, C's or D grades do they give for efforts that would at one time have been considered unacceptable, even failing? It amounts to how realistic are their evaluations?

"Trout says, 'Growing numbers of college students are unprepared for the rigors of higher education. Many cannot read, write, or compute. They have a weak grasp of historical and cultural information. Students with such handicaps often enter college with 'exalted high school grade point averages, and an outward display of excessive self-esteem. They are incapable of extensive reading assignments, and do not write and reason cogently when they reach college level.

"'According to a UCLA survey, 40 percent of each freshman class is 'disengaged' from educational values and pursuits. This means that they have almost no desire to learn, to know and understand things outside of their narrow vocational interest, if indeed they have determined a major interest.

"'Such students are inattentive, easily bored, and unwilling to work hard, especially on difficult or abstract material outside of their interests. Students themselves report that many of their peers 'just get by, and are more interested in socializing than taking the academic responsibilities seriously. One student said that about half just don't care.

"'Frustrated students with negative attitudes give zeros as merit marks for their teachers. One untenured faculty member admitted to watering his course down. Another in a different university said he complied with student demands for comfortable, less challenging classes.

"'What sort of heroic resistance can be expected from those who have given their life to a deteriorating field? Their hopes, after so many years, are to be able to last until retirement, because they don't have any answers to the problems. One study suggests that 'a third of the 900,000 instructors in higher education may have eased their requirements and standards.

"'If this system is ever to be corrected . . . it is up to taxpayers, parents, legislators, public-interest law firms, and alumni to correct the system.'"

"Thank you Cliff Collins for sharing the article on 'Merit Marks' with our listeners, and our thanks also to its author, professor Paul Trout who teaches English at Montana State University, for this reputable data.

"This is Igor Connifer, Station KABC signing off until 3:30 P.M. when Kirk Collins will be here to interview a mother who will tell us about her experiences with home schooling."

Chieko had listened intently to the program. She had put aside the planning she had wanted to do. Everything she had heard made her mission more important . . . the educational center she intended to design, the tutoring at the library, and Apple A Day.

Cliff Collins. She remembered meeting him. He was one of the tutors at the library. He had said he was an automobile mechanic. Quite a change in his career.

[1] Paul Trout, "Low marks for our top teachers," News Commentary Special to *The Washington Post,* reprinted in *West Hawaii Today,* March 21, 2000.

Chapter 38

Life's Bounty

"This is Station KABC signing on for an afternoon and evening of information with music to dream by. Your host is Kirk Collins. The time 3:30 P.M., and we have a guest from our community. Thank you, Miriam Heffner, for being here. Please tell us about home schooling."

"Well, I teach my own two children, a girl 14 and a boy 12. I have also taken in the children from two other families. Their ages range from 6 to 13 for a total of eight students. Three from each family. Four boys and four girls."

"It sounds like a page right out of the little red schoolhouse. That's quite an age range, 6 to 14. How do you manage the different subjects, and how do you know what to teach?"

"We cover all the subjects the Department of Education requires for each grade. Students take a test at the end of each semester, so we use the books assigned, until we are sure they can pass the tests. Then we get into our own studies."

"Your own studies? You mean that you get the public school classes done, and have time left over for other subjects?"

"Oh, yes. That's why we are doing home school. It is so much more efficient and effective."

"Watch out now! You'll have all the kids dropping out of public schools to have you teach them."

"The kids tell me that we spend more time studying, writing, and reading than they did in school."

"Are they complaining? How is it that they let you get away with that?"

"Well, I'm no miracle worker. I do have some very special kids. They all learned at home to like reading. The youngest one is only six, but she has been reading for more than a year. They like to learn. That's about all there is to it."

"Did you teach the youngest to read a year ago?"

"We all did, and we're still teaching her. The parents and her siblings had taught her the alphabet. They also taught her that each letter has a name, and each has a sound. We are still working on the vowel sounds, and the combination of vowel sounds. At first the combined consonant sounds are confusing in English."

"I'll bet they are. Like 'ph,' 'th,' 'ch,' and even 'rh.' English is a very complicated language when it comes to spelling."

"Say, you're good. Don't forget the problems with spelling double consonants. Would you like to join our teaching staff?" Miriam appreciated Kirk's ingenuity and awareness, the same traits she depended on in herself to accomplish the home teaching tasks. This prompted Kirk's next question.

Kirk laughed at her invitation. "That's very tempting. I can see that it's rewarding to you. But, tell me, considering the wide range of knowledge we need in this complex world, how do you decide what needs to be taught at each of their respective ages?"

"Time is one of our most important commodities. We don't have enough of it to learn everything there is to be learned. We won't learn all about everything. We can't even predict what information each of us will need in life. Our culture is leaning toward lifetime continuing education, isn't it?

"Learn it now or learn it later. Learn just enough to be aware of it, or study it in depth. We may as well allow the student to make those decisions. He will then give full attention to what interests him, so it is more effective to provide what he is ready to learn. When he needs that knowledge, he will be open to it."

"So it is the student who narrows down the subjects he or she will study," Kirk said.

"Except for the required subjects that they need now, yes. The basics such as: communication, math, social skills, and health are required and ongoing. We have a curriculum that covers a broad range of knowledge that is a guide for a lifetime of learning."

"What would be included in your lesson plans?"

"Reading, then sharing by writing and speaking, and of course listening. Not just listening to the teacher, but also hearing what classmates have to say. We learn most by doing. Doing requires thinking. Knowing that we must share, sharpens our attention to the reading. It requires arriving at some decision, even if it is only the awareness of how complicated an issue is."

Kirk could relate to that. "My best classes in school were with teachers who made demands of me. The teachers who worked the hardest to lecture or to correct papers, didn't teach me the most. It was the ones who kept me interested and involved. Is that what you do in home school?"

"Exactly. We are all taking responsibility to read, write, speak, listen, discuss, and evaluate."

"Who, and what do you evaluate?" Kirk asked.

"The subject, issue, or problem we are discussing. We question our sources. We evaluate our own reasoning and that of the others, and also statements by people who are considered authorities, because we want to know how they back up their opinions."

"How much education does a person need to start a home school?"

"We need more education, more experience or learned skills than the children have who are being schooled. I have a high school diploma. I've learned a lot since we started home school, and I continue to learn. It's important to be creative and intuitive. We must start where the student is, and not skip over what may seem obvious. I try to get into each student's mind by asking a lot of questions in the beginning of a subject."

"Can you give an example? Are you referring to vocabulary they lack?"

"Vocabulary is part of it, but I can't assume that they have concepts needed to understand new material. While I was learning to do arithmetic in isolated exercises, I never applied it to life. When I teach fractions and decimals now, we talk about why we are using a fraction. Why not a decimal?

"We write our own problems, and then solve them. We make up problems about sharing money, or a pie we have for lunch, or dividing a recipe in half for our lunch . . . We decide whether decimals or fractions are better. We work it both ways.

"We take the mystery out of fractions. Students may forget whether the top of the fraction is a denominator or, uh . . . or the other." Miriam laughed at her lapse of memory. "They will not forget that the bottom number shows how the pie is divided . . . how many equal parts and the top number is what part of the whole thing each person gets. And how big a share Eddie got if I let him eat my share, too. Then he understands why we reduce the fraction, and what that means. Everything we divide we make a lesson out of it before they get to eat it."

"Great incentive!" Kirk said. "It's a lot different from studying math out of a book."

Miriam smiled, and continued. "We go shopping, and their assignment may be to write some problems that need a whole price, a sale price, and a percentage price of something. We see how many ways we can write a problem using any two of the known figures to arrive at the answer, the unknown figure.

"Sorry, I get carried away, but I remember how much some teachers assume their students already know. The smarter teachers are, that is to say, teachers who caught on to the concepts by themselves, the less they can see why their students don't understand. Then, they are not as able to help the kids."

"I always thought that my teachers must have been scholars, smart kids who learned everything without much effort. It's true that the smartest ones often can't bring the information down to the kids' level. Mrs. Heffner, where do you get your books, and how do you use them?"

"At libraries, including school libraries. With any subject, we learn the vocabulary, the spelling, and definition common to that subject. We can get that from a textbook or encyclopedia. As I said before, we use our time to read, write, listen, and discuss. We summarize stories, or something we have read. We try to change activities, but it is pretty much up to each of us. I make sure they have some experience in all of the communicative skills, so I don't exclude any of them.

"We take all the reading material we can get hold of, that interests us. I vary it with classics and other good literature, poetry, science, current events, magazines, and newspapers. We have a video once a week, and tune in on good television programs on science or travel. We make our own flash cards and make games out of them, or help one another drill for vocabulary, spelling, definitions, timetables, arithmetic problems, or whatever.

"We almost wear out our dictionaries. We use them constantly. The big dictionary and the enlarged edition have loads of student information such as" (she read from a scrap of paper:) "English, literature, mathematics, reference for business office, music, geography, civics, history, astronomy and space, biology, chemistry, physics and education. I jotted those down in case you asked. They're all in there."

"We also have a well-thumbed set of encyclopedias. Some details are outdated, but we compensate for that by getting new publications to bring us up to date. If we could read everything in our own home, we would be very well educated, I believe. Current events require a lot of our time. They apply to our own lives and the world around us."

"What about foreign language?"

"Because we have fewer vacation days in home school, we have time for some of that. We are deciding which foreign language to start with. We have plans for Hawaiian, Spanish, and an Asian language. We have to agree on which is to be first, probably the Hawaiian to learn how to pronounce names of streets, islands, towns, and commonly used words.

"That would help us with Spanish, because the pronunciation is similar. We will need some tapes to hear it spoken."

"Well, hang in there while we pause for station identification, and we'll continue with this. Station KABC. We are learning about learning today. That is, we are learning how the children in one home school, directed by Mrs. Miriam Heffner, use their time and the results they get."

"We'll accept calls from our listeners. This has been very informative. Okay, Igor says that Malia is on the line. Your question, Malia?"

"Have your children passed the SAT tests?"

"We are ready to begin taking the tests scheduled in the schools. Third and fifth grades will be taking the SAT in May. There are two parts to the test. Reading, math, and other problem solving. First, second, fourth, and sixth are given what they call a "Field Test". Second graders receive a reading test. After each reading selection, the children write down what they understood about the paragraph. The Field Tests are for the school's use only. I think they are to make the children more at ease taking tests, and get some measure of how the children are progressing. But, to answer your question, we expect to do very well on the tests. I forgot to say that eighth grade students take a PSAT. I think that is for the schools use in order to recognize who needs special help before graduation. Then twelfth grade takes the college-based SAT."

"Why did you take your children out of public school?"

"I am convinced that they will learn more at home. We use our time more wisely. They get the attention they need. They are acquiring confidence and learning to take responsibility, even for their own education. In public school, all kinds of tests, the holidays, and other special activities deduct a great deal of time from the school day. We don't have breaks. We can get up any time to get a drink of water or use the bathroom. We can have some healthy snacks while we study. If we feel restless or need to relax, we get a book and curl up in a corner to read until we're ready to join in again."

"I wish you had brought the children so we could hear their side of it."

"I decided against it for today because I was asked to speak to my side of the question. They would like very much to be guests on the program. They are not in the least shy."

"Do you think that anyone can school children in their home?"

"I don't think everyone would enjoy teaching home school. The teacher must have good rapport with the children. I get very tired, but it is a good feeling of accomplishment. I did say that it helps to know more than the children one is teaching, but on the other hand I am learning at least as much as they are. It seems to me that many people who decide to become teachers do so, not because they are so intelligent or knowledge-able, but because they have discovered that they have a knack of knowing how to make others understand. That's the way it was with me. I have seen aides in the schools who were as good or better than the teacher, when they were explaining lessons to the students.

"When I decided to do this, I had a few doubts about my ability. Then I remembered reading about mothers in colonial and pioneer times. They taught their children to read, to write, and to do simple arithmetic. Many school marms or masters had very limited schooling. Many famous and successful people attended a school for only a few years and were self-taught from then on. I knew then that I could teach them, and I haven't regretted it."

"Greta, a grandmother whose two grandchildren live with her is on the line."

"Thank you for the home school information this morning. I have something to share with all teachers and parents. I read about it in a maga-zine and sent for materials to help me raise my grandkids. I'll read this to you.

"The Mega Skills program helps children with academic and emo-tional challenges. It helps us to instill attitudes, behaviors and habits needed for successful learning. It stresses confidence, motivation, effort, responsibility, initiative, perseverance, caring, teamwork, common sense, problem solving, and focus.

'Mega Skills program was developed by Dorothy Rich, an educator. Her ideas coalesced in The Home and School Institute, a not-for-profit organization in Washington, D. C. in 1972. Her book *Mega Skills* [1] was pub-lished in 1988. The third edition appeared in 1998. There is a web site: www.megaskillshsi.org. Her workshops have trained more than 125,000 families in 48 states.

'The founder, Dorothy Rich, believes that kids learn as much at home as they do in school when parents get involved.'"

"Thank you Greta. This is valuable information. The U.S. Census Bureau reports nearly 5.5 million children living with grandparents. I'm sure they and parents can use 'Mega Skills.'* "

"Trudy on line. Your question, please."

"I think that home school would be deadly. What about the social interaction kids get in a public school? Your kids are missing out on them. What about music, art, health, exercise, or competitive sports?"

Kirk gestured to Miriam to reply.

"Art? I get an artist to visit and they all take painting lessons. There will be exposure to other art skills, such as clay later, but we don't use our school hours to complete the artwork. It's just an introduction to the arts. They can bring it back to show us after they complete it at home. We have videos for art and architectural appreciation. We go to art exhibits.

"We study a health textbook. They read whatever applies to them. I test them on vocabulary that I feel they need. We visit health, career, and science fairs.

"We parents are all alert to students' expressed interests. Some are into music or dancing lessons, as well as martial arts, soccer, outrigger clubs, Four-H membership, Boy Scouts, religious and cultural classes or activities. We are open to putting them into any sports they show an interest in. These kids are as competitive as they wish to be. We leave a lot of that up to parents to supply."

"This is break time, Miriam. I want to thank you and we invite you to bring the eight children when you come back. This has been most interesting. I would enjoy being a student in your school.

"Thanks to our listeners and today's callers. Stay tuned in for good listening music. Hope you are enjoying our choices. This is Kirk Collins bidding you a good afternoon, and keep listening."

[1] Jane Durrell, *Real Life Lessons*, What kids can learn from doing the laundry. *Modern Maturity*, Jan–Feb 2000

Chapter 39

KABC Home School Kids

"So who made the decision that you attend home school, and why?" Kirk asked the scrawny, serious, redheaded kid who chose the name Aaron for the radio interview.

"My parents and I. We decided to try it. It wasn't working at public school. I enrolled mid-semester. Kids are real cliquish when they get to secondary school. Some kids like to push each other around. Like, they look for kids who have the mark of 'victim' on them, and pick on them. I guess I am just one of those kids they like to pick on, or at least in this time and place I was It."

"What's your story, Debrah?"

"It isn't any different for the girls. Haoles have to learn how to behave to be accepted. I didn't have any warning about what to expect, and how to react, so I was the sacrificial lamb. Later, all the adults were giving me different advice: To turn the other cheek. Be friendly to them in spite of the way they treated me. Get so mad that I could go at them like a tigress, and beat one of them up. Said they'd leave me alone if I did that. I didn't know how to fight, so my parents put me in a martial arts class, but I just couldn't do it."

"Paul? What's your story?"

"I just couldn't take it anymore."

"But you look Hawaiian, Paul. Why did anyone pick on you?"

"I am part Hawaiian. Teachers tried to explain to me that the kids just wanted to be my friend cause I'm so big. But the way they went about it was weird. They'd wait for me after classes, and tease, call me names, push me around. They threw things at me and hit, pushed, pulled and tugged. I guess I didn't measure up to what they wanted me to be. I think they wanted me to push or hit them, but my mother had taught me not to fight. I didn't want to get into trouble so I tried to avoid them."

"Didn't teachers talk to them?"

"Sure. It didn't do any good. The more they got into trouble for it, the more they tried to get even with me. I didn't tell on them. I did stay in a teacher's room until the bus was almost ready to leave every day, but sometimes I waited too long, and missed the bus. Then the teacher would take me home, or my mother would come after me."

"I get the general idea. Did all of you have trouble like this?"

"Not the little kids. It would start about fifth grade, sometimes earlier."

"Did all of the older haoles get picked on?"

"No, some of them had lived here a long time. Spoke Pidgin English. Or they acted tough and mean. They fit in okay. It was mostly the new kids."

"Aaron, someone told me that you got hurt. Do you mind if I tell our radio audience about it?" (Aaron shakes his head to give Kirk permission.)

"I was told that one afternoon a group of your classmates, boys, waited for you just past the school grounds. They started picking on you. You talked back to them, then they attacked you, and a couple got you into a brutal wrestling hold that wrestlers are forbidden to use in the ring. Some teachers broke it up. You were taken to the hospital in an ambulance because you couldn't walk. You spent several days there, then time in physical therapy to recover.

"Would you tell us how it made you feel, physically and psychologically? No? May I go on? Correct me if I'm wrong. I'm guessing that you felt humiliation, extreme anger, and confusion as to why you were so badly treated. Have you recovered?"

"Physically, I'm okay, but I don't want to go back . . . not even to take the tests at the school. Mrs. Heffner says I should take them when the school offers them."

"Did your family sue the parents of the boy?"

"No, we try to live peacefully. My mother thought that if she went to school and talked to the classes, that it wouldn't happen again. I think it helped, for a while. I think it embarrassed the boys who had tried to act so tough. Later, the schools started social skills and sensitivity classes. We finally moved. I didn't want to walk in the neighborhood again. I didn't know who I was anymore or how to act. It isn't easy to pretend you are mean. It doesn't seem like you're being honest and true to yourself. Mrs. Heffner has helped me to understand myself and our culture . . . like what those kids see all the time on television and try to copy, 'cause they don't know who they are either."

"Do you think that movies and television should be censored, Aaron?"

"No, but schools should understand that some kids and some grownups don't know how to separate fantasy, fiction, and reality. We've talked a lot about it in home school. We should choose good people as heroes, instead of the rough and tough ones."

"Well, that's one side of home schooling. It seems that some kids feel threatened in the public schools, and the home school is a haven for them. This is Kirk Collins. We'll be back after station identification to hear more about home schools."

Chieko had tuned in late. She was horrified at how much children had changed since she had attended the same schools a decade ago. Kids loved to tease each other even then, but they would not have thought of doing physical harm. They would have been shamed by their elders and their peers if they had hurt anyone, or acted mean. This was indeed opening her eyes.

She was torn between the desire to give all of her attention to her architectural sketches, or to listen to the rest of the program. She wanted to know more about the children and the schools so she stayed tuned in.

Cliff Collins listened to KABC as he worked under the hood of a Chevy pickup that was running on borrowed time. He worked in a friend's garage. The friend had appreciated Cliff's ability even though he had only recently taken up auto mechanics as his livelihood after leaving the field of education.

He heard nothing that surprised him in today's KABC program. It was as he remembered it on the mainland before he moved here. Animosity of some adolescents was the same. Did the attitude come from the adult world.

It did provide a different slant to hear about the attitude toward 'haoles,' Hawaiian for "stranger, foreigner, or white-skinned people." Many local kids resented newcomers to the island. They spit out the word *haole* as one would an epithet, contrary to the aloha spirit of love characteristic of Hawaii

People from all over the world have learned to work together in Hawaii, but usually socialize in the bosom of their own culture. We all search for a comfort zone where we feel accepted at least, appreciated at best.

Cliff's two sons were opposites. Neither was a 'bad kid,' but, they were trying to find their place in the world of adolescents. His older son had blended in with the tough kids, who were themselves trying to fit in somewhere. Now Cliff did not know where his older boy was. He feared the worst, because he had been experimenting with drugs before he left home without notice.

Whether to reject the tough crowd or join them? That seemed to be the choice for many of the wayward kids who wanted to suck others into their self-destruction, and to pick on those they saw as different, or weak.

Cliff's son Kirk was a different matter. Kids like him had done well in their early grades, then coasted as they became confused and unhappy with the complicated social atmosphere in high school. Yet outwardly they demonstrated a mature self-confidence.

They were capable of a surface amiability with the 'underworld' kids, who were in school under protest until they were of an age to legally drop out. But, Kirk and others of his sort did not join in if they were invited to any after-school escapades. They were friendly to all, and liked by the extremes. Yet sometimes they were living on the blade's edge, especially if their home life was unstable. Cliff worried that his son could easily shift to a different life style as his older son had done.

When Kirk's brother left home, their world was in turmoil. Kirk could not seem to function. His mother had died before they moved to Hawaii. There were just the three of them. Then just as suddenly there were only two, Kirk and his father. Cliff tried to put it all back together again. The meeting of Apple A Day, which they had attended by chance, offered a fortunate turn in the road. Kirk asked Igor intelligent questions about broadcasting. Igor would need a partner for the new station.

Why not employ this kid with the wonderful deep voice who had a head on his shoulders? It would give him no earnings, just the apprenticeship under Igor's tutelage. Igor offered, and Kirk became a community celebrity at age seventeen. What had saved him was having a purpose, an interest that captivated him. It provided an identity, at a time Kirk was trying to discover who he was.

Cliff got behind the steering wheel of the vehicle he had been working on. He turned the key in the ignition. It roared courageously and then purred as it idled. Good for another few hundred miles, thanks to Cliff's expertise. He turned back to the radio as KABC returned from the station break.

"We are back with our group of eight home-schooled students. The first part of the program made it clear that, at least for some students, the public schools have not provided a feeling of welcome and safety. A few of today's student participants turned to home schools because of an unpleasant, and sometimes unsafe, environment encountered in the public schools.

"Aaron you were telling us how home school study helps you to understand why some people become violent."

"Before I was attacked I liked people. In home school, we study a lot about man's inhumanity to man, but we counter it with heroic things that people do as well. We discuss things like psychology, or how people react and why; and philosophy, which makes us think on higher levels of thought and conduct. We look at principles that regulate human interactions, which are a part of all reality. Mrs. Heffner makes us realize how complicated life is, how we make it more difficult if we just react emotionally, instead of making wiser realistic choices."

"Well stated, Aaron. We can see that you have given a lot of thought to constructive ideas. They seem to have replaced the unpleasant negative reactions that your experiences caused. So now you are rid of the fear, anger, and anxiety you had after you were attacked?"

"I'd rather say that now I have the ammunition to get rid of those reactions in me when they reappear. I know that if I don't put what I am learning to good use, then it is my fault if I let my experiences destroy me."

"Okay, it's clear that those of you we have heard today are well read and well spoken. How is it that you express yourself so well? Most kids your age don't have your broad vocabulary. They fill their speech with vague, meaningless words like 'stuff', 'junk' or 'you know.'"

One student spoke up for the first time. "I've changed a lot at Mrs. Heffner's because we write a lot and talk a lot. You can't write much without a lot of vocabulary choices."

"Thank you, Gail." The shy child seemed to be part Asian. She lowered her eyes and smiled. "I want to hear from the youngest. Odette, you are six years old. Do you understand the things your older classmates say in class? For example, what Aaron was just saying?"

"Well-ll-l, at first I had to look up an awful lot of words. Mrs. Heffner says I don't have to learn how to spell them all, just understand the meanings if they interest me. I keep a notebook of new words. We all do . . . and we try to use them. Usually after I add a new word to the list, I know the spelling and the meaning, even if I don't try to memorize it. Sometimes, I just want to read my books, but while I'm reading, if they get all excited talking about something, then I can't concentrate, because I want to know what they're talking about.

"I read a lot. Then I have to tell someone or all of them about what I read, or I write about it. Then I read it to someone; that person or someone else will correct my spelling or punctuation. They make me read what I write until it sounds right. If it sounds funny, then I can usually tell what's wrong, and correct that myself."

"What is the longest word you know?" Kirk asked.

"Superfragilisticexpialidocious."

Kirk released a slow, shrill whistle of appreciation. "Do you know how to spell it?"

She grinned and shook her head.

"Why not, Odette?"

"Mrs. Heffner says we don't have to learn to spell every word we know, unless we expect to use it. . . . Where would I use a word like that?"

"I agree, Odette."

"Who else has something to share with us about your school?"

Gail's brother raised a hand. Mrs. Heffner nodded giving him permission to speak.

"We drill each other on multiplication tables, and addition. We have to do that without a pencil by looking at the problem. Mrs. Heffner shows us shortcuts to use when we add. And we're learning to use the multiplication tables to divide. Did you know that you can do a lot with those tables when you memorize them? We work with pennies, or rocks, beans, or whatever. So now I understand why the multiplication tables help make it easier. And I can choose which way to figure out a problem. Any way I want . . . as long as it works. Mrs. Heffner says, 'There's more than one way to skin a cat.' (Do you know what that means?) I just love 'rithmetic problems."

"Eric, you're seven. What do you like best about your home school?"

"Well-ll-l . . . I was going to say reading but what I really like best of all is that we love each other."

Everyone smiled. This teacher was doing a lot of things right, Kirk decided.

They all showed the same enthusiasm. They all were helping to teach anyone who needed help, especially those younger than they are. They seemed very proud of that. Discussions always included everyone who was interested.

They talked about interesting current news. They used the news to expand on their knowledge. They liked to research place names and locations, do map reading, and read about foreign places. Some follow-up was very limited, while others led to reading books about history, famous places and people. Students took turns with researching a subject, then reported on anything of interest to the others in the class. Sharing was a great way to learn.

"I have one more question for all of you. Do you ever get bored with your home school?"

Paul raised a hand, then proceeded when Kirk gave him the nod. "I don't get bored because we have the choice of how far we want to go in researching something. Sometimes Mrs. Heffner has reasons for thinking we should know something, then we have to do it as an assignment. But that doesn't happen often. Usually if she thinks we need something, she prepares the lesson, and it's a listening exercise for us."

"All of you say you don't get bored. Did you ever get bored with your public school classes?"

Five negative replies. Three got bored if only the teacher did the talking; when they couldn't hear what the teacher and classmates said, when they had to finish assignments on things that didn't interest them, and when they were just not in the mood.

In home school, they said that they have more freedom in the choice of activity, except when Mrs. Heffner insisted that they all must listen to whoever was reading, because the subject was important. She was the boss, they all said, and students must be good listeners.

"I thank you all for being here to share your experiences with our radio audience. I'm sure that we all are enlightened about your home school. You are very bright and dedicated students, a very good example to children who may be listening in. Keep up the good work.

"This is Kirk Collins. After the station identification please call in if you have comments about our program today. This is Station KABC coming to you from a community in Kona."

"First call is from a public school teacher who does not wish to be identified."

"I was impressed with the presentation today, but I want to caution the listeners that the children we just heard are not typical. Every home schoolteacher doesn't have the imagination, or awareness of what children should be learning. This is the only home school teacher I have heard of who takes the students to be tested when the various State SAT's, (reading, math, and problem solving), the Field Tests or the high school PSAT and college-based twelfth grade SAT's are given. Home school teachers are notified of the tests, but they don't show up.

"The children on the program today are obviously above average intelligence, and a one to eight ratio for teacher-student hardly provides a fair comparison to public school classes." (Click. Buzz.)

"Thank you, caller. Your comments emphasize the importance of making changes in the way the public schools are teaching. Different ages grouped together do not seem to hamper students if they are all eager to learn. It would seem that Mrs. Heffner's students are eager, which seems even more important than whether their IQs are comparable. Perhaps they are not. Perhaps they are progressing because they are motivated by their interests, by feeling useful, by teaching one another; by feeling free to discuss and write about their feelings and opinions. And many other differences that are resulting in a love of learning.

"We have a call from a middle school student who says he is at home sick today. Jacob, what is your comment?"

"I think those jerks are all dorks, and I'm glad they aren't in my school."

"Thank you, Jacob. I tried to get an explanation from Jacob, but that is all he would, or could say. One more caller before we bid you good day. This is also a teacher, and an avid union member. He prefers not to disclose his name."

"I am appalled that our state permits children to leave public school, and it allows just anyone to teach children at home. We have worked long and hard to get schools to require certified teachers. Now even people with no training are being allowed to teach. This is a step backwards in educating our children."

"Thank you for calling, sir. I have only one question for you. Not too many generations ago, children were often not able to stay in school for more than six to eight years, if that long. That was the total of their academic education. How do you explain that they went out into the world well able to read, write, and solve mathematical problems after that length of time? Unlike many of today's students after ten to twelve years in public school. Do you have an answer, caller?"

"The difference is in the complexity of today's world compared to former times."

"Then why is it that children of some cultures, such as Asians, who have to struggle with a very different language and are entering a highly complicated society when they arrive here, are excelling, even in our public schools? Why, is it that the Asian, the Jewish, and other cultures are successful in instilling a love of learning in their children?"

The caller answered the question with another question. "Do you have an answer to that, Mr. Collins?"

Mister Collins! Kirk loved the sound of that. "Yes, there are two obvious reasons. Their families expect excellence, and the children respect their elders enough to be determined to please them. Education here is the fulfillment of a dream that may not have been possible for them in the culture they emigrated from. In their homes learning is a way of life from birth to death. It is so ingrained in their culture that it may now be genetic. To say it in one word, the answer is 'attitude.'"

"Attitude? You're trying to say that those cultures have more intelligence, Mr. Collins? That is ridiculous, you know."

"No, sir. I'm saying that an appreciative and accepting attitude is taking the children of those and some other cultures to a higher level of education. That is what Apple A Day is working toward. They hope to start with the most eager students, then work toward larger numbers, as student attitudes change toward a desire to learn.

"Thank you, listeners. Your interest in our station is spreading the word beyond our own community. This is Kirk Collins signing off KABC with our best wishes."

Chapter 40

Night Stalkers

A full moon glowed over Kona. It cast a shimmering golden path on gentle waves ending at the sandy shore. Two dark figures disembarked from a fishing boat that had anchored in the bay. With a lantern to help them cross the treacherous lava field, the two made their way mauka[1], toward a forest of ancient twisted eucalyptus trees. Hidden in the shadows of the trees was a coffee shack that had once sheltered workers who picked coffee beans. Rows of coffee trees covered the hillside beyond the forest as far as one could see.

The planting ended at the Mamalahoa Highway, which did not carry much night traffic. An hour before, a truck with one passenger, and the driver, had turned into the road above leading to the coffee farm makai[2] of the highway. The driver had maneuvered the truck into a space off the road. He and his passenger covered it with palm leaves they had brought in the truck bed.

With only the moonlit sky to guide their steps, the two men walked stealthily toward the slits of light oozing through cracks between boards of the shack. One man held a small black object in his hand. By the time the two boatmen had reached the shack and entered the rickety structure, the two men were entrenched outside in the shadows.

The older man stifled an urge to cough with deep breaths. The black box was balanced on a ledge, beside a large hole through which they saw light and heard a radio playing reggae. He hoped that whoever was in there would not be able to hear them above the music. The volume was turned down low.

"Where the fuck have you been?" a voice growled as the door opened, and the two young boatmen entered the shack.

"Climbin' over the damn lava." someone answered angrily. "It ain't always easy gettin' away from a boat without bein' seen."

"Watch your mouth, kid. You wannabes[3] need ta show some respect for the bangers[4]." The authoritative voice hesitated. "Here's the stuff. You know where to take it. Help yourself to some butts. When you're big boys, you can roll your own."

Through a crack, the outsiders smelled the pakalolo[5] drifting on the air currents. The two arrivals hung their heads and did not respond. They heard a lot of voices inside.

"Don't come down so heavy on 'em, Goose. They ain't had no trainin'."

"'Bout time dey get it den," a whiney voice said. "When's da 'nishation?"

"Gotta talk 'bout dat. Either a you packin' a gun?"

Silence. "Speak up. Answer. Can't hear ya shakin' yer head."

"No, yer not shooters, are ya?"

"Shooters? We aint got a gun."

"Den ya gotta work on dat."

"How?"

"How he says. Where'd ya get deese guys, Goose?"

"Yer first assignment, gooney boys, is ta find out where ya can steal a gun. 'Till den make a weapon, a club, anyt'ing, 'cause we gonna need ya for some jobs. We want cha ready. Get it?"

"Speak up!"

"Yeah, we get it."

"'Till den you're a 'tagger'[6]." Their silence indicated lack of comprehension "Spreadin' graffiti, ya dumbhead. Ya gotta git yer rags,[7] too, so the OG's[8] and da udda bangers'll know ya. Yeh, and Poki's right: we gotta have a jump in[9]. We'll tell ya when. Any questions?"

"Yeh, what's a 'jump in'?"

"It's a 'nishiation. We's gonna 'nitiate you greenhorn wannabe's. Don' look so scared. You'll love it." Laughter. "Now git yer asses outa here. Ya know where ta dump the stuff?"

"Yeh. Somebody'll contact us at the Hale 'tween nine and ten tomorrow."

"And his name? Boy, this one's sure quiet. We gotta liven you up, brah[10]. You! Not him. Don't you talk?"

"Yessir. The name's Waterboy."

"Yeah, that's your contact. Gotta get a moniker for you, too. How about 'Junior,' boys?" Guffaws of laughter. "Now git goin', an' don't light that damn lantern till ya get to your boat."

The door slammed. Laughter followed the boys, who beat a hasty retreat makai to reach the shore. Shadows on the lava caused them many slips and stumbles, even with the moonlight overhead.

Outside of the shack, the two men lay so quietly their muscles cramped. One stretched his legs and hoped they weren't lying in the middle of a nest of scorpions. Maybe those don't venture out at night, he hoped. They heard laughter inside, then voices.

"Shee-it! What a couple a greenies. Who brought them in?"

"Never mind the jump in 'll bring 'em around. Let's git ta da good stuff. Here's da plan?"

"Why we goin' for da library, Goose?"

"'Cause dats da order. If I knew, I'd tell ya. We don't ask da OG's questions like 'why'. It's like we gotta have faith in da big picture, which we don' always know. Deres plenny stuff comin' in here. Some a duh action's ta get da cops busy wit' da' divershuns."

"'Divershuns'? What's 'divershuns?"

"Diversions ya shitheads. Diversions are things that scare people an' take their minds off a the big stuff comin' in till we get it all distributed."

"So we're gonna bomb the whole building, or just a part of it?"

"We'll get our orders on that. It's ta scare them, not ta kill anybody. First, they're gonna have a fake bomb scare some night. Den when they're calmed down, we'll let 'em have it."

"What a we use for explosives?"

"Don' worry yer pretty head 'bout dat, Gopher. I got some powder hid real good. It'll be there when we get the word. Now, if you're stayin' the night, shut up an' go ta sleep. If yer not, then get outa here. Meeting adjourned. Gimme da sign."

Sounds of hands slapping, chairs scraping, the building shaking from heavy footsteps across the floor. When the door burst open, the men hidden outside pressed their bodies into the soil and lava rock. A camouflage cover over them concealed their presence as the door closed. Several men and boys of all shapes and sizes walked up the trail.

The outsiders waited an interminable amount of time under the cover, until from mauka they heard the sound of a motor. With a squeal of tires, a vehicle roared toward town. Only then did they consider stealing away, but suddenly the door burst open again. The two men fell silently back into the shadows.

Oh my God, the intruders realized, they're going to pour themselves out to piss. The trespassers froze in place, hoping no one would turn their way. Fortunately, the gang members walked a few steps makai for the process, and did not go toward the mauka side of the shack, where the men remained cramped and chilled by the night air.

They were greatly relieved that their timing to leave had been delayed. They would have been in full view walking away from the shack, had they left earlier. All clear now, they crept, testing every step before trusting their weight on the path. They did not uncover their truck until they looked around for any other vehicles belonging to the few still in the shack. They couldn't find any. Tough luck. It would be helpful to know the license plates and car models.

"I hate like hell to leave here without knowing who those birds are, but neither of us can camp out all night. We've got a start toward identifying them, though. And we know who the boaters are. With any luck those are our patsies. I hope we can save them in the bargain. I don't think they knew what they were in for until tonight. I think they are two scared kids after that meeting. Let's get out of here."

The moonlight on the water and the plankton near the surface created a green luminescence too beautiful to go unappreciated, but the two young men in the boat had no eye for beauty as their craft carried them back to the pier.

Kawika had scarcely spoken a word in the coffee shack. He was numb with fear. Only when he had been taunted and forced to answer had he spoken up. Now with his best friend and cousin safely aboard and headed home he scolded Keoki.

"I told you not to get involved with those hoods, Keoki. I should never have gone with you. Now we're in real trouble. We know who they are and they'll never let loose of either of us . . . alive, that is." Kawika shuddered. "We've got to do something. We can't go through with this. Our parents will kill us if the Hoods don't do it first."

"Shut up, Kawika. I'm thinking. Even if you're right, I don't want to hear any more about it. We've got to get rid of the pakalolo, or whatever it is. Maybe it's crack, or ice. Whatever it is we can't get caught with it or we won't have to worry about the Hoods at all. The law'll take care of us."

"Oh, God." Kawika moaned.

"Shut up, Kawika. We haven't said our vows yet so we're not officially members."

His cousin stared at him, unbelieving. "Jesus, Keoki, have you lost your fuckin' mind? We're not talkin' about joining the Marines, ya know. We're in because we know too much about them. Just tell them that we don't want to say the vows, and see what happens. You jerk!"

Keoki sighed and hid his head in his hands. After a few moments, he looked up. "They just wanted to look tough to us tonight. After we're in and part of the gang, then we'll all be like brothers. Listen Kawika, you gotta realize that your friends will turn on you, and your family will turn on you, but once in a gang, we're blood brothers, loyal to the end."

"Oh, Jesus," said Kawika, this time more in prayer than as an oath. He was dumbstruck that his dumb cousin believed that gang crap.

As soon as the truck on the mauka road was underway, the passenger rewound the tape in the black container and pushed the 'play' button. They both held their breath until they were assured that the recording was clear and audible. Then, greatly relieved, they listened in silence as the voices from the coffee shack echoed what the two of them had first heard under less comfortable circumstances.

Occasionally they paused to discuss what was happening, or who was talking. "We've got three of the names in the group: Gopher, Poki, and Goose."

"Four, in fact. They mentioned someone called "Waterboy." Might just be a code word for identification though."

"There are always a lot of drugs coming in, or floating around. They gave no hints there."

"Right. There was no clue as to which library they're planning to bomb either. They were real cool about waiting until the novices had left before mentioning that."

"I'm trying to figure out how to go about this since I was not there under official orders. I could get into a lot of trouble for going over my bosses' heads in this. I don't even want to report it or use the tape as evidence, until after you turn it in to the police. They don't need to know I was there. I was really sticking my neck out."

"Yeah. I won't let this get you in trouble, Glenn. Thanks for going with me. I'd like to work alone for a while. I could talk to the two kids who were there tonight. I'll bet they're squirmin'. Probably wishin' by now they hadn't gotten involved with this crowd."

"I can't allow you to wait on this, partner. You've got to report the intended bombing right away. We don't know when it'll be. We can't take chances. I know you've had more undercover experience than I have, Igor, but right now you aren't legally qualified to follow through."

"Guess it's hard to get an old firehorse to stop. We just keep on reacting to the alarm bells. Okay, buddy. Thanks for going with me. I'll turn the tape in . . . tonight maybe . . . no later than tomorrow. No mention of your part in it. But I am going to have a talk with those two kids to try to get them on another path." Igor pulled over to let the detective out in front of his home.

He didn't know why he had turned toward the pier, but it was a lucky move. There at the boat ramp sat two dejected boys staring at the ground. No one else was around.

He approached them. They threw their arms across their eyes, blinded by the headlights.

"Need a ride, you two?" he asked.

They were likely to be picked up in an hour by an uncle who would be getting off work. But what the hell. They were dog-tired. "Where you headed?" Kawika asked.

"Toward Kau. Where you goin'?"

"That'll get us there," Keoki said. They pushed the already open door to climb into the cab of the truck.

Igor drove in silence for nearly an hour before he reached a stretch with no buildings. Just wild brush and huge trees. Unimproved land. A tall lava cliff ahead. He slowed his speed and drove on the shoulder until the passenger door was almost flush with the lava abutment leaving no room for the passenger door to open. Then he stopped, put the keys in his pocket, turned headlights off, and put his right hand just inside his jacket, nearly under his arm. He had no weapon, but it wouldn't hurt to make them think he did.

"What the hell? What are ya doin', mister?" Keoki sputtered. Kawika just watched.

"Not to worry, boys. You don't know me, but I know you."

Keoki felt for a knife he carried in his pocket.

"Don't make any dumb moves. My trigger finger gets nervous. We're just gonna sit here an' talk."

"Who the hell are you? What's goin' on?"

"Maybe I should make myself understood. I'm gonna do the talkin'. You are gonna listen. I'll tell you when to talk. Now shut up. We ain't got all night. Got it?"

The boys looked at each other, then watched and waited.

"Good boys. I know you because I've trailed you. Looks like you're hangin' around with a rough crowd. You're way out of your league. We find bodies all the time on this island, bodies of people who thought they could deal with these guys. Some poor jerks even tried to outwit them. It ain't gonna happen.

"What did they give you tonight? You can talk now, Junior." He used the name one of the Hoods had hung on Kawika tonight. He wished he could see their faces. "Come on. I know you've got somethin' to deliver to 'Waterboy', isn't it?"

"Who the hell are you?" The boy's voice quavered ever so slightly.

"Let's see it. You've got it with you. I don't want to work you over."

It was an idle threat, but it worked. Keoki pulled the package from his clothing and handed it over.

Igor slid it under his seat. "Now, it seems that, as the saying goes, you're between a rock and a hard place. You thought you would like to belong to a gang, right? Now what do ya think? What? No reply? Okay. Maybe you're gettin' smarter. How about if you go with me to the police station?"

"When?" Kawika asked.

"No way!" Keoki protested.

"Tonight." Igor said. "Either that, or we go talk to your folks, and we all go tomorrow to the police. What would your parents say to that?"

"Don't know." Keoki almost whispered.

"They'll kill me," Kawika said.

"Can't we make a deal with the police to pick us up when we deliver it to Waterboy? Then the gang won't be able to blame us. And our folks will think we're helping the law catch crooks."

"Might be a good plan, but we still have to make the deal with the police. Then you'll be undercover detectives. And then you'll have to go on with the charade and pretend you're one of them until they catch on, and we find your bodies in a gully somewhere."

"Which library are they planning to blow up?"

"Library? We don't know nothin' about any library. Blow it up? Where'd you hear that?"

"After you left tonight Goose, Gopher, Poki and the others were planning it. Which library?"

"You were there listening tonight then. You had to be. It was kinda dark, and some of them didn't talk. You were one of them, weren't you?"

"I was there, but I wasn't inside," Igor said. "And I had someone with me. So eventually everything is gonna blow sky high . . . including one of the libraries if you don't tell me."

"Honest. We don't know anything about that. They must not want to tell us until we've been tested."

"Yeah, and initiated. Unless they kill us because we don't say our vows of loyalty. We've got some choices." Kawika's voice was laced with sarcasm.

"Library. Wait a minute. They may be planning to blow up the Kailua Village library, where I take my kid brother for tutoring. It's a good bet. Damn them. If Keola got hurt because of those creeps, I'd kill every damn one of 'em." Keoki raged in the darkness.

Igor smiled. "Got 'im!" he thought. "So which will it be, boys? Tonight? Tomorrow? When?"

Keoki looked at his cousin. "Let's go home and tell your folks.

They'll handle it better. Then we'll get them to help tell my Pop. He's gonna kill me. That's okay. Then it'll all be over. I'll be dead, and out a this mess. Hope you can help hold back a wild tiger, mister."

Only one stop was necessary. The two large families shared a property with other kin. Igor had seen many parents when they were confronted with their children's transgressions. It didn't surprise him later when Keoki's father, instead of ranting and raving, sank into a chair as if his knees had given out when he got the news. His face was contorted as if to hold back the tears, but he said not a word. The effect on Keoki was tragic. He realized how much he loved his old man, and really wanted to please him. He had expected to be slapped around and yelled at. It would have been more merciful than seeing his father like this, sensing his disappointment and fear.

Igor cautioned all of the parents just in case. "The trouble your boys will have with the police is minor. It's the danger they've placed themselves, and you, their families, in, that we have to worry about. I'll send a police car tomorrow morning, or you can all drive to the Kailua station tomorrow. I'll be there as soon as I can. Just ask for Detective Glenn Asato. He'll take care of you."

"You two get off to bed." Igor ordered the boys.

As soon as the two were out of hearing, Igor put a hand on the old man's shoulder, patted the hand of the mother, and shook the hand of the other father, with one hand on his shoulder. "I guess you all recognize that this is not the time to scold or lecture them. Just be glad they turned to you before it was too late. Shall I send a car for you tomorrow?"

"We'll drive in ourselves. Don't know about Keoki's mother. She's working the night shift. Not home yet. She's gonna be needin' some sleep. What time should we be there?"

"Any time after 8:30 A.M. There's no deadline, but try to make it before 10:00. I'll have to inform Detective Asato that you'll be there.

"And listen, folks, we've caught this in time to keep it from being a disaster. The boys haven't broken any laws yet that we can't get leniency for. I think they have both learned a lesson. Good night."

As he drove away, he saw the elderly father of Keoki still seated in a rocker as if too weak to move.

[1] *mauka* (rhymes with how-kah) a direction meaning inland, or away from shoreline.

[2] *makai* (sounds like maw-kah-ee) toward the sea.

[3] Wannabe. Gang slang for youngsters who want to be a gang member.

[4] Gang slang: Active gang member.

[5] Hawaiian for hemp, or marijuana.

[6] Gang slang for someone who uses graffiti.

[7] Colors to identify each gang with same color scarf or wearing apparel.

[8] OG: original gang member.

[9] Jump in: gang initiation

[10] Pidgin for brother, close associate, or friend.

Chapter 41

Follow Up

It was late when Igor got home, but he called Asato anyhow. It was all right. Asato needed time to unwind after such a night.

"Can't come down, eh Brah?" Igor teased. "It's the curse of police work." Then Igor told him what happened after the detective had been dropped off.

"You don't let any grass grow under your feet, do you, partner?

"'Course a cop wouldn't have dared to trap them in the truck, and let them think you might blow their heads off. They didn't know if you were a gang member or what. By the time they found out what you wanted, it must have seemed like a trip to Disney Land compared to what they had imagined."

"You got it." Igor smiled, proud of his flair for underworld characters, and kids teetering on the brink. "So you'll bring in everything early tomorrow. They'll be booked, but the tape will save their necks. At least I think a judge will see them as dumb kids who almost got trapped into a pattern that would have led to destruction . . . theirs."

"How you going to explain how you got the tape? Just tell them you wanted to play cops and robbers?"

"Oh, I think they've got a record of my work. If not, it won't be hard to run it down. They know that undercover cops are nuts and that they never get over the disease. I'll just tell it like it was. I saw Keoki leave his little brother one night, then swagger down the street like the big boys do. I said to myself, that kid is lookin' for some action that may mean trouble for some citizen. I followed him. Watched him get into a car. Followed the car until we got out to the coffee fields where we were tonight. Did some snooping around, and you know the rest."

"We sure did, but I think you ought to become an official undercover cop over here. You're good, man!"

"I know it, but I'm gonna do it as a hobby from now on. Never again the pressures you guys are under. See ya tomorrow morning."

Igor secured the evidence in his apartment, then he called a friend to fill in for him at KABC tomorrow morning. Broadcasting was a healthier occupation than police work, but a little shot at this once in a while wouldn't hurt. Little by little maybe he would wean himself away from it for good. Unlike the old days on the mainland when he was so used to the tension and lack of sleep that he thought of it as normal. Tonight he was asleep almost before his head hit the pillow, and he slept like a bear in hibernation.

The sun wasn't up yet, but the sky was light from the sunrise on the other side of the island. Hualalai, and the other volcanos, Mauna Kea and Mauna Loa, blocked it for a while. The air was cool and refreshing. The mynah birds were already chattering in the big banyans. The cooing of the doves relieved the harsh sound, and a cardinal and its mate chirped their happy song from a plumeria that hid its naked boughs under an onslaught of creamy blossoms.

Igor walked up to the front desk at the police station and introduced himself. Best not to ask for Asato. Better to tell the cop on duty the story, turn in the tape and the package of whatever drug . . . he hadn't tried to open it. The guy he talked to, who also took the evidence into the locked room, got pretty excited.

Igor explained Kawika and Keoki's part in this. He said that the boys and their families would be in sometime this morning. Igor wanted to leave then, to return to his radio station, but they would have none of that. They weren't accustomed to a civilian walking in with a case they hadn't even heard of, now apparently solved.

They were checking on his credentials when Detective Asato happened by.

"Good morning, Igor," the detective said as he approached. They shook hands. "What are you doing here?" The policeman at the desk explained, as he had heard it briefly explained by Igor. Then Asato stepped in.

"Well, well. You are up to your old tricks. Did you check this man's background, Sergeant? Here." He wrote some numbers down for them to call on the mainland. "So, it looks like you beat me to it by getting a lead on this new gang over here. We do a pretty good job keeping them off this island, but they keep trying to move in and recruit our kids. We keep trying to send then back to Honolulu or L.A."

"I guess, we better listen to the tape, Sarge, but I'm sure it's all right to let Mr. Connifer get back to his work. We know where to reach him if we have any more questions. I want to hear that tape before the families and the kids get here."

Of course he did. He knew that it was imperative they get word to the libraries. They shook hands. Igor left, and Glenn Asato pitched in to complete the work they had started.

Chapter 42

Architect At Work

"This is Chieko, Cliff." She stammered, in an attempt to explain, when his response wasn't immediate. "We met at the library tutoring."

"Yes, of course, Chieko."

"I have a problem with my car, and I do want to be there to tutor tonight. Are you going, and would you possibly be able to bring me home after the tutoring session?"

"Sure, Chieko, but I'll also come to pick you up on my way there."

She was hoping he would offer, but she lived only a few blocks away from the library. It was reasonable to ask for a ride home when it would be quite late, but she didn't want him to get the idea she was making a play for him, which maybe she was.

"That's very nice of you. I live in the Helani condos."

"Perfect. That's near Sandy's apartment. She's going to join us tonight, and I'm picking her up, too." They exchanged details of time. "Perfect!" He said again as he wrote down her last name, in case he needed to ring the buzzer.

"Yeah, 'perfect'," Chieko sighed after she hung up the phone. Another live one, already as good as caught by someone else, before she had a chance to get his attention. It wasn't that she was hunting for a man. Well, shopping a bit, yes. That was to be expected. Her years of schooling had left her little time or energy to even think of the opposite sex.

This current slowing down, a transition period, had awakened her interest in men. She liked having their eyes follow her down the street. What was the matter with women who were so antagonistic when a man expressed appreciation with a glance, a wink, even a discreet whistle? Women have the option of disregarding them, or responding with a shy smile. She had been too shy to acquire the art of flirting, but it wasn't too late to learn. It was good to be an American girl who could make choices. Her Japanese grandmothers would be horrified. But theirs was a different world.

187

She spread out the plans on her workbench. Creativity and practicality were still battling to gain a foothold. She was ready to embrace new
ideas she might introduce or to fend off impractical notions. So, maybe
he isn't taken. Maybe he and this Sandy person are just friends. Anyhow,
she couldn't afford to get involved. Relationships require time, time she
didn't have with this new architectural project. She regretted that the
Shower tree's season was almost past. She took comfort in the fact that
every season had its own beauty. Hawaii's ever changing flora and foliage
never failed to inspire her. She was soon lost in her work.

New ideas came quickly. She was mesmerized with rapid sketching
and note taking. The morning sun rose high enough to streak across her
drawings.

The blessings of the sun. She must put windows, and skylights in the
buildings to allow a play of filtered light to ease into each room at some
time every day. The sun and Kona trade winds must be caught up into the
architectural content as mutual partners in the plan. And she must specify
the use of magnificent trees to filter the sun's rays. There must be space for
them to spread their ample boughs casting enormous shadows that danced
with the light on grounds, paths, ponds, and gardens. People should have
benches to rest on, while enjoying nature's bounty.

The sun's rays had alerted her to the passing of time. Hunger had
not interrupted her work. She had not even thought of lunch. Her
fatigue was not due so much to her work or a need for food, as to her
thirst. The tendency of dehydration was a foe to be reckoned with in this
climate. Her attention had been riveted for enough consecutive hours to
be considered a day's work for most people.

Hurriedly, Chieko put her combined desk and workbench in order.
A glance at the clock, and her image in the mirror determined that there
would be little time to change from the white blouse and black tailored
slacks she was wearing. Her hair would have to do with a quick brushing
and a hair clip at the nape of her neck to hold it in place. A dash of natural
lip gloss, and the buzzer sounded.

"Who is it, please?" Chieko was always cautious.

"It's Cliff."

"Be right down," she said, reaching for the shoulder strap of her
purse.

The short ride to the library scarcely allowed Chieko and Sandy
time to get acquainted. Chieko remembered Sandy from the night she
attended her first meeting of the 'Apple' group.

Pretty and pleasant. Probably smart, too, Chieko observed, studying Sandy. Sandy was sitting in front, very close to Cliff. Chieko was in the back seat.

"What's wrong with your car?" Cliff asked.

"If I knew, I would have fixed it. Just kidding, but I don't know. It just wouldn't start."

"I'll look at it if you'd like. I should have gotten here earlier to do that, but Sandy took so long to pretty herself up that we don't have time now."

"Don't blame me, Cliff Collins. I was waiting at the curb for you."

"So you were, but you do look pretty. Two pretty women!" he added quickly. "I hope everyone sees me drive up tonight."

Chieko was getting the message that it would be wise to scratch Cliff off the list she was mentally compiling of eligible men. The way he stole glances at Sandy convinced her of that by the time they entered the library.

Chapter 43

Architect Turns Tutorial

The librarian beckoned them to approach her desk. "You're with the tutoring group, I believe?" They nodded. "I'll need your help tonight. So glad you are here. The police have some plainclothesmen around. I don't even know who they are. They're worried about a bomb being planted," she added as though that was an ordinary message.

The tutors' eyebrows were raised. Surprised and curious, they gave her their full attention as she rattled on. She appeared to be enjoying her position. She even seemed to strut, as if she were a character in one of the shelved books. Her behavior calmed any concerns they might have had.

"Now don't get excited. The police have looked through the whole building, inside and out. They haven't found anything, but we are going to have a practice fire drill. It won't hurt. It might flush out whoever has made a threat," she added with the wink of a conspirator.

"Please inform the children you are tutoring about the drill so they won't be frightened. No need to mention a bomb threat. Just ask them to follow you outside. We'll all stand about a hundred feet away from the building. The chief will look around, turn off the alarm, and we'll come back in. Nothing to it," she smiled coyly. "My staff and I will get the other people out."

"Thank you." Cliff bowed slightly and smiled. "We'll do you proud, ma'am." It was his best Rhett Butler imitation. Why would anyone threaten to bomb a library, he wondered. It must be a prank. Pretty extreme. Certainly not playful.

"You got your orders from Miss Priss, I noticed," said one of the tutors. "Hey, gang, Miss Sandy's back. Say good evening to your tutors, boys," he told the children.

"Good evening." The boys grinned at the unfamiliar greeting. Their tutors tousled some of the shaggy heads before settling down.

"Keola isn't here tonight, Chieko. Did you scare him away?"

"I hope not. Someone just tell me where I can help."

"I need help," several young voices pleaded, gazing at the pretty tutor.

"Down, boys. We are working on our nines in the multiplication tables. Any of you know them already?" No show of hands. "Each tutor will coach two of you, and review the twos, fives, tens, and elevens as well. Then we'll have learned all of the easiest ones in the tables."

"Nines ain't easy," a dark-skinned boy with large brown eyes complained. He and another boy near Chieko had each grabbed one of her hands to claim her as their coach.

"Hey, Albert. He who says 'ain't' gets tongue cut out. 'Ain't' is only used by people who don't know any better." The tutor whispered the warning in a mysterious, dramatic, not quite threatening tone. "The word 'ain't' is not to be spoken by our students."

"Okay, every coach to your corners with your contestants. Remember, if there is ever a fire alarm in here it is just like school. Everybody out, and stay with your coach. We come back in when the fire chief says it's okay. Then, we'll divide into two teams. The winning team gets a prize. Next best team gets a consolation prize."

Chieko led the two nine-year-old boys into the children's section located in a front corner of the building. There they could sprawl and squirm on the beanbags in a carpeted pit. Chieko reviewed the two's, fives, and elevens as a warm-up. Did they understand what they were doing, and why multiplication tables are important, she wondered. Well, she would soon know.

It was an easy transition from elevens to tens. Then the nines. "Nine times zero is . . .?"

"What does zero mean?"

"A zero means no number?" Nate ventured, his voice rising to a questioning tone.

"Right. Always start your tables with a zero, because we multiply many zeros and must write the answer down. So, nine times zero is . . .?"

"Nine!" shouted Albert.

Back to square one, thought Chieko. She pretended to place something in his palm and closed his fingers. "What did I just put into your hand?"

Albert opened the fist she had closed. He scratched his head and looked bewildered. "Nothing."

"Now, I'm going to give you nine of the same." She repeated the same action nine times while she counted, "one nothing, two nothings, three nothings, . . ." they watched her, until she said "nine nothings. How much did I give you? How much do you have?"

"I ain't . . . I mean I don't got nuthin'."

"You're right, Albert. Repeat after me: I don't have anything."

"That's what I said teacher."

Chieko decided not to overdo the grammar thing for the moment. She made a mental note to cover that lesson another time.

Chieko grabbed him in a hug. Then seeing Nate's face, she hugged him, too.

"What about our nines, teacher?"

She realized that she had gotten sidetracked. "Okay, team. Let's go!"

"Nine zeros are . . ." (the pause was painful for her) "that means the same as nine nothings are . . . ?"

"Nothing!" Albert shouted. "Nine zeros are zero, which means nothing."

"Wonderful, Albert." He looked like he thought it was worth another hug.

"Albert and Nate, why do we memorize the multiplication tables? What good are they?" Silence. "Why do we need numbers?"

They both shrugged. "To count with?" Nate ventured.

"Cause that's what they do in school?" Albert answered.

"Boys, we're going to pretend that we lived thousands of years ago."

They brightened. That's what they like to do . . . pretend.

Chapter 44

The Magic of Numbers

"Now, team, we're going to pretend we are cave men."

"You have to be a cave lady." Albert said.

"Okay. We lived a long, long time ago. Thousands of years ago. We were very smart. We had to be to stay alive. We had a big brain. Everybody was a student. We studied animals, and plants and other people. When someone learned something new, he or she had to be teacher. Everybody was a student sometimes, and a teacher sometimes, so they all would learn and understand."

"Why don't we build a house, Miss Chieko?"

"Good question, Nate. They did have shelters other than caves, but they could draw on cave walls. For now, we live in a cave and we don't have numbers. But we could sure use them to say how many of something we traded or shared with the other cave people. Can you imagine what they used instead of numbers?"

They shook their heads.

"Look at these pictures. These are called petroglyphs. Hawaiians, before they had numbers, drew simple pictures like this in the sand, or on rocks. We're not sure what they mean. We study them, and we guess.

"Here's a picture of writing done by people in Egypt, a country far away in a part of Africa. See this animal?"

"It looks like drawing, not writing. It looks like a deer." Nate volunteered. "I could draw that."

"Sure, if you wanted to leave friends or family a message, like a letter, saying you saw two deer, you could just draw two box shapes, four lines for legs, and antlers on their heads. Show me." They each drew the shapes and held them up for her to see.

"But what if we saw one hundred deer? Not so easy to draw a hundred, right? What could we do then?" They shrugged their shoulders, waiting for her answer.

"We would have to make some kind of mark that would mean one hundred to us. Draw a line, or circle, or any shape you can think of that's quick and easy to write." Chieko looked over their shoulders. They peeked at each other's paper, and copied. They drew a check mark, a tiny circle, a dash, a curved line, and a lollipop shape.

"Those are good ideas for our tribe of cave people to use. We need symbols, shapes like you just drew, because we don't know about numbers or the alphabet yet.

"Numbers are symbols. They are just curvy lines that someone made up. Each person who learned the symbols taught someone else, so that everyone, when they saw a shape like that, would understand what that mark meant. So it was hard to draw how many fish we caught, or how many spear heads we made."

"Too hard to draw many fish, instead of only one or two," the boys agreed.

"Do you think that we cave men and women had multiplication tables?" Chieko asked.

"Nope, don't think so," Albert said.

"Do you think life would have been easier for them if they had known about multiplication tables?"

"Yeah."

"Why? What good are they? What do they do? What are you going to do with them?" she persisted.

"Well-ll-ll..."

"It's always okay to say, 'I don't know.' Then someone will explain it to you. It's a smart person who will admit that he doesn't know. Don't ever forget that."

"First, we are going to make a list of one of the tables. Which is the easiest table to do? One you already know very well."

"The two's are easy. Why do they call them tables? They ain't tables." Nate protested.

"No, they aren't tables. Repeat what I just said, please."

"You said, 'No, they ain't tables.'"

"No, I said, 'they aren't tables.' I mean that they aren't tables like furniture, but a table also means a tablet, even a piece of board or a rock to write on."

She sat between them so they could copy what she wrote. They snuggled up to her. "Write the symbol that tells us to multiply." 'X', they wrote. "We cave people didn't have that symbol, instead we can make as many dots as the number equals. Why do we need a symbol for zero? What does zero mean?"

"Nothing." One boy said, and the other echoed. "But we don't have numbers yet so we can't write a zero either."

"But cave men are smart. We'll invent a symbol for it. Let's draw a doughnut. A small circle that has a hole in it. It has nothing in the middle. How's that for a symbol of zero? Okay, write two lines, like this '. The two lines look the same. What a good symbol. That's what equal means. Equal means 'the same.' And the answer to two times zero equals . . . what?"

"Zero . . . nothing," they both shouted.

"Write the table of two's like this," and she showed them by making dots to represent each number.

"I'm tired of making dots. Two times 10. Gosh, I'll have to make twenty dots for the answer."

"For ten times ten you'll have to make a hundred dots," Chieko said. "Which do you think is easier, writing dots to show how much or writing the symbols people use now instead of all of those dots?"

"Numbers are easier." Nate said. Albert nodded agreement.

"Aren't you glad you memorized numbers so you can use them? But we're cave people for tonight, and we don't know numbers yet, so we are going to travel far away now in time and place. It is now many, many years later. We aren't cave people now. Our people have built cities. Cave people didn't have cities. We are in a faraway place called India." Chieko bounded over to the world globe on a shelf.

"Here is where we are now." She pointed to Hawaii. "See, we are really on this tiny island with miles of the Pacific Ocean around us. But with our make-believe time machine, we have traveled far away to a place called India, where Hindu people live. Here is India on the globe."

"Wow. It's a lot bigger than our island," Nate said.

"Yes, and we Hindus are very smart. We have invented numerals that we now usually call numbers. We Hindus have invented these squiggly lines." She wrote: 1, 2, 3, 4, 5, 6, 7, 8, 9, as they copied them onto their papers. "Only the 1, 4 and 6 are the same numbers they used."

Chieko smiled. She was having a good time. It appeared that they were also. "The numerals were such a great idea that other people wanted to use them. In Arabia people were called Arabs. They were very smart too. They were so smart that they improved on the numerals. It was such an improvement that since that time, about 1400 years ago, they have been called Arabic numerals.

"They had nine numbers, but what did the Arabs add to that to make it easy for us to write any number. What was missing?

"Here we are. Arabs in this place right here on this globe, far, far away from Hawaii. Maybe we are on a desert, riding on camels." She flipped through pictures of such scenes, as she described them. "The sun is very hot, and we wear clothes that cover our heads and our bodies, clear down to our ankles. Some of us live in tents that we put up, take down, and even move from place to place. Some of us live in cities in Arabia. And we have learned a lot since we were cave people. Now, no more dots or dashes or marks for numbers. We have symbols called numerals. And the whole world is going to copy us. But what was missing that the Arabs invented?"

"She means a zero. Like this," Nate said.

"Zero," shouted Albert.

"Yes. So we now have a zero, and with just nine numbers and a zero we can write any number we want: 10, 20, 30, or one hundred, or a billion, or trillion. Isn't that a wonderful invention we Arabs have given to the world?"

"How do you write a billion?" Nate asked. Chieko wrote 1 followed by nine zeroes.

"Wow. I wish I had a billion dollars," he sighed, and wrote the number down. "How do you write a trillion?"

"Just write three more zeros on the end of billion. What would you have a trillion of, Nate?"

"Stars maybe?"

"Five-minute break," Chieko relented. "Go get a drink of water and stop at the restroom." She stretched out on the carpet in the reading pit until they came racing back to her.

Chapter 45

Close Call

Chieko figured that the other tutors and their students were equally engrossed. She didn't even feel tired. She was exhilarated, and the boys appeared alert and frisky as kids are when at play. "Let's add some numbers. Here are nine twos." She wrote each number placed one below the other with a line under the stacks. They copied them to their own papers. Albert started counting on his fingers, then was confused and started over. Nate had memorized the two's.

"Zero, two, four, six . . ." Nate counted to himself to eighteen. Albert looked ashamed. "Good job, Nate. This time you're the teacher. Show Albert and me how you did that."

Nate repeated the two's of the multiplication tables. "You memorized them." Chieko exclaimed. "How many twos equal eighteen?"

"Nine twos equal eighteen," Albert said.

Chieko blew him a kiss. With a wink and a nod of her head, "And, how many nines equal eighteen?"

"Nine twos and . . . ," Nate began. "And two nines," finished Albert.

"I wonder if it always works when we change two numbers around like we just did." It was becoming a game instead of study.

They shrugged, and had soon discovered that multiplication did indeed work that way. "See," Nate gloated, "two times three is the same as adding three and three. And three times two is the same as two plus two plus two, both add up to six. Multiplying is like adding, only it's easier to multiply when we get to the big numbers."

"Maybe, but memorizing them is hard," Albert complained.

"Do you remember how much you practiced learning numbers and the alphabet when you were little kids? Now it's easy for you to write them," Chieko said. "When you memorize the tables and practice using them, all arithmetic problems will be easier. Congratulations. You got it! It's about time to go, boys."

"But we didn't do our nines teacher," said Nate, who didn't want the evening to end.

Chieko groaned inwardly. She had failed the mission that all of the tutors had been asked to do. Now it was too late to rush the boys through it. She decided on a mini-lesson.

"Here's another quick way to add nines, and you can add them to any number. See how the 'tens' place number gets one bigger," (she pointed to it) "and the 'units' place number gets one smaller when you add nine to it. Watch: 36, to add 9, the 3 changes to 4, or 1 more, and the 6 becomes 5, or 1 less. See how 36 + 9 = 45. List the rest now. After 45, what?"

"Fifty-four! Then 63, then 72, then 81, 90. The next number doesn't work the same, but you know your elevens."

"Ninety-nine," they both shouted. "That's nine times eleven." Nate was happily chattering to anyone who would listen. "Boy, it's just like magic!" He looked at her adoringly.

"The important thing is that you understand that there is more than one way to figure out answers to number problems. Boys, I have an assignment for you. Make flash cards of the nines. Memorize them so well that you can skip around."

"Can I add 10 to 45 and subtract one to add nine?" Albert asked. His answer was 54.

Chieko clapped her hands and gazed at him in wonder. He was reasoning, not just echoing. It was like watching a light come on. "Show Nate how you did that."

Nate copied Albert's answer of 63 on the next line. Albert spoke aloud, with authority, to his friend "And 63 plus 10, equals 73, but take away one because you need only 9 of it. Ten is easier to add. That's why you do it that way." Albert explained to Nate. "Get it?" he asked.

"Yeah, I got it."

Chieko could only watch dumbfounded, as they checked their answers. She hugged them both at the same time. "Albert and Nate, I congratulate you. You listened, you used your brains, and you learned." Chieko shook their hands as if she were a politician looking for votes. They were amused because teacher didn't know that shaking hands wasn't done that way. It should be a ritual ending with a slapping of each other's hands, overhead, and a holler. "Yeah!" They'd have to teach her how. They basked in her appreciation for their achievement.

Chieko was elated with their progress. They had been attentive all evening.

At that moment, a deafening sound shook the walls, and seemed to echo through her body. She was thrown off balance. Surely her heart must have stopped. Then it pounded wildly. The two boys, mouths open, watched her face so they would know how to react. There was the sound of people running. Dust, smoke, and stench hung in the air. Plaster had fallen from the ceiling.

"Chieko, are you all right? The boys? Is anyone hurt?" Cliff and Noah were calling to her from the doorway.

The boys were clinging to her, their eyes wide open now, in shock. "We're all okay," she shouted. As she turned to run with them toward the exit, she noticed a wide gap in the wall not far from the corner where they had been curled up together. As if all was blurred, she saw books spilled from shelves. Standing shelves near the outside wall had tipped over. Running toward the door, they stepped carefully over art objects that lay smashed on the floor.

Noah picked up Albert. Cliff took Nate in his arms. Chieko could scarcely keep up with them. In a matter of seconds, they reached the outside door. Firemen were already on the job. They succeeded in putting out flames before they had time to more than scorch the wood. The firemen must have been very near when the explosion occurred. They were combing the inside of the building to be sure that everyone was out.

Miss Priss, standing some distance from the entrance, was shivering and wringing her hands. A bystander threw a jacket over her shoulders. Noah led the way toward the other tutors standing with the children they had been in charge of. They counted again to be sure they were all out of the building.

Just before the bomb exploded, one of their students had returned from the restroom. Some of the fire captains were already questioning people who had been in the library. The police had run yellow tape around the grounds to mark the limits, to hold the curious observers back, to lessen confusion, and to avoid destruction of any clues.

It soon appeared that no one had been injured. No bodies were under the shelves that had toppled from the blast. The expected alarm drill had not been sounded. But the instructions given earlier by their tutors had helped to quell panic. Everyone reacted favorably. None of them were crying, yet there was a look of horror in their eyes.

Parents heard the explosion and the sirens from some distance away. They saw the dust in the air and hastened to its source. Tutors were relieved that the children were all picked up early. Parents hugged their children.

The police and the fire captain tried to get everyone's name on a list before anyone left the premises. It was difficult. Chieko and Sandy leaned against a rock wall in stunned silence. The other tutors were in a group discussing it with the officials.

"Which boy had been in the restroom just before the blast?" One of the tutors supplied the child's name. "No, he had said nothing of seeing anything strange when he returned," someone answered. It was possible that the child had seen something, or someone. That information might be significant to the investigation. Perhaps there was more than one person responsible.

The building had been under scrutiny due to the threat someone had reported to the police. With plainclothes policemen around, how could anyone place the bomb without being noticed? The building had been searched. Someone must have penetrated the police surveillance and arrived just before the bomb went off.

Noah had arrived late. The library parking was filled, so he had parked some distance down the street. Cliff was grateful that he had parked on the far side of the lot. Three cars near the corner of the building where the bomb exploded were badly damaged. Everyone was amazed that Chieko and her two students were not hurt. It was the most damaged part of the library.

Chieko was suddenly too weary to wait much longer for a ride home. She was almost ready to leave, to walk home, when Cliff and Noah finally approached.

"Would anyone like to stop somewhere for coffee?" Noah asked.

Tired though she was, Chieko's nerves were too on edge to allow her to fall asleep anyway. She was agreeable.

Cliff and his two passengers arrived first at the late night franchise restaurant on the hill. They were settled at a table clutching menus when Noah entered. He had almost decided not to bother going to the library tonight. There was very little time left to work with the students. But he wondered if the petite brunette with silken hair and feline, languid eyes would be there. Now, due to the nightmarish explosion, he would be spending the rest of the evening with her.

"I'm famished, but this is a terrible hour to eat a meal," Chieko said, scanning the menu. She opted for a quick energy dessert. Pie heaped with whipped cream. Sandy just stared enviously.

"It is unfair that some people can eat high on the calorie list, and not gain a pound." Chieko grinned like a teenager, but didn't say that pie was a choice that she rarely made. It gave her a wicked satisfaction to know that someone as attractive as Sandy had to work hard to keep slim.

Sandy and the men ordered vegetable soup for Noah and chowder for the other two. They lingered over coffee, loathe to leave for what would probably be a sleepless night. Yet they seemed unwilling to discuss the explosion.

Finally, "Why would anyone choose a library as a place to vent their anger?" Cliff asked.

"And who in Kona would see any point in doing such a thing?" Sandy spoke up.

Shaking his head slowly, Noah added, "It's not something a sane person would do."

"Would he be after a person, or a group of people in there? Or would the building be a symbol of the establishment?" wondered Chieko.

"You're wondering if this had anything to do with our Apple group activities?" Sandy had wondered the same. "It would be a rotten thing for anyone to choose a time and place where kids were gathered."

"It's not the act of a person who would care about that." Noah insisted.

They had so little information that it was futile to continue the discussion. There was no way they could arrive at reasonable conclusions. Suppositions seemed pointless. They hungered for more facts.

The awareness that they all might have been killed closed in on them like a dark cloud. And why? Because some idiot is running around with dangerous explosives. So many children were at risk. Silence reigned. Each lost in thought, they could not yet express the thankfulness each felt that all lives had been spared.

The bomber had wanted to frighten or intimidate someone, to destroy only the building, not people. If so, from his perspective, he had succeeded.

The food, relaxation, and sharing made them feel at ease with one another. They had been scarcely aware of their appearance until after they had relaxed. Chieko's hair was sprinkled with white plaster and a smear of soot spread from one eye to the opposite cheek. Sandy's hair was standing on end. Cliff's shirtsleeve was torn, maybe from the boy clinging to him while being carried outside. Noah's dark suit was covered with plaster. His tie and collar were askew.

They looked more like actors from an action movie set rather than residents in paradise.

The foursome was now aware that people in the restaurant were staring at them with curiosity. Their fatigue, relief, exertion and confusion bonded them. Their emotional turmoil expressed itself in a nearly hysterical, breathless giggling fit. It started with Sandy. The contagion spread to Cliff. Their guffaws, especially when they tried to control themselves, affected Chieko and finally Noah. The gasps of uncontrolled laughter dwindled to chuckles, then flared again to giggles that they could not stop. Surely people thought they were drunk or crazy. It was a night to remember.

Chapter 46

Getting To Know You

The weeks following were full of ongoing investigations by the police and the fire departments. The bomb placed at the library left evidence that allowed experts to identify it as a bangledore torpedo, a device used to make holes in wire and fences. Many soldiers were familiar with it from their army service.

A possible clue, decided the investigation team. "But how is it that the teacher and two children were not injured?" someone asked.

"The bomb wasn't as large as usual. If it had been placed on the ground, the full force of it would have been going away from the ground surface. It appeared to have been placed in the branches of a bush. The library wall behind the bush took the force of the explosion, but it deterred some also, so that the majority went outward, away from the building. Anyone nearby felt a tremendous amount of pressure. You could feel it going down your back. You could hear the air pressure coming from the explosion."

"I suspect the purpose was to frighten, not to kill . . . but the people inside were lucky. The explosion could have crushed those inside the building. We might start looking for someone who has been in the service. Someone who has a screw loose. Maybe has a nutty cause to uphold."

"Maybe he was hurt in the explosion or was covered with rubble. I think we can count on someone to call in a report of suspicious behavior or talk they've heard. Our Crime Watch system has been a great help in getting the public involved."

"Yeah, just put a generous reward out there for information. No name to identify the caller, just give the person a number to call in. Then claim the bucks if their information results in the arrest of a guilty party. Works like a charm."

The foursome of Chieko and Noah, and Sandy and Cliff met periodically. Since they all worked and volunteered a large part of their own time, they met for exercise and light lunches. Each occasion resulted in added respect for one another. There were so many things for the foursome to talk about. They were well matched, having enough traits in common to be compatible and enough differences to be interesting.

After a tennis game, Sandy took them to a place she had discovered that served old-fashioned malts. She and Cliff shared one to salve their guilty consciences. They avoided talk about the explosion.

"How's the car running?" Cliff asked Chieko.

"Oh, it's fine now, Cliff. Thank you so much. You are a genius." He had refused to take any money, and she was still wondering how to show her appreciation. She didn't want to say that Noah had been chauffeuring her around so much that she hadn't driven her own car since before the night of the bombing.

Chieko was surprised and pleased by Noah's attentiveness. He was a gentleman and did not seem to want a relationship. He was just considerate. He would call when he was going to the store, to see if she needed anything, and always seemed to be available to drive her anywhere she wanted. It seemed that a close friendship was growing without any conditions. The result was an ever-increasing amount of time spent together, with no demands being made by either. Chieko found it to be a very pleasant arrangement.

Noah recognized this as a convenient and appropriate way to be with the woman he adored. She showed no signs of the same feelings toward him, but it was a great improvement over the way she had reacted toward him after that first day.

That day she had been on guard. Well, he was a stranger to her then. She was a bit haughty, too. Noah didn't handle rejection well. He had moped around for days after that. He felt foolish. What made those movie idols so smooth? Well, they spoke from a script, for one thing. No help to Noah's cause to win fair lady, he thought.

Chieko labeled her work as "Project CC," for community center, so Noah didn't know anything about it. She answered his questions briefly without revealing much about her goal. He sensed he should not intrude on her territory. She would tell him in good time as he gained her confidence.

He took to arriving early and finding an excuse to remain afterward. Chieko liked having him there. He would sit across the room from her and pretend to read. He watched her every move. The way she tucked the pencil behind her ear. Her sighs when she sought answers to problems she faced. And tapping one finger on the desk when deep in thought. He teased her when she was searching all over for her glasses, while they rested on top of her head.

Lately he had been getting bolder, taking a glass of water to her, so she would drink fluids while working. She was even coaxing him to stay longer, with promises of a simple snack or light meal. By helping her set the table or to prepare the food, he became comfortable using her refrigerator, and doing routine household activities. If he saw a task that needed doing, he just did it without comment. He was tempted to even buy some delicacies and fix a meal when she was busy, but held back. He didn't want to overstep his boundaries with her.

Sometime preceding this newfound friendship, he had learned her last name. He had not connected it to his boss' until he saw her picture on Ross Ota's desk. At first, it seemed that might be a barrier to dating her. Then there were other complications. It just hadn't been mentioned. Well, the current situation was a very agreeable one without any of the hassles that often accompanied dating. Noah's score in romancing techniques was zero.

Chieko did not yet know that her uncle was Noah's employer. The current slow-growing relationship was much better, Noah decided. Except when they sat close together in the car, and he detected the slight scent of Kahili ginger. Except when he heard her laughter, and looked into her eyes. Eyes that seemed to change according to whether they were mischievous or enticing. And the enticement: was it her intention or his imagination? No matter, it struck him speechless, so in awe was he of her fragile beauty.

What was it she had just said? He almost dropped the dish he held while gazing at her.

"You weren't listening, Noah! I said that I got an invitation in the mail from Guy and Amy Benson. It's to invite all of the tutors for an afternoon at their house. Here, you must have one in the mail at your place. Shall we go together?"

Noah brightened noticeably. He didn't even ask when. If he had anything else scheduled, he would change the former plan. And she had asked him! "Together, yeah . . . sure . . . let's go together . . . to the Benson's I mean."

He is nonplused, Chieko told herself. He certainly is. And trying all the while to cover it up. She just smiled sweetly.

"It's potluck. Maybe we could fix something together." It was the beginning of their acknowledging a certain togetherness. People may assume a romance, she thought, yet there was none. Oh, well, she wasn't ready for it, although a little flirting is fun, Chieko was thinking. He never seemed attracted to her as men usually were. Well, so be it. She didn't have time for that, she decided as she tapped her pen and peeked at him through the silken curtain of her hair.

Noah had seen Guy only at work since Barry had been found. Guy's dedication to the cause of education was strong and deep. Yet now marriage would come first. Guy had phoned after the bombing to make sure that Noah was all right, but they hadn't talked about any matters other than what was happening in Apple A Day. Noah had been voted to lead the group when Guy refused that honor and responsibility.

Noah phoned Guy from his apartment. "I just got the invitation from you in the mail. What can we bring?" Noah asked. "Never mind. Ask Amy what we can bring. How would you know?"

"Amy just left to go to the store. I'll have her call you. And what do you mean by 'we'? Are you bringing a friend?"

Noah ignored the question. "I don't want to be nosy, Guy, but I'm hoping all is going well between you and Amy. Work isn't the place to discuss it. Is everything working out now for all of you?"

"It couldn't be better, Noah. Well, it will be better. I'm trying to think before I react. Habits are hard to break. Both the counselor and Amy are working on me and it's a hell of a lot more peaceful around here.

"Amy is working on her own ways. She kept her hurt and anger inside instead of telling me so we could confront it. Problems arise in a marriage, but there is nothing that we can't learn or relearn to save it. We have one happy boy here too."

"That's good to hear, pal. The way so many marriages are going downhill, we bachelors are getting cold feet. Too cold to even test the waters."

"Okay, Noah. Who is she? You didn't call just to find out how we are doing. You're thinking about diving in, aren't you? Who is it? Where did you meet her?"

"No, no, no, you know me. Confirmed bachelor. I just wanted to know that everything is okay in spades with you and Amy. Bet your Dad is delighted, too. I'll see all of you at your house. Tell Amy to call me now, so we'll know what to bring. So long, Buddy."

A very abrupt leave-taking, Guy thought as the receiver clicked. And who is the "we" Noah referred to? He's hiding something. No doubt about it.

Chapter 47

Best Way to Have a Future

"Education is the great equalizer of the conditions of men . . .
the balance wheel of the social machinery."
—Horace Mann

"The best way to have a friend is to be one," somebody once said. The best way to have a wife is to woo one, Noah thought. The best way to have a future is to plan one, by taking the initial steps.

Noah was playing with words. Words concerning the future. That was the subject discussed at the Apple meeting last night. The organization had taken on a life of its own. It seemed a long time ago that a few friends had gathered several times a week to get it off the ground. Yet things had moved fast, "as if they were meant to be," his mother used to say.

The broadcasting had given their group the momentum that was needed. Local newspapers had publicized the new radio station KABC even though it only had a five-mile transmission radius. There had been a burst of response in the community when neighbors began talking more to other neighbors. The community suddenly was empowered. There was now both agreement and disagreement about what must be done. More of the former than of the latter.

The meeting last night demonstrated that people believed in themselves enough to know they could make some of the necessary changes. The rest of the problems, well, the ball was already rolling. Everyone was finding a niche in which they fitted to help their cause.

There were reports of efforts being made in the schools among the students to make them more aware of their role. Emphasis now was on conversion. That seemed to be the right word for the transition from students' lack of faith in their schools, in the teachers, and in themselves to strong belief in their capacity to learn and a heartfelt desire to educate themselves. They knew they were responsible for that.

They couldn't expect large numbers of students to adapt to this positive approach at first. That would take time. A slogan as powerful as "Black is Beautiful," which once was a magic potion that changed the attitudes of both black and white people across our nation, would be necessary. Once that was raised as a banner, the transition was jump-started. Apple A Day needs such a slogan, one that will catch on. Put out on the airways a powerful, all encompassing slogan, which will be accepted by the multitude, and there will be a miraculous turnabout in the attitudes of America's children.

Only in America could this be happening. Noah recalled yesterday's KABC broadcast. A student from Mrs. Heffner's home school called in to read his report on education over the air. Igor asked Aaron's permission to make copies to use as a handout to inform the community. Noah buzzed Chieko's apartment and identified himself. He was eager to share the report he had picked up earlier in the day from Igor.

"Noah," she sounded surprised as she opened the door. "I thought you weren't coming over tonight. I've already eaten."

"I'm late. Sorry. Do you have a cracker for a hungry man? I want to read something, and I think you'll enjoy it, too . . . that is, if I'm not interrupting."

"Come in. I think I can do better than a cracker."

The light behind her formed a halo around her head. Noah had never seen her looking more beautiful. She was usually in jeans or shorts, and comfortable T-shirts. Tonight she wore pale pink silk pajamas that showed beneath a belted embroidered silk wrap-around top. Her hair hung long and loose. Although she used makeup sparingly, the absence of it tonight made her look like a teenager.

"Whoa. I guess I am later than I thought, Chieko. You're ready for bed. I apologize. How about if I come tomorrow, and let you get some sleep now."

"Don't be silly. I'm going to fix you something to eat. An egg sandwich? How does that sound?"

"Like Ambrosia. Food for the Gods."

"You're staring."

"You're beautiful."

Chieko looked at him wide-eyed. "Well!"

"I'm sorry. I shouldn't have said that. I'd better go."

"Sit down!"

As she prepared the sandwich, he explained the report he had brought. Suddenly it seemed a foolish reason to invade her privacy tonight. But he relished the sandwich and milk. They settled down to take turns reading aloud James Aaron's report about education, and other factors he had included concerning the Revolutionary War. Chieko was curled up in a huge armchair that made her look lost in its comfortable upholstery.

Noah explained that the student who wrote this was another red-headed teenager who left public school and is now doing well in a home school. He had been interviewed on KABC with his home schoolteacher and classmates. The students had not used their own names for privacy's sake. He had given his name as Aaron. That was his surname according to this report.

Noah sat on a footstool in front of Chieko's chair, insisting that he was quite comfortable, they could share the light and . . . Actually, he just wanted to sit as near to her as he dared. She smelled fresh with a faint scent of lavender. Noah began to read.

Report by James Aaron
Subject: World History—Emphasis on America
June 2001

Colonial America in Early Revolutionary Times
As reported by Alexis de Tocqueville in *America: A Narrative History*, by George Brown Tindall with David E. Shi. W. W. Norton & Co., New York, N.Y. 1992. pp. 240, 503–508,
(*Comments concerning this source are by James Aaron.*)

The ideology of Americans after the revolution and the formation of a new government was of great interest to the Europeans. De Tocqueville was a great statesman and author in France. He told his countrymen about the changes in the Americans after they had won their independence.

John Adams had said that "the Revolution was already in the hearts and minds of the people before the war had begun . . . . This radical change in the principles, opinions, sentiments, and affections of the people, was the real American Revolution."

When de Tocqueville came to America in the early 1800's, he said that "Americans had been born free, and that the Revolution had merely been a defense of liberty and property, which they had already become used to. After the war, they had to reason, and examine things about freedom that they had once taken for granted." Political thinking had to catch up with colonial institutions and practices. Americans began to see themselves in a different way. As free citizens, they wanted to change their ways to bring about virtuous ways.

Colleges and universities were started. Then, very early they decided that public schools would be the best way toward moral and civic development. At first the state-supported schools just wanted to "make children literate, and learn to choose the public good over all private interests and concerns." Jefferson agreed that public education would serve as "the very keystone of our arch of government." In 1779 he established a plan to fund elementary schools for all free persons, and higher education for the talented, up through the state university.

These well-intended plans did not work out because wealthy critics refused to spend tax money on schools that would "mingle their sons in a vulgar and suspicious communion with the masses." Public schools had to wait until the attitude of people of influence would be more democratic.

Yet people were finding ways to get education, and it was strengthening nationalism. Spelling books were widely used. One person wrote, "The American national consciousness is not a voice crying out of the depth of the dark past, but is proudly a product of the enlightened present, setting its face resolutely toward the future."

By 1830, people were demanding public schools for all children. They argued that popular government required "a literate and informed electorate." They claimed that it would reduce crime and poverty and improve manners. There was opposition only from taxpayers who wanted education to be a family matter, and from church groups who supported their own schools.

The great lawyer and educator Horace Mann started a drive for statewide school systems. From that beginning a state board of education was formed, and a "normal school" which was for training teachers. A minimum school year was six months. He said, "Education is the great equalizer of the conditions of men...the balance wheel of the social machinery."

Some difficulties with public education were: There was not enough funding for buildings, books, and equipment. Teachers were poorly paid, and often were poorly prepared, being not much ahead of their pupils in reading, writing, and arithmetic abilities. Most students going beyond elementary grades went to private academies supported by a church and public funds. A Boston High School opened in 1821. In 1860, there were fewer than 300 high schools in the whole country.

A form of "popular education" was growing to inform, therefore educate the populace. There were workingmen's institutes, young men's associations, debating and literary societies. Philadelphia had the Franklin Institute in 1824 to inform in the fields of science and industry. Some philanthropists sponsored institutes. Some cities had night school for those who could not attend day schools. The lyceum method was the most widespread and effective means. Knowledge was shared through public lectures. Professional agencies provided speakers of all kinds in literature, science, music, humor, travel, and other fields.

The movement that reached most people was the growth of public libraries. Ben Franklin's Philadelphia Library Company began the trend in 1731. By 1851, there were about 10,000 libraries. Not all were free.

The coexistence of state and religious schools raised problems over funding and curriculum. Many church schools emphasized theology over science and the humanities. The University of Virginia, Thomas Jefferson's school, in 1826 introduced a curriculum emphasizing pure knowledge with "all the branches of science useful to us."

Technical education grew slowly. Usually people were trained by practical experience, apprenticed, according to their field of study to doctors, lawyers, agriculturists, mechanics, manufacturers, or merchants. Railroad and canal companies trained their engineers.

In 1835, in de Tocqueville's report on American Society he wrote that the intellectual and moral associations in America deserve special attention. In 1831 he heard that 100,000 men had pledged to abstain from alcohol. "Why?" he wondered. Then he understood. "Americans of all ages, all stations to [sic] life and all types of dispositions are forever forming associations. There are not only commercial and industrial associations in which all take part, but others of a thousand different types religious, moral serious, futile, very general and very limited, very large and very minute."

Ralph Waldo Emerson, essayist and poet of the early 1800's, asked: "What is a man born for, but to be a Reformer, a Remake of what man has made?" The nineteenth century in America was rooted in all types of missions stemming from their faith in the expectation that humans dedicate themselves to self improvement. There was a belief that intuition led to right thinking.

I believe it does also, but only if we are educated in ways to broaden our knowledge to a degree that we can exercise wisdom in the choices we make.

It is worthwhile to examine literacy in those times considering that illiteracy is becoming more of a problem in our country today. The author says that literacy in the Jacksonian era of America (President Andrew Jackson's time) was "widespread." An interesting phenomenon considering the condition of public education in our time.

Census data of 1840 shows that about 78 percent of the total population, and 91 percent of the white population could read and write. Since the Colonial period, Americans had the highest literacy rate in the Western world. Children learned to read and write from church or private schools, tutors, or from their families.

In 1830, no state had a school system in the modern sense, but for 200 years, Massachusetts, preceding that time, had required every town to have schooling. New York had started a system of free schools in 1805. By 1853, the society of schools had 600,000 pupils. Rural systems had more problems, and different ones, because the population was so spread out.

I researched this subject because I wanted to know why we are not getting good results in today's schools according to national tests. Several things surprised me about the schools during the Colonial period of our history, and following the Revolutionary War.

(1)   Many people learned to read and write without public schools. The book also pointed out that many people read books, magazines, and newspapers at that time.

I credit that to: a driving desire to raise oneself to higher levels of ability in order to have a more rewarding life. Often before that time they had the desire but there was no opportunity.

It was possible to learn without schools as long as there was desire for self-improvement, encouragement and confidence. As soon as they learned to read most people read extensively. It broadened their knowledge. They learned on their own because there were libraries in the bigger cities. There was also, what the author called the "Lecture Circuit." They were experts, famous people and speakers with a message who traveled all around the country to speak. Listening to these travelers was a good way to learn about things outside of their experience.

There were several quotations in this book that expressed the importance of public schools in a free society. For example, "Uneducated people are likely not to take their responsibility to vote, and to shirk other responsibilities of citizenship." This seriously weakens a country.

The qualities characteristic of the people who came to our shores to become free, and to build a new government, seem to be similar to traits of many of our people today, who take up a cause that they believe in, and see it through until they succeed in making this a better country, and a better world.

I am sharing this with you, the members of Apple A Day, Inc., to thank you for your efforts. I know that you will succeed if we rethink public education.

My reference book America *is called a narrative history. It begins with pre Columbian Indian Civilizations and goes through the 1990 census. It includes the Constitution, Declaration of Independence, and many tables and lists that relate to our history in its 1488 pages, and the appendix.*

In this book, I referred to the pages in the index under the subject of education to prepare this report. I have since listed many other subjects on these pages that I want to read later. I will choose those that interest me most to report on. I expect to read most of, if not the entire book, by skipping around and breaking it down into subjects.

Chieko looked sleepy. "Say, I'm impressed by the work this young man is doing. If he and his classmates consistently turn out reports like this, they'll make great progress in their education."

Noah was lulled into drowsiness by the warmth of the one light focused on the copy she held. A brief hint of gardenias drifted in on a breeze. The aroma, the seclusion, and the semi-darkness accentuated the late hour. He yawned and stretched.

Chieko could scarcely believe herself when she said, "Noah, you look exhausted. I'm very tired, too. If you care to stay the night, I'll grab a blanket and pillow, and you're welcome to stay on the couch."

Surely Noah had misunderstood what she had suggested. He usually left her at the door downstairs when they were out in the evening. His visits here were in the daylight hours. He must have hesitated, surprised at her words.

"Well, say yes or no, my friend, because I am going to bed before I drop."

It was so out of character for Noah. "Why, yes. I'd welcome not having to drive home. It has been a very long day."

Chieko tossed him some bedding from the nearby closet, threw a kiss goodnight, walked into her room, and shut the door behind her.

Noah lay on the couch, watching shadows of the leaves on the wall, and hearing the sound of the tree branches brushing against the window. In mere seconds, he was asleep.

Chapter 48

No Fury Like a Woman Scorned

When the telephone rang, Chieko had already washed the sleep from her eyes and groomed herself. As she picked up the receiver, she turned to see if the sound had awakened Noah. He smiled a good morning greeting and arranged the cover around his shoulders.

"Oh, good morning, my dear. How are you this beautiful morning?" she said into the phone.

Noah was contemplating how he was going to maneuver toward the bathroom wrapped in a blanket, while carrying his pants and shirt, which he had removed last night. He turned to look at Chieko, when he became aware of the tension in her voice.

"You're calling from where? Downstairs? You're in the lobby calling on your cell phone?" Chieko and Noah's eyes met.

"Yes, of course you may come up. Hold on and I'll push the buzzer to let you in." Then, directing her words to Noah, "I'm sorry, Noah. I couldn't tell him to go away. This may be awkward for you. As for me, he will not intimidate me. If that happens to be his attitude he will be out of line."

He? Who is she talking about? Noah grabbed his clothes and was in the bathroom in one leap. This was no time to ask questions. Chieko took a deep breath, reminded herself that her conscience was clear, and pushed the button to release the lock at the building's entry. She snatched up the pillow and sheet from the couch, tossed them in a heap into the closet, and arranged the decorator pillows neatly.

Noah was hurriedly combing his hair. He was in shock. Did Chieko have a male friend that had just arrived in town? He knew her schedules well enough to know that she had no current lover here in Kona. As he came out of the bathroom someone was tapping lightly on the door, and Chieko was opening it for him to enter.

Ross Ota leaned toward her for a kiss on the forehead. "Well,

Chickadee, I haven't seen or heard from you, so I thought I'd come by to take you to breakfast." Chieko kissed him on the cheek. Then, a sound...or a shadow, Ross wasn't sure what, made him turn toward Noah, who stood wide-eyed, not knowing whether to be relieved or to panic upon seeing his boss in the doorway.

Noah was clumsily shifting his weight. An interminable silence reigned while all three struggled for composure.

"Good morning, sir."

"Good morning, indeed," Ross said, stretching his short stature to its utmost height, and glaring at his employee. "And what the hell are you doing here, may I ask?" He enunciated each syllable.

"Chieko," Noah said, turning to her in his feeling of helplessness, "would you like for me to leave so that you can explain this to your uncle? Or would it be best that I stay? This must be very awkward for you, and I apologize."

Her eyes flashed. "You apologize? For what are you apologizing? There is no need for an apology. Better that I ask my uncle what it is that he is assuming. You and I are adults, Noah. This is my apartment. If I decide to invite you to stay overnight, it is our business. Yours and mine. There is no need to explain, Uncle, until you apologize for your insulting, mistaken imagination and your reaction."

"Apologize? I should apologize? You disappoint me, and a person I trusted has betrayed me. And I am asked to apologize."

"Sir, I have not been disloyal to you. Except for staying over last night, I have followed your wishes to the letter. I admit that I should not have stayed, but I give you my honor that nothing happened except that I slept here . . . on the couch."

"Did I have to delineate every do and don't regarding our agreement? You knew it was not acceptable regardless of what is going on between you. I wasn't born yesterday!" Ross's voice had risen to an angry pitch.

"What are you two talking about?" Chieko snapped. "Stop treating me like a child, Uncle." Frustration teamed with confusion. "Noah, what agreement is he talking about?"

"He will have to tell you, Chieko. Or, he will have to ask for your trust, if he chooses not to tell you yet. It seems to me that we could benefit from some trust on all sides. Sir, your niece is a lady and does not deserve your insinuations. As for me, Chieko, I am not entitled to speak in answer to any accusations yet. I am leaving."

"If someone doesn't explain, you are both leaving! Uncle, tell me."

"Chickadee, I hired Mr. Solomon to watch over you. There is so much that I can't tell you yet, but I have an involvement that is a possible threat to both you and me. It was not by chance that you encountered suspicious people following you, or around the building here. Since Noah has been driving you and accompanying you places, especially at night, there have been no such threats. That is why I hired him."

Chieko could only stare at each of them in turn. "Noah, you were only seeing me because my uncle was paying you. I thought you were my friend. I thought . . . "

"I am your friend, Chieko. Under the circumstances I could show no more than friendship, you understand?"

"I'm trying to. My God, you were as unresponsive as a . . . as a fish. I was beginning to think you must be gay when you continued to treat me like . . . like I was your sister. How much did he pay you? Was it enough to make it worthwhile for you to carry out such a . . . a difficult task? How could you deceive me like this? How dare you!"

Noah smiled weakly, unable to respond. Ross Ota just stared back at them. He was realizing that some of his assumptions must be incorrect. Still, he did not like the look of this.

"Don't you smile at me, Noah Solomon. The best thing you both can do is to get out of my sight. I will not be treated like a child. I am an adult. I am a woman. I have earned the right to your confidence. This is an insult to me." Her voice rose, trembled, and broke as she dissolved into tears, covering her face with her small hands.

Both men wanted to take her into their arms, but with a glance at the fire in her eyes, first Noah, then Ross backed away from her, walked out, and shut the door quietly behind them.

Chieko leaned back against the door, sobbing. She slid down slowly to the floor until she was able to stem the flow, bursting as a dam, confining tons of indignation.

Noah and his employer had switched positions from being wronged, to justification, to becoming coconspirators, both having lost Chieko's respect.

They scurried down the stairway. They were about to pass Ross Ota's well-maintained old Cadillac, he called to Noah, opened the passenger side of the Cad, and gestured for Noah to get in.

"We need to talk," Ross said.

The younger man conceded by getting in. "Where are we going?"

"To the office." Ross smiled painfully.

They rode in silence until Ota pulled into the parking lot facing a building with a sign overhead that read "The Office." Ota drove to a far corner of the lot to park. They walked back to the building. Using his own key, Ota unlocked the door. It was too early for it to be open. "Another business?" Noah asked. He had a hard time seeing his employer as the owner of a bar.

"One can't have too many varied investments," Ota replied. "It is early for a drink, but perhaps we can talk over a bloody Mary, and lick our wounds, while we get things out in the open." He busied himself by mixing their drinks. They sat on the stools at the corner of the bar, facing each other. The faint early morning light rays barely came through the plate glass window. He did not turn on the electric lights.

"Well? You're on. Are you waiting for a spotlight, gigolo? What is going on between you and my niece? If I read you both accurately, I may owe you an apology . . .a partial one anyhow. If my first impression was correct though, I'm going to kick the shit out of you."

"Good. I'm safe then," Noah said almost able to grin at this threat, but chafing at the "gigolo" barb. "I told you that your niece is a lady, and I like to think of myself as a gentleman. I have always been a bumbling fool with women, and she seems too innocent to be believable. Has her entire life been spent studying? Both of us are clumsy as hell, and completely unsure of ourselves when dealing with the opposite sex.

"Don't think that I'm going to confess to you the feelings I have for her, when I've never been able to tell her. First, you and I have an agreement, one I take seriously. You wouldn't even have to pay me to protect her. . . but thanks a lot. If you hadn't told me about the potential dangers, I would never have known. It's given me the opportunity to do what I would have done on my own. Except that now I am in hot water because, how could I tell her that I was only with her because you hired me, and how will she ever believe that I wanted to be near her, and to keep her safe . . . money aside?"

Ota eyed Noah suspiciously. Can this man be so honorable when faced with temptation of romancing a beautiful, innocent girl? He had thought so, or he would not have hired him. However . . .

"What the hell were you doing in my niece's apartment at that hour? Why should I believe you? It isn't acceptable." He poured another drink into their glasses from the pitcher he'd prepared.

"I know that. I should never have accepted her offer to stay over. It was given in all innocence. I will say no more except she went to her room last night and I hit the couch. The next thing we knew you were phoning her from downstairs."

The men were drinking the tasty tomato juice cocktails with no regard for the amount of liquor Ota had spiked them with. They had gone down fast. Too fast for a before-breakfast drink.

"That's all you have to say?" Ota slurred the words slightly.

"Right. End of story. Do you want my resignation, Mister Ota?" Noah's tongue was tangling a bit also.

They glared at each other. A bit wobbly on their respective bar stools. Neither was accustomed to heavy drinking.

"I'll think it over. Meanwhile, continue as usual, but stay out of my niece's apartment."

"I can't imagine I'll have any choice now. I doubt that she'll be talking to either of us. Nevertheless, I will be either driving her or tailing her everywhere she goes."

Ota reached out his hand, which Noah accepted as a gesture of truce, if not forgiveness.

Chapter 49

Truce Rejected

Shortly after they had parted, Noah and Ross Ota phoned Chieko. She did not answer, but listened to Noah's voice on the answering machine. Then she didn't answer any phone calls. She heard her uncle's words pleading with her through his recorded message. She played both messages back, listened intently, unsure of whether she was angry or wanted to cry. Right on both counts, she decided as she listened again to Noah's words.

"Chieko, you are probably there. Please, don't make it hard for me to keep watch over you. Yes, your uncle hired me, but if I had known that you were in danger, I would have done it anyway. When I discovered you were his niece, I should have told you that I work in his office. As your uncle's employee, I had to keep my relationship with you on the level of friendship, and no more than that. Besides, you are so shy. I didn't get any signals from you that you might be interested in me in any other way. It was pleasant just being your friend. I liked the hours we spent together. Someday I would like to talk to you about the possibility it could be more than that.

"Meanwhile, please understand. So, I've talked about the present, and the past. Now, for the future . . . You and I have a date, if I may call it that, to go together to Guy and Amy's picnic. What shall we take for potluck? I have a few ideas. Please answer next time I call. Your friend for now, Noah calling." Click.

Chieko wiped tears from her eyes and waited for her uncle's message to be repeated on the machine.

"Chickadee, it is your obstreperous old uncle calling. Please forgive me for loving you too much to use good judgment when I was afraid. Even though the fears were unfounded, please understand that love and fear are never reasonable emotions. I should have told you that I had hired Noah. I only knew that I could not go everywhere with you to protect you. I knew that the two of you were involved in the same activities, so I gave him permission to leave work any time you needed transportation. It was working well.

"We won't talk about last night, or this morning. I never intended to ever invade your privacy or to try to rule your life. You were right: you are a grown woman, not a child. I trust you to make wise decisions. I promise to always phone ahead when I am going to your home.

"Chieko, are you listening? You understand more than other people do how difficult it is for a Japanese-American male to grovel for forgiveness. I'll call again tomorrow. Please answer. You and I are all there is of our family. We must stick together. I love you, Chickadee."

Noah phoned the next day. No answer. He left a sad message: "Chieko, please do not be cruel. Pick up the phone. If you do not have any ideas to suggest for the picnic, I will make a huge bowl of potato salad. No one makes it as good as I do. I will call Guy and Amy to tell them what we are bringing, and I will pick you up Saturday. I miss you. Your tongue-tied friend, Noah."

When her Uncle Ross called that day, Chieko waited until he started to leave his message, then she picked up the receiver.

"I'm here, Uncle Ross. Thank you for your message yesterday. I'm sorry I got so angry. There's nothing going on in my home that I'm ashamed of so you need not feel that you must call before coming over."

"Chickadee, I love you. I hope we will never again be angry at each other. Thank you for answering the phone. Now I can get on with my work. I could not concentrate on anything."

"We will promise to never be angry at each other, never again, Uncle."

"Has Noah called? I know that he is still watching over you. He is probably sleeping near your apartment in his car, fearing to have you go out anywhere without his protection. Forgive him, too, Chickadee. He is a good man . . . a trustworthy man."

"I will consider that, Uncle. I must say that I don't understand him. He seems so unlike other men."

"Perhaps that is to his credit. Some male traits are less than honorable. How is your architectural plan coming along, my dear?"

"At a standstill the past few days, but I will be getting back to it. I want to discuss building materials with you someday."

"Any time, my sweet."

"Goodbye, Uncle. Thank you for calling. I love you, too."

Chieko placed the receiver in its cradle. The red sun was setting in the west. It was the loneliest time of day.

Chapter 50

Artist at Work

The world appeared to be a better place when she awakened to the touch of a gentle breeze. A little Japanese White Eye was perching on his favorite branch outside her window. He is so tiny and delicate, she thought. Not much bigger than a hummingbird. The white ring circling his eye makes him look so wise. A slight breeze played on the leaves, and White Eye flew to a calmer part of the garden, out of Chieko's view.

"Fickle little fellow." Chieko complained. She wanted his company, and was annoyed to be rebuffed like that.

She took her breakfast coffee and toast to her drafting table to review the work she had been doing. If she only knew the plot of land, where her buildings were to be placed. Then her plan could be more specific and creative.

Something on the television caught her attention. Joaquin Perot. Nice sound to it. "Wuah-keen Pey-rro," she said aloud, enjoying the Spanish name, and especially the trill of the 'r'. He was the guest artist, a raku pottery expert on the home show. She was attracted by his good humor, free from affectation (like Noah), she added, immediately trying to tame her ardor.

This man was obviously very skilled and original. His smile and his laughter lit up his face. His posture even reflected his Latin humor.

American though, no accent. And a resident of this island. Heritage? Perhaps some Negro, Spanish, or maybe French Canadian . . .Cajun.

Her attention was drawn to his demonstration. The raku pottery was not easy to make. Fifty percent of the pots might not survive the firing. Several times it must be refired.

His artistry changed a delicate, blackened pot into a work of exquisite beauty. He showed the chemicals and colors he added to the piece between each of the firings. With each one, the pot glowed with lovely, light touches of color, and metallic or white emphasis.

His kiln was in his yard, a shallow depression he had dug into the soil. A straw like substance was stuffed around the pot's base, and poked into the top of the pot. The surprise was the simple metal trashcan turned upside down over it after the fire started. The artist then sprinkled sand around the base of the can to seal the heat and smoke in, and to keep the air out.

Such an artist could be of use to her in creating natural, understated, yet awe-inspiring art for the community center she was designing. It required very little time and effort to find out how she could reach him.

His phone was published. He lived in the beautiful Koloko region above the village of Holualoa, he explained when he answered the phone. He was puzzled, but agreed to meet her at the quaint outdoor Holualoa café for a cappuchino, to discuss his possible interest in her current project. She would say no more over the phone.

What the heck, Joaquin decided. This lovely voice belongs to a woman architect. Nice voice. It would be worth the time spent to drive makai, and the time to meet her for a pleasant hour in a quiet garden café. He took his art seriously, but never let his art crowd out potential women in his life.

He shaved and tamed his salt and pepper, short and wiry Afro. His jeans and a silk aloha shirt would do. His posture was that of a man continually in motion. His body was well proportioned.

In less than an hour, he was sitting across the table from Chieko. He had envisioned what she would look like. Her name was of a heritage that greatly appealed to him. Very attractive, he noticed immediately when she walked into the garden. Her nature had been stripped of the old Japanese cultural traits. This was a modern American woman. Very intelligent. No wedding ring. Very self-sufficient. Well worth a time away from his dedication to raku.

Chieko had come dressed as she was when she phoned him, in her well-worn jeans and a cotton camisole. She had wound her hair into a swirl secured with an elegant clip.

They exchanged introductions and niceties, ordered espressos, and seated themselves by the lava rock wall. A jade vine bearing scarlet blossoms trailed from the lattice overhead. Each of them analyzed the other. Chieko saw a tan face, neither handsome nor homely. Eyes dark and jovial, under dark, expressive brows. Must be about fifty years old. On the television show, he had boasted of thirty years experience in art.

Chieko was telling him, as succinctly as possible, her purpose in calling him. That entailed telling him about the proposed educational center, the contest and prize for the winning plan. The latter had not yet been decided. In fact, the contest had not yet been announced either. Chieko was so interested in the Apple A Day endeavor that she felt driven to contribute in the way she knew best. Now she was probably ahead of any potential competitors.

"And how do I figure into your plan?" He smiled winningly.

"Well, of course this is premature. You may think me a fool, but it is your fault." She smiled shyly. "Your work impressed me this morning as I watched on television. I am a devotee of Frank Lloyd Wright and I want my work to blend with nature as his did. You also work with a natural product that reflects nature. I want the buildings to be of natural substances. We must be able to construct them with volunteers. Many will not be craftsmen, just regular folks providing labor.

"But I don't want the buildings to be crude inside or out. I have wondered how untrained people could create beautiful interiors and exteriors with limited labor. When I saw your raku pots, your artistry seemed to explode from clay into images . . . equal to rainbows, reflections in a pond, or blended blossoms and leaves in a garden . . . well, I just had to contact you." Chieko was getting flustered. Perhaps it had been foolish to call him. He would think her impetuous.

"I am so pleased that you called me," he stated as though he had read her mind.

Chieko was startled by his candor. It seemed that he knew her thoughts and empathized with her situation.

"But I know nothing about this organization, so I can't say yet that I want to ally myself with it. I doubt that it will make me more prosperous."

"Only in a social and moral sense. Perhaps you have no concerns about public education. In that case, my approach to you is premature. But if you do care to contribute something of yourself to this island community, then this is an opportunity to do so. We enrich ourselves in many ways. Much enrichment has nothing to do with monetary gains."

Chieko stood to indicate that she had no more to say to him.

"Wait Chieko. Sit down please . . . Chieko." Her name was sweet on his tongue, sweet as a chocolate bonbon. "What a lovely name," he said. Her name had never sounded so good to her as when he spoke it.

"It is not often that an angel confronts a man with a message intended to enrich his soul," he continued. She sat, and cleared her throat to regain composure.

"I did not say, Chieko, that I was not interested. I only need information from you, and time to learn more about this organization. Tell me how and where I can find out enough to determine whether I can become as excited as you are. Then if all is favorable to me, we can talk about how I may contribute to your project."

Chieko was so mollified that she was on the verge of inviting Joaquin to the Saturday picnic. Just in time, she realized that it was not an activity for the entire membership. Rather, invitations had been sent only to the originators of the group and tutors who met at the library. It was the Benson's party, purely social. She had no right to invite anyone. Thank goodness, she had stopped before blurting out the invitation. Where was her mind?

Chieko promised to get as much information as possible to him. She wrote down the time and location of the next Apple meeting. Then she also wrote the phone numbers of Guy, Noah, and Sandy, in case he had any questions before the appointed meeting time.

They both stood. Joaquin's eyes sparkled. She wondered how to interpret his slightly raised eyebrow. They shook hands. Perhaps he held hers a bit too long. She knew that he was watching her walk away. Why did that not anger her as it usually did?

Chapter 51

What's Going On?

Joaquin could not get the young woman out of his mind. He had pots to fire, but he would only work on them when he was at peace with the universe. He must be wholly in tune with the process. His raku pots were like women. They must be given his total attention when they needed it.

Women! After his adored wife died, Perot had worked fiendishly to avoid the pain of thinking about her. Had he ever grieved normally? No, he had just escaped from the gnawing emptiness in him. Time, the merciful healer, finally allowed him to think briefly about her, but never had he given in to his deepest emotions at her loss. He came to accept bachelorhood. There was always a woman who would appear and succumb to his needs. But no commitment, and there would be none. His life was just the way he liked it.

Maybe it was not the woman who was the reason for his preoccupation. Maybe she was caught up in the cause. Maybe he did need some kind of a commitment. Contacts through an involvement of that kind might help his business. Maybe he should investigate the group that wants to reform public education. He was already at the phone, reaching into his pocket for the phone number. Hmm. Three of them. He called the first two. Received no answer at either. At the last number, a woman answered.

"Yes, my husband can tell you about Apple A Day, he is not here now. Maybe I could help you," Amy said. She answered his questions.

"Thank you. That is enough to satisfy my curiosity," he said, "but I don't see how I could be of any use." He was ready to forget the whole thing.

"Public education affects us all," Amy said. "The ability and the desire to receive effective education is a major requirement for our future as individuals and as a nation. What do you do, Mr. Perot?"

"I'm an artist, a potter. I dropped out of school and have done just fine without the blessings of the halls of education."

"I'm sure you have," Amy said. "Some in our group have done equally well, but we all agree that we cannot gauge our needs for the future based upon the patterns of the past. Why don't you join us at a picnic Saturday, Mr. Perot? It is short notice, I know. It is not a formal meeting, but you will meet some of the people who originated the ideas for changing public education." Amy gave him the address and the time. "You will be our guest. Joaquin Perot, is it? And you are not to bring anything."

Joaquin thanked her again, and agreed to be there. Was he being sucked into something he would have trouble getting out of? He would probably not go at all.

"Hello, Chieko. If you are not going to answer your phone, I'll stop bothering you. I'll be there at 9:45 to pick you up for the picnic on Saturday. Call me if I can do anything for you until then. Please do not go out without someone to drive you. I am available. Your Uncle gave me a cellular phone to use." Noah gave her the phone number and wished her a good day.

His cell phone rang. He brightened. Hopeful. He recognized Ross Ota's voice. "Oh, it's you, sir." Disappointment registered in his tone when he knew it was not Chieko. "No, she is not talking to me yet, but I am picking her up for the picnic Saturday."

Ross indicated that Noah did not know Chieko very well if he expected her to give up the grudge she was carrying. "She is nurturing it for some reason that we mere men cannot understand, but we had better try if we expect to be near her in case any of the threats are carried out. I don't like it Noah. You are no use to me if she continues to avoid you. Did you know that she was running around in secluded areas this morning?"

"Yes, sir, I knew she was out. I followed her, and then I lost her in the traffic. Don't you think I should know more about what or who I am protecting her from?"

"Agreed. Tomorrow morning at 7:00 A.M. at The Office. Don't park your car near there."

It was misty the next morning. The moisture felt good on his face. Noah followed his boss's directions. He saw Ross Ota walking toward their meeting place and lingered a moment to allow him the lead. As Noah approached, Ota had the door opened. Noah had barely entered when Ota closed and locked the door. Ota scanned the parking lot. He saw no activity.

"All right. Let's be brief, and on our way." Ota said, wiping the moisture from his face with a linen handkerchief. "I have decided that I must trust you with this information. It is to go no further." He peered at the younger man to verify he had been understood.

Noah didn't like the sound of this mystery. He had not been involved with crime and violence for a long time. He had not carried an automatic weapon since his had misfired, wounding an innocent bystander when he was with the Federal Bureau of Investigation. Noah had wanted to leave that all behind him, but when Ross hired him for the office job, the process had revealed his former investigative work with the FBI, on the mainland.

"You remember the old Perkins estate, Noah?" A nod of his head, and Ota continued. "We felt lucky to get it rented, you'll recall. Well, it seemed a successful transaction. The owner does not want to return here to live in it. The place is too shabby to get the high rent Perkins wants. The renter has paid regularly. He never bothers us to fix this or that, or to clean, or paint, or remodel. It was my idea to get old Perkins to agree to some work on it. Just for maintenance, you know.

"When I spoke to the renter about sending a crew there to do minor repairs, he got belligerent. Said he never asked for service, and not to bother him. Not the usual reaction of a renter, wouldn't you say?

"Then the police got a tip-off about the biggest drug operation to hit our island. You guessed it. As the police investigation progressed, there were suspicions about the old house and property. People coming and going. Police know now that the drugs have been stored there, with more to come."

"Good Lord, I remember the place well. No one even knew it was there until construction began nearby. It's surrounded by about ten acres of overgrown foliage. Even the entrance to the driveway is angled so it's out of sight. It's in terrible condition. But why are you being targeted, or Chieko?"

"Because these are hoods who need to get others involved so they can use them. I'm the landlord. When they tried to put me off from sending a work crew in, I was persistent. They have to keep everyone away from the property. I was about to interfere with that. They thought that a large amount of money would tempt me, and I would turn away and ignore them. I took the money, told the police, and put the money in my safe deposit box. Then I wrote a check, which my lawyer is holding in escrow where it will stay until it can be used as evidence in a big trial. When this thing blows, it's going to expose a major drug ring.

"Of course, I said no more to them about sending workers in. This is big potatoes to these guys. They aren't sure they can bribe me or intimidate me, so they are trying make sure that I'll cooperate by threatening to harm Chieko if I don't. I'm pretending to play along with them. They never told me what they were up to, but I'm working on the side with the undercover policemen assigned to the case."

Noah was holding his breath as he listened. Damn! Here he was, right back in the game. Big time. He exhaled forcefully. "Christ, man, you don't know what you're up against. You're playing with the big boys now. They need all tracks greased to make this happen. We're going to have to walk on eggshells. Jesus! They have connections in every pocket, maybe even on the police force or political wheels."

"Well, you're either with me or against me. You are no use to me if Chieko won't let you get close to her. I'd send her away for a while. A nice quiet retreat where she could do her project. However, she'd never go. I'd rather she didn't know too much."

"I can't believe it. Here I am getting right back into this business, but I'm going to level with you. I told you before that protecting Chieko isn't a job. I haven't told her that I love her. Now, here I am telling you before she knows. I feel like a damned lying hypocrite. As of now, I am off your payroll, except for the office job, and I don't know how often I can make it in to do any work there and still watch over her.

"I'm going right out to order a bouquet of the most expensive roses. I'm going to woo your niece and do my utmost to spend as much time with her as she will allow. We are not going to tell her anything about the drug operation. Obviously, when she finds out, she is going to think I'm an insincere bastard and, probably will refuse to have anymore to do with me. Well, I'm not going to think about that. All I want is to keep her safe, and happy. Do you have anything else to tell me that I should know?"

Ross felt as though he had been scolded mercilessly. He and his employee seemed to have reversed roles. "No. Thank you for watching over her."

Noah paced across the bar room. "I want to be informed of everything you learn. Everything, you hear. Tell me what happens. Who did it or said it. What and who you suspect. We will have to develop a kind of code, and find ways to meet, and I don't know what all." He sounded annoyed. "I haven't played this game for a long time."

Noah saw Ross nod as if trying to avoid eye contact with him. It was enough of a signal for departure. The boss, a man who was always in control, was suddenly not as sure of himself. Was it shame he felt? Noah grabbed his car keys off the bar and stalked through the door.

After a stop at the marketplace where they wrapped up the long-stemmed red roses, Noah bought a card with a message that spoke his heart's desires. Inside the card, he wrote: "My dearest Chieko, I cannot bear another hour away from you. Please let me in so that I can tell you in person the feelings I have for you, or I will have to announce them to all of your neighbors. I can sing them in the lobby, but must I? Your devoted friend," (he paused, then wrote) "and whatever other honors you will bestow on me."

On the way to Chieko's condo, Noah called her on the cell phone. When the answering machine came on, he said, "Good morning. You look beautiful this morning. No, I can't see you, but you always look beautiful. I am on my way to talk to you. I will not take No for an answer. I will be outside your condo door in ten minutes. I will remain there until you open the door."

Noah checked to see that her car was there. Then he rang her buzzer from the lobby. No result. He rang all the buzzers except those on the first floor where residents could open their door to see him. He knew some tenant would push the button to release the lock without knowing who was there. Sure enough. At the sound of the lock being released, Noah tugged quickly at the lobby door. It opened. He raced up the stairs and down the hall to her door. He tapped quietly. No sound inside. He slid the greeting card under the door and waited long enough for her to read the card at least twice.

"Chieko, I will settle down here on the floor beside your door if you don't open it, and I will talk to you until your neighbors gather around to hear what I have to say. Then I will plead with them to beg you to let me in. I have a gift for you. You will have to guess if the gift will spoil, melt, or wither if I have to wait too long." Silence. "If your neighbors don't come to my rescue before night falls, I will sleep here until tomorrow morning."

Chapter 52

A New Start

The door opened. Chieko folded her hands and bowed her head as though she was close to tears. "I didn't know that you felt that way about me, Noah. Please come in."

That was much easier than Noah expected, but he would take no chances on saying the wrong thing now. Action maybe. But he had better move cautiously. As he entered, she turned to walk away. He caught her wrist to detain her, and put the roses into her arms.

"They're beautiful, so fragrant and delicate," she said.

"They are overshadowed by your beauty, Chieko."

"I don't know what to say. Let me put them in a vase. I have some wine. We should drink a toast. Get the glasses, please."

It was good to move, to have an objective other than grabbing her into his arms. A little warning bell sounding in his head signaled him to tread lightly. He had missed an opportunity by handing her the roses first. No time for a kiss then. Too awkward. God help me, I am not good at this, he thought.

Together they opened the wine bottle and poured the glasses. They stood side by side, glasses in hand. (Clink) The time-honored symbol of unity, of togetherness, of victory. Two glasses touching to announce an occasion. "Slow down you fool," he told himself. "Don't push it."

They smiled at each other. The tension vanished. "To us, Chieko. I meant what I wrote on the card. To us, together, in friendship or in love, wherever the future leads us."

Their glasses clinked again. With eyes drinking in the moment, with heads reeling, they sipped the wine. Now, instinct told him, now! He took the glass from her hand, set the two glasses on the table, and took her into his arms. He buried his face in her hair, kissed her ear, her neck, and her lips. It was a lover's kiss, but prompted by wonder, not passion. She returned the pressure of his lips on hers. Only their sighs indicated the exchange of an unspoken promise. His lips moved to her temple, her forehead. He kept his emotions and his behavior in check. They held one another close.

Desire warmed the blood pulsing through his veins. He stepped back, his hands on her shoulders. "You are headier than the wine, my beauty. I think I can handle the wine, but it is harder to resist your charms."

"We must sit, Noah," she giggled. "I have never been so affected by one sip of wine. We have so much to talk about." They picked up the wine-glasses and she led him to the sofa. "Now, you must tell me what you and my uncle have been up to. You left here like coconspirators, and since then he has been defending you, encouraging me to understand and forgive."

"And do you understand, Chieko? I must tell you that I am going to try to keep up with my job in his office, but I will need your coopera-tion to do that. I will be continuing to protect you, but you must tell me every time you intend to leave your condo and I will drive you wherever you want to go. I will take no money from your Uncle Ross for watching over you. I will do it only because I love you. I will not permit you to be in danger. Don't make it difficult for me."

"Well, except that you have taken a vow of poverty instead of accepting pay, nothing has changed. But both of you seem overly dramat-ic about it all, don't you think? You carry a gun, don't you? I could feel it when my arms were around you. Is that really necessary? I don't like guns."

The spell of romance had vanished. Reality had moved back in. But this time there would be communication, and honesty between them. As much as was needed for now, anyhow. No need for her to be frightened by the details, Noah reminded himself.

Chieko pulled her feet up under her on the couch as she used to do, but now she sat very close to him. She used to be careful not to stare at him. Now she let herself look at his face. The dark brows. The face, not chiseled, yet rugged. A slightly aquiline nose.

"Why the gun, Noah?"

"Because some of the big boys carry guns. It's an equalizer. Don't worry. I know how to use it, and I will never use it except as a last resort. Trust me."

"I trust you, but I'd feel better if you would take it off, hide it . . . or whatever . . . while you're here. I don't like it being on your person, when we're together."

Noah removed his shirt and unfastened the harness and holster with the revolver. He hung the harness strap over the back of a barstool, tossed a dishtowel over it, and returned to her side. "Better?" She nodded, studying his muscular arms, and hairy chest while he slipped the shirt over his head and combed some of the curl out of his almost jet black hair.

"Yes, ma'am, any more requests, before I ask some questions? No? Then would you tell me about your work, the drawings you do at your worktable all the time. I didn't want to pry, and you didn't ever say anything about them."

Chieko unfolded her plans and spread them on the tabletop. His arm rested on her shoulder. They leaned over the drawings while she explained them to him.

"Well, I'll be damned. You're an architect, a full-fledged architect," he said, noting her credits written in the corner of her work. She had not yet shown her plans to anyone. Noah was impressed with her knowledge and skill. She explained how she wanted the community center to be. Constructed of island materials as much as possible, which ruled out lumber. Lava rock mixed with cement to mold concrete forms, perhaps.

She explained that the island did not yet have the means to accomplish this. That was part of her plan to convince islanders that they did not have to pay for imports. It would call for a new industry to carry out her plans. Cement houses were being built all over the world. Scandinavia, Mainland USA, Europe, the Middle East.

"We can't afford wood on the scale we have used it in history," she said. As she spoke, her excitement was contagious. Noah glowed with pride.

"And electricity . . . ," she continued, "each building would have photovoltaic cells instead of standard roofing to supply their own electricity. Their community would have more than enough electric power for their own needs, and the government requires public utilities to buy excess production from their citizens."

"There is much more in my plan, but I am not going to tell you all of it now. It is too wonderful to have you here with me again." Noah was immensely pleased to hear her admit that. She had said nothing yet that he could construe as stronger than friendship, although that kiss had almost been a breakthrough of some kind.

"Oh, what time is it? I almost forgot that I promised to have the potato salad made for tomorrow. It's better if it rests overnight to meld the seasoning. Is that all right with you, or is there something else you'd prefer to take?" Until a short time ago he had feared that she might even refuse to go with him Saturday.

"It's a good choice Noah. You can teach me how you make it." A quick check of ingredients showed that a trip to the store or to his apartment would be necessary. The store was closer. That way he could get some delicatessen foods, so they could eat in style tonight, candles and all. He scanned the contents of her cabinets to see that she had the necessary things to set a romantic mood for dinner.

The shopping done, they worked together on the salad. The afternoon passed quickly. The spud salad as he called it, was in her refrigerator ready for tomorrow.

Chieko put on background music. The table was set with her best china and the candles lit. Noah poured another glass of wine to sip with the selected delicacies he had bought. They talked in the way lovers do when they are just discovering each other.

The glow of candlelight allowed them to slip into Kona's daily performance. A tropical sunset. The light changed from mellow, to golden, to roseate hues announcing twilight. A quiet settled over them. They held hands across the table.

"Do you think a man and a woman can be friends without becoming lovers, Noah?"

The question jarred him. The smile slipped from his face. He let go of her hand. "What a question. I suppose so. Why do you ask, Chieko? Do you want that for us . . . to just remain friends?"

"I don't know yet. I hate to see our friendship ruined."

"Why would you think it might be ruined? It is just gaining ground." What is the matter with her, Noah wondered. I was afraid that I would be the one to say, or do something to spoil this moment, this magical day!

"Never mind. I guess, . . . well, for all the years of working toward my degree, I was so on guard I didn't even date. Never mind, I shouldn't have said that." But she had said it, and he was obviously disturbed, and confused. She reached for his hand, but he was already on his feet.

He strapped on the gun over his shirt, and slipped into his jacket.

"You're going." Chieko said.

"I got up very early this morning, after a sleepless night. What can I do to help you," he offered, clearing the table, and blowing out the candles.

"Nothing. Leave it alone. I'll clean up . . . you're angry."

"No." He didn't know what to say. Her question hung in midair. He imagined all kinds of obstacles. He smiled at her to ease her concern.

"I'll be here at 9:45 to pick you up. Don't let anyone into the lobby, and don't open your door to anyone until I get here. You have my cell phone and my apartment number. Call if you notice anything unusual. Meanwhile, don't eat all the potato salad." He must leave on a light note, or he would not sleep all night.

He moved to where she stood and slipped his arms around her. He tilted her chin up to look into her eyes. "I do love you. It is you who will have to decide whether we remain just friends. I like the idea of friendship as a foundation for love." He kissed her nose, then her lips. It was hard to end the kiss, and walk out the door.

She watched the door close behind him. There were tears in her eyes. Tears of self-reproach? Tears of love? Both, she decided. What is so wrong about loving a dear friend? Can't friends ask any question of one another without feeling threatened? That should be true of friends, but lovers seem to be forever on guard.

Chapter 53

Picnic

Morning. Billowing clouds fringed with sunlight and rosy hues seemed voluptuous, as if ready to burst into the cerulean basket of sky. The world appeared tinted by an artist. Each leaf, each flower, competing for the most vivid hue. Mornings are for lovers, Noah smiled. The whole world is for lovers. It is all about renewal. He didn't want to wait to see Chieko.

En route to Chieko's condo he was invigorated by the world around him. The mood stayed with him as he entered the room, hugged her close, kissed her quickly, waltzed to the refrigerator, and piloted her down to the garage carrying the huge bowl of salad.

"Well, Noah Solomon. You are certainly bright and cheery."

"Why not? I get to spend the day with my best girl, in the midst of other best friends. With no responsibility except to eat heartily, I might add."

"Best girl? And who are the 'good' and 'better' girls in your life?" she teased. "Thank you for placing me at the peak."

"They are my mother and my sister," he lied, wanting this to remain on a fantasy level.

"You have a sister? There is so much I have to learn about you."

"No, of course I don't have a sister, or I would know more about women. And mothers never teach their sons about women. They want their sons to love only them, so they don't even talk to us about women."

He was joking, at first, and then he realized why he had always been ill at ease with women. Where did all that come from? Well, this was no time for self-analysis.

"So where did you learn about women?"

"I'm only kidding. Must I say it? You are my one and only girl. I love you. And haven't you noticed that I know nothing about women?" He gazed at her. "Teach me, Chieko."

"You men. You pretend to be so innocent. And your mother, where does she live?"

"Died many years ago, when I was small. And we are almost to the Bensons," he concluded, returning to the present time.

"I'm sorry, Noah. I lost my mother when I was young also. Uncle Ross has cared for me ever since."

"He has done a terrific job, Chieko."

He turned into a driveway, unloaded Chieko and the salad, received a hug from the hostess, then backed down to park the car on the street. When he returned Chieko was already holding a glass and looking over Guy's shoulder as he played chef, flipping barbecued hamburgers.

As Noah turned to join them, someone called his name. "Sandy, where's Cliff?" He felt a hand on his shoulder and turned. "Oh, there you are. How's it going?" They shook hands. Noah waved at Ike, the amiable school custodian who was having a serious talk with Igor Connifer across the yard.

"Hey, who's holding down the responsibilities for radio communications, Igor?" Noah called.

"Cliff's son. I'm going to leave soon to replace him. What a kid! He'll be here later," Igor shouted.

"I want to say hello to Guy's dad and find out if I can help with anything." Noah excused himself.

Sandy and Cliff dismissed him with a wave of their hands. They were busy attacking the potluck goodies.

"Hello, Mr. Benson. Hi, Barry. What are you two up to?"

The old man looked up, squinting. "Oh, it's you, Noah. Do you suppose you can call me Ben, at least during a picnic? Good to see you. Say hello to Mr. Solomon, Barry."

"Hello. Can I call him Noah during the picnic?" Barry asked.

"You can call him Uncle Noah if he agrees to it, Barry."

"May I?" Barry asked Noah. His eyes wide.

"I would be honored to be your Uncle Noah."

The boy thought he knew all of the guests, until he saw a stranger enter the gate. "Who's he, Papa?" Both men looked, and shrugged. The man stood there for a moment as though searching for a familiar face, then headed directly for the barbecue. Noah saw Chieko turn, smile, and take the hand that the man was offering her.

"Hello, Chieko. Maybe you can introduce me to this gentleman whom I am guessing is our host."

Chieko sputtered. Surprise had blocked her memory of his name for the moment.

"I'm chief cook and bottle washer." Guy laughed, and held out his enormous padded hot mitt for the man to shake.

"Joaquin Perot, Guy. Your wife was kind enough to invite me." He gingerly shook the end of the mitt, laughing.

"So, you and Chieko are acquainted, I'm tied down a bit at the moment, and Amy is in the kitchen, I believe. Chieko, could you introduce Joaquin to the others? How do you like your burger cooked? I'm not sure I can guarantee to get it right, but I'll try."

"More or less medium, I'm easy. So," he said, turning to the disconcerted woman by his side, "we meet again." He took her hand, placed it on his folded arm, as side by side they walked toward the nearest group. To anyone watching, it appeared that the two had a well-established friendship.

Noah was watching. He didn't miss a move as they worked their way among the guests. Amy came out of the house, so Chieko detoured to introduce him to their hostess.

To Noah's appraising glance, the man looked too slick, too good looking, too well dressed to be useful. A silk aloha shirt, unbuttoned at the top to expose a silver necklace. A narrow red silk scarf, tied in a knot around his neck. Must be worn to use as a tourniquet in case someone slits his throat, Noah snorted. The Afro? Noah did not usually indulge in prejudice, but his animosity was aroused by the familiarity the man had shown toward Chieko.

"Oh, Mr. Perot, so glad you made it," Amy purred. "Come, let me introduce you. Who have you not met? Thanks, Chieko, for filling in for me." And she waltzed away with Joaquin in tow.

Noah noticed that the guest did not place Amy's hand in the crook of his arm as he met the remaining guests. Ben, Barry, and Noah were sitting on a bench at the far side of the yard as Amy and her guest approached. Noah liked him less and less, the nearer he got.

Ben, a shrewd student of human behavior, had observed it all while he and Barry were playing checkers. "Papa, that was not a good move." Barry scolded him.

"Oh, you're right, my boy. Your old Gramps must pay attention." He looked up and smiled at his daughter-in-law.

"This is Joaquin Perot, Dad. Guy's father, Ben Benson, and our friend Noah Solomon, Mr. Perot." Amy indicated, gesturing toward each one. "And this young man is Barry, our son." They shook hands. The man shook Barry's hand also, showing him the same courtesy he showed the adults. Barry loved that. He loved it that the man didn't ask his age, or about school, or any of the silly questions adults usually asked.

"Guy has the hamburgers ready, everybody. Grab a plate and git goin'. Barry will serve you, Dad, won't you son?" Barry was already on his way. Amy excused herself to get everyone moving.

"Well, we have the choice of standing in line over there in the hot sun or waiting here in the shade. What's your choice? Perot is the name?"

"Yes, Joaquin to friends. Makes sense to wait here," he said.

Noah could not wait to find out more about this man. Wears a nice ring, but his hands are not manicured. More like those of a laboring man. It doesn't fit. In the few minutes they waited for the line to get shorter, Noah discovered that he was an artist . . . and that was all.

Perot had taken control of the conversation. In a very short time, he had Noah discussing Apple A Day and its purpose. How it had gotten started. "And how is the project progressing now? What are your hopes for it?"

"Whoa, I think we had better fill our plates," Noah said. "It has been a while since the last meeting, and we all need some feedback to answer your last question." They walked together slowly. "The meeting scheduled next week will provide some answers. Also questions. It should be lively. We are getting to the action stage."

"Interesting," said Joaquin. "Let's eat."

Before the afternoon ended, Joaquin Perot had spent time with each of the guests, the host, the hostess, and their son. He seemed to be talking and eating less, while listening more. Igor was trying to talk, while hurriedly eating his lunch. Finally he filled another plate to take with him and said goodbye. He could eat it on the way to the station. Kirk would be awaiting Igor's return thus releasing him to enjoy his turn at the food and fellowship.

Sandy, always well organized, had started a newsletter to help everyone keep informed. The organization had grown so much. Meetings that had begun in Guy's living room were now being held in the neighborhood theater. Sandy had a form to distribute at the next meeting to have a better accounting of people. She wanted to know the membership's greatest concerns, their skills, the talent and the labor they could contribute toward the building of the community center. Also, how much time would they pledge.

The way volunteers had turned out to build a playground, a few years ago, she knew they could do it. But it hadn't been easy. People are like cattle and sheep. They have to be led and they must be prodded when they slow down. Well, step by step it would be done.

At the next meeting, they must get some leads on property to build on, and how they were going to finance it. The public school system had not yet shown any interest in their plans.

Noah stayed by Chieko's side the latter part of the picnic. He held her hand as if to announce an alliance between them. Most people noticed. Especially Joaquin Perot and Kirk, who had a young man's crush on her. He was more quiet than usual.

The picnic was a success in reestablishing the camaraderie between these people who had given birth to the initial ideas, formed an organization, spread the word, and had gotten it all rolling. Now their burden was lightened by others willing to add their strength, effort, and creativity.

Chieko and Noah collected their empty bowl, now filled with leftovers they were happy to take with them. They thanked their host and hostess, promising to get together soon, just the four of them. Hugged the others who were also on their way out. Noah shouted, "Bye. Ben," pleased that the old fellow treated him like family, or a very close friend.

"Bye, Uncle Noah," Barry called.

"Goodbye, nephew." Noah winked, swooping him up for a big hug.

Chapter 54

"Getting to Know You...."

Noah swung into the driver's seat, beside Chieko, and reached for her hand. He placed it in his own palm, smiled at its exquisite details. Too perfect a work of art. He felt euphoria at her touch. He gazed at her in a way he hadn't dared before.

She warmed to his touch, unaccustomed to this intimacy. The togetherness they had formerly enjoyed was reborn. "Lovely picnic, wasn't it?"

"Late afternoon. Would you care to go anywhere, Chieko? A movie? A walk on the beach?"

"Home sounds very good. Noah, I would like to see your home. Could I?"

"Sure, Sweet Stuff. It isn't a home in the sense that your condo is, but it is comfortable. We'll stop there."

It was about a mile from Chieko's condo. A large apartment complex. The kind in which the residents seldom are acquainted. Not the best decorated exterior, but when Noah turned the key and pushed the door open, she entered as if she were in a holy place.

Beautifully blended earth tones. She looked at the furniture, the bookshelves, and peeked into the bedroom, feeling almost risqué. She returned to the living room to read the names of the books. Biographies, travel books, police manuals, many reference books, atlases, dictionaries, state, county, and town directories.

On the wall, no paintings, only one large photograph of a wave curling, just at the moment a surfer might enter it for the ride of his life. Good taste. Strange, that there were no photographs of friends or family about. She was pleased that he kept it neat, especially because her visit was impromptu. She sat down in the big brown leather chair.

"You look like a child in that," he said with a smile.

"I don't like to look like a child, but I like your chair. I hate looking like a child. I am..."

"I know . . . you are Woman!" He laughed. "How well I know it."

He sat on the footstool in front of her. "You do look sweet in that dress. I should have mentioned it before. You made the other women look tacky by comparison. I love the way you look."

"You called me 'Sweet Stuff.' You never called me that before."

"There are so many names I want to call you, like 'dear' because you are dear to me, like 'honey' because you are sweet, and like 'sugar' because that is how sweet you are. Did you mind that I held your hand at the picnic?"

"Did I pull away from you?"

He smiled, recalling how pleased he had been. "Speaking of sweets, how would you like some ice cream with some Kahlua poured over it?"

"Is it good?"

"You are going to find out. Sit right there."

"I want to watch you fix it." She followed him to the galley kitchen. It was small, but efficient.

"Would you please not stand so close to me."

"Am I crowding you?"

"No, you're melting the ice cream."

"Oh, Noah," she giggled. "You are so silly. I love it when you make me laugh."

"I have to hold you, Chieko." He pulled her close.

"It was you who was accusing me of melting the ice cream. We'll have to drink it if we don't get started on it."

He sighed. They took their dishes to the balcony where they could see a little bit of the ocean.

"Delicious, Noah."

"Good. I've got to get you home. I don't want to, but we have a problem."

"We do? I'm in no hurry."

"The problem is me. My thoughts when I'm alone with you are not, well, . . . they are not appropriate. All I want to do is to grab you, hold you close to me, and kiss you until our knees give way under us and . . . I think I had better not go on."

"Why not? Have I tried to stop you?"

"That's what bothers me most. I know we could, and I know we are not ready. We need some time to know each other if we want this to end happily. You know that too, Chieko. Let's go, we'll talk in the car." Would he have been ill at ease if Chieko were not his employer's niece? They had the same thought.

"So, Mr. Solomon, are you all talk and no action? I thought you were about to sweep me off my feet."

"Stop teasing, Chieko. You're acting receptive because you know that

I'm on guard. And . . . so far, I'm not letting it happen. Am I right? Are you putting the whole burden on me?" She smiled. "Yes, you're right. I was afraid of you until I discovered that you are even more afraid of me."

"Well, don't misinterpret my fear, fair beauty. You know now that I am not gay. I don't think I should have to convince you that I am not celibate either."

"Maybe I shouldn't ask you," Chieko wasn't sure how to interpret that, "but if you are not celibate, then . . . are you active?"

Noah laughed, grateful to get all of this out into the open. "No involvements, not for a very long time. And you? Is there anyone else?" He wanted to ask about Joaquin. Strange she hadn't mentioned him.

"I told you that while I was attending college, I was tempted, but that isn't the way I want to experience love. I can't understand the way some of the women behave. But you talk of your emotions and being on guard . . . don't think that I am without normal hormonal reactions. You arouse strong desire in me, Noah."

She looked so serious that Noah had to laugh. He doubled over trying to catch his breath. "I can't believe I am hearing this in this day and age. Any other two people would have been in bed long ago."

"Are you laughing at me, Noah Solomon?" She was annoyed.

"No, my sweet." Tears of laughter ran down his cheeks. "Not at you, but at us. Just listen to us. We sound like a psychology textbook chapter on sexual responses."

Chieko laughed with him. They held each other close, laughed until they both were gasping and crying, then fell back against the couch pillows exhausted, struggling to catch their breath, their ribs aching.

Chieko heard the song "Smile" being played on the radio. She closed her eyes, her cheek against Noah's chest, where she relished the sound of his heartbeat. She heard a feisty little gecko chirping as she drifted comfortably into slumber. Noah's arms surrounded her. He closed his eyes. His mind played with the recall of the words to the song he was hearing. He was asleep before the gecko's chirp sounded.

Chieko awoke to see Noah staring at her. Neither of them had moved.

"How long have you been lying there looking at me?" she asked.

"I don't know. When I woke up, I thought I must have been dreaming. I still think I am dreaming. I'm not sure I ever want to wake up. One thing for sure, if we tell any one that we're sleeping together, they'll never believe that it's a literal interpretation."

Chapter 55

Meeting of the Minds

The active members of Apple A Day, Inc. had done their best to assure a good turnout at the meeting. Station KABC broadcasted continuous announcements. Not to be outdone the other stations announced it, as did the local newspaper. The Department of Education and School Board continued to ignore any activities of the "radical" group, as they laughingly referred to it. But sitting in the auditorium seats, facing the stage, were about four hundred residents. All were not yet committed to this cause. They wanted more information.

Noah had just greeted the audience, thanked them for their attendance, introduced himself, and asked for questions from newcomers. He was flanked by committee members seated on the stage to help him explain their cause. The questions came thick and fast:

Question: "Is your intention to revise education in all grades?"

Answer: "Not at first. It's a pilot plan aimed at high school students. We have expectations of later expanding and perhaps modifying the best features of the plan to include middle school. Finally, we hope to apply what is practical to elementary grades also. Some public schools on the mainland are asking successful pilot schools to help them design new curricula and develop teaching methods."

"One example is KIPP Academy (Knowledge Is Power Program). This academy has been the highest-performing middle school, grades 5 to 8, in the Bronx for three years. It has maintained the highest margin of improvement every year for test scores. Two-thirds of the kids read above the national average; 70% are above the national average in math. It's in a high poverty area. Their prior records therefore were not used to determine their enrollment. It proves that attitudes and

ability can be improved, and that we can make an Information Age, manifest destiny idea come into being." [1]

Question: "Will the school be open to all students?"

Answer: "No. Students will have to qualify, not by grades they have received, but by their ability to express themselves in writing and speaking. The subject they will be expected to discuss regards their sense of responsibility, what motivates them to read, and how they hope to apply their knowledge.

"Their reading level must be standard for their age. The essay they write need not be perfect in grammar, punctuation, and organization. It must show thought and sincerity. Writing skills improve with constant use, aided by time and guidance."

Question: "What about preparing our children to fit into a world in which our economy depends on technology?"

Answer: "We will neither exclude technology nor give it emphasis. Students will have opportunities to investigate technology. They will be encouraged to broaden their knowledge in that direction, because it is a modern tool. However, it is not the only or the most important educational goal or tool. It is frightening to imagine what the future holds for us if we have leaders and followers whose minds are filled only with technology. We do not minimize its importance, but it is not the whole of what is needed in education. Our country is becoming weaker due to inadequate preparation for basic skills, knowledge, and the wisdom to assess and apply what we learn."

"In the 60's, 20 percent of our jobs required higher education. Now 65 percent of the jobs require a college degree. In the future that percentage will rise. Secretary of Education William Bennett[2] states that our colleges and universities receive many students from government schools who are not well prepared. This requires that those institutions spend less time on what used to be called 'higher learning', and more time on remedial courses. In 1995 one-third of college freshmen were enrolled in remedial courses."

Question: "What will the curriculum include?"

Answer: "Our system requires interaction with other students to
             acquire people skills, self-confidence, sharing, and teaching
             one another. We must encourage an awareness of all that
             defines us as Americans, as inhabitants in space and on this
             planet as humankind. This requires a wide range of subjects to
             study. Liberal Arts provide subjects to prepare us for a future
             we cannot predict.

             *"The weakness in current public schools lies in our children being
             unprepared to learn how to learn, therefore lacking ability to educate
             themselves. That comes first and is foremost in our goals.*

             *"One of the dire weaknesses in public education is the attempt to
             include everything. It may dilute the most important subjects, or
             unnecessarily expand on subjects to fit them into a quarter or semes-
             ter course when a video would be adequate. It varies with each stu-
             dent but, for many only an awareness of some subjects is necessary.
             Students can study in depth if they choose to.*

             "Ongoing education is a necessity for adults and children. Our
             learning center will be for the community, all ages. I refer you
             to literature on the back table so that we can proceed with
             new business. You are welcome to stay. Thank you for your
             questions to get us started."

"The purpose of this meeting is to report on progress, to receive any
suggestions, and to encourage volunteers to join us. Our committee heads
are prepared to share what is happening to move us forward. I'll direct
questions to them for the remainder of the meeting. There is a question
involving our progress in writing grants. Sally Adkins and her group have
been working hard on this. Sally."

"Good news, Noah. Two grants have been approved One from the
United States Government for $2.5 million to begin our community
learning center, where the first students will begin classes as soon as we get
our building plans finalized. We can, of course, begin classes before construction starts and we are looking for a location.

"We have received another grant from the National Library
Association for $500,000, to purchase books for the library to be built in
the center. In addition, we are expecting grants from other organizations

we have written to regarding needs for our project. We turned one grant down because it was too explicit as to how the money for supplies was to be used. Most of it was to go to textbooks. We will not need to purchase large numbers of textbooks."

Some people seemed elated about the grants. Others seemed surprised. Perhaps it was the remark about textbooks, or just that they had not expected the group to gain so much momentum. Noah waited for the applause to diminish before calling for another question.

Question: "I don't like to rain on your parade, but do you really expect our youth to take the kind of responsibility you require of them? And how can you expect them to work without receiving grades?"

Answer: "Sandy, may I pass this to you? Miss Sanders will answer that." Gail Sanders approached the microphone. Her voice commanded respect. "I assume you are saying that our youths have neither the stamina, desire, character, pride, nor initiative to take responsibility. In the first place, some students have all of those qualities, but some of them have become convinced that we expect less of them, so most of those at this higher level of skill, intelligence, and interest give only as much as we expect. They are capable of more, but we have made them lazy, as even adults become lackadaisical if they are allowed to be.

"They are that way because we have taught them that it is accepted. Each generation conforms to what it is taught. As parents and educators we have failed to require their best efforts. We can change that. Our media has the means to praise and to motivate the achievers. When our nation shows our children that we value people of high character, those who are achievers; when we give attention and respect to the worthy people in our society, our children will act in accordance with our expectations.

"Some of our students have been able to resist destructive messages they get from our society. Some do enjoy learning and they are excellent students. Others are as capable and choose to take a path unlike the hype and stereotypes the media presents.

"As for grades. They are false indicators of achievement. Actual achievement requires time, thought, investigation, analysis, sharing, and reporting on the information. Educators have misused grades so that now they are meaningless. Please pick up information at the back table as to how our students' work will be assessed." Sandy sat down.

Noah looked down the line to see who else wanted to volunteer. "Mrs. Ng. what do you have to add?"

A petite Vietnamese woman came forward. She spoke slowly to compensate for her accent. "Our committee has contest entry blanks ready for contractors, draftsmen, architects, or anyone else who wants to compete for the honor of designing our community learning center. It will include a library for adults and children, classrooms, and meeting rooms. The applications and contest rules are on the table where you can pick them up as you leave tonight. Thank you."

"Our thanks to you and your committee, Mrs. Ng. Help us spread the word, folks. Soon we are going to need many volunteers to put this all together."

Noah surveyed the crowd for other questions or contributions. Ike Epstein stood and waved a clipping from yesterday's newspaper. Noah nodded and adjusted the mike for the big man.

"Mr. Ike Epstein is another member who is prominent in the schools. We teach by example, you know, and everybody at the high school loves Ike. He's a friend and counselor to the students."

"Don't butter me up, Noah. I'm a custodian, folks, so, yes, I get around the school and observe a lot. I'm an informal counselor from Hard Knocks University." He paused and was rewarded by laughter. "This article is about student improvement. What works, according to research, and what doesn't.

I'm about to get myself into hot water with teachers, and with unions, by even calling attention to this clipping, but I agree with the results based on what I've witnessed for many years. This is it:[3]

"More research. The Rand Study shows that 'States (Texas and California are two examples compared to demonstrate extreme results)...' *States that reduce class sizes, enroll more kids in public preschool, provide more classroom materials, and target additional money to poor children, are improving the lot of all students. Regardless of how much money parents make or what race they are, those children are likely to do better than counterparts in other states.*

"This private study concluded that 'The Rand study ranked the 44 states that participate in the voluntary national test program, by average test scores, by average* *score improvement, and by directly comparing scores of students with similar race and socio-economic backgrounds"*.

"That means that kids with those four advantages in school: smaller classes, preschools, classroom materials, and money for the poor kids will do better 'regardless of how much money their parents make or what race they are, or how low their scores were before' . . . they will do better."

Ike wiped a finger across his shaggy moustache and stared at the faces to be sure they were listening. Assured of that, he continued:

"Rand compared scores of students who shared similar family circumstances, such as whether their parents were single, were teen parents, or had finished high school. All factors that have generally affected a child's ability to do well in school. The conclusions were still found to be valid. And this is the clinker, folks, I quote: 'What did not necessarily help children's scores was having teachers who were highly paid, or with advanced degrees."

"That is all I have to say except, I told you so. Most of the teachers I have known work hard and continue their own education throughout their careers. They determine which classes will help them to do a better job, but they don't necessarily go on to get advanced degrees. It is the union and the universities that try to convince us that higher pay and more degrees will mean better teachers.

"Teachers are dedicated. Our aides are also dedicated. They all should be paid a good salary that is determined by supply and demand. When there is a shortage of teachers, their salaries rise to attract more. That's enough said." Ike moved heavily, like a big bear, across the stage as he favored his painful back.

Question: "In what other important way will your school differ?"

Answer: Noah searched the faces on stage to determine who was ready for that one. He saw Guy's father lift his hand. Noah motioned to him. "Come up here to answer this." He met him partway and spoke before handing the mike to him. "This is another long-time educator, Alf Benson."

Ben cleared his throat, and stood tall. "The government schools are failing to teach compassion for other beings to counter what our children witness in our society and the media. I cut this from a newspaper report this week. It is concrete verification from 30 years of study duplicated by four major health groups. You'll find this in detail with names of these four prestigious organizations on our information table by the door. [4]

"From their 30 years of research they have concluded that *'viewing entertainment violence can lead to increases in aggressive attitudes, values and behaviors, particularly in children.'* We have known that, but this leaves no doubt. This leaves no room for the excuses, argument, and denial from producers of entertainment media. They go on to say that *'children who see a lot of violence view it as an effective way to settle conflicts . . . are more likely to assume violence as normal behavior.*

This decreases the likelihood that children will take action on behalf of a victim when violence occurs, and they have a higher tendency for violent and aggressive behavior later in life.'

"These health organizations put the responsibility on parents to *'police children's entertainment,'* but I remind you that as educators we must also find ways in schools to teach children to be humane. The Golden Rule is still the best and most inclusive rule to teach. It must be instilled into their minds through good literature and logical discussions, to be woven into everyday life patterns." Ben shook his fist in the air for emphasis and jutted his jaw forward. "Children and all of us are being desensitized. Making our children into creatures without sensitivity before they learn to reason is a crime, an aberration to the future of the human race. You, who abhor the smut of pornography, can't you see that unlimited exposure to violence has the same deteriorating effect on the quality of our lives?

"A few seconds more, please . . . just as parents police what children eat, and schools teach health classes, this article made it very clear that our children's mental health must be guarded. One entertainment violence monitoring group, called 'The Lion & Lamb Project' cheered at a meeting in Bethesda, Maryland. They cheered statements at the meeting of the Health Organizations, and that group which has been trying for years to convince the entertainment industry stated: 'Right now, the message we're sending children in the media is that violence is OK, that it is a part of life, and that sometimes it's even funny. We're even using violence for humor now."'Ben shook his head. as he turned to walk slowly back to his seat.

The audience was silent. The full impact of Ben's report had been like a blow to the solar plexus. Quiet reigned for some moments. Then they burst into applause.

"We will stop on that note if there is no other new business."Voices sounded to make the necessary motions and votes. "Thank you all for coming. The newsletter will capsulize the meeting. Goodnight all." Noah breathed a sigh of relief, already eager to compare notes with other members on the effectiveness of the meeting. He saw Chieko talking to Mrs. Ng, who was giving her the architectural contest rules.

[1] Stanley Crouch, Special to *The Los Angeles Times*, News Commentary, August 25, 2000 of West Hawaii Today.

[2] Cal Thomas "School vouchers are dead, but school choice is not with K12" 2001 Tribune Media Services, Inc., Printed in *"West Hawaii Today"* May 20

[3] Associated Press Education Writer, Anjetta McQueen "Rand Study", July 26, 2000

[4] Associated Press Writer, Jesse J. Holland,"Health groups directly linking media to child violence." American Medical Association; American Academy of Pediatrics; American Psychological Association; and the American Academy of Child and Adolescent Psychiatry. A joint statement released July 26, 2000.

Chapter 56

Hostages Held

Chieko had worked on the plans since dawn. Now feeling tense and restless, she needed a break. Just to get out and to walk would help. Maybe to window shop in the village. She should call Noah, but he was behind on his work. Anyway she was tired of being dependent. After six years at the University, where she had become a "liberated woman," she was pleased and proud of her independence. It was hard to be cooped up so much. She needn't stay out long, just enough to stretch her legs.

She brushed her hair letting it hang loose. She glanced in the mirror: her shorts were just fine. She would blend in with the crowds of tourists who had embarked from the ship. After scooping up her keys and purse, she fairly flew down the stairs. It felt so good to get out that she almost skipped as she made her way down the street toward the village shops. It would be a treat to get a sandwich where she could look out at the ocean waves crashing against the sea wall. Then she began her shopping in the village mall.

The sheer joy of it lifted her spirits. She was almost to the end of the mall when she noticed two young men leaning against the wall near the storefront. Hadn't she seen them in the same posture outside a store near the other end of the shops? They seemed unaware of her as they talked and laughed, but as she stared at them, they pulled their caps down to their dark glasses, stopped chatting, and studied the paving stones under their feet. One had a sparse beard and hair pulled back in a braid. The other had long hair worn loose and uncombed.

A store across the mall had two entrances, one from the mall and the other from the street side. She reversed her direction and entered that shop. When she looked out through the window they had moved about fifty feet in the direction she had taken. Was she imagining it? Well, she could soon find out. She walked to the clothes racks. The clerk was puzzled when Chieko then moved like a streak past her, through the shop toward the street entrance, and paused to peek through the clothing displays. Seeing no one following her, she slipped through the street side door.

People stared, and seemed annoyed that she was weaving, in and out, running through the crowds, dodging pedestrians, and very nearly knocking them down. She didn't take time to glance backward until she reached the shady trees of the palace grounds. Breathing heavily, she stopped to lean against the wall, and turned to look. In the distance, were those the same two dark figures? They were running in her direction. She didn't linger to find out.

"What-a-ya mean, she gave ya duh slip? Can't you goons do nothin' right? So go find'er. Ever'body else has brought some chicks in already. It's like a zoo here."

Moose shoved the cell phone in his pocket. "Come on, Wart. We're gonna find 'er."

Chieko entered the Kam Hotel before the two rounded the curve by the sea wall. She bypassed the wall phones. Too visible from the lobby. Moving past the service shops, she saw a beauty shop sign ahead. Perfect, they'd never look in there. She entered, and leaned against the door too breathless to speak.

Kitty, the shop owner, looked up expectantly, but it wasn't her next client who stood there. "Yes, may I help you?" The girl was under stress.

"I need a towel and, . . . and a cape." Her breath came in gasps. "I'll explain later." As she spoke she moved to the back of the shop. The towel stack was within reach. She took one and wrapped it around her head into a turban. "Please, act natural," she said. "Tell me if you see two men, teens or older, go past the door." She was slipping into a cape that was hanging on the barber chair.

Kitty put a "Closed" sign in the window and locked the door. Chieko sat in one of the stations with her back to the door, her face in her hands. Kitty made an effort to look busy and kept one eye on the entrance.

"So what's going on?" she asked.

"I have to call my uncle, please." Kitty handed her the phone. He wasn't in. She waited for the answering machine beep. Chieko left the phone number of the beauty shop. "Please call, Uncle Ross." No one answered Noah's phone.

"The number of the police station is taped on the phone." Kitty offered, sensing the urgency of the situation. Only then did Chieko notice the small television. The volume was turned down very low. She heard the newscast reporter say something about the Perkins House, and hostages being held. Chieko hesitated. "Police are not revealing any information yet. A man is issuing ultimatums and threatening the hostage's lives if his demands are not met. The man has requested a helicopter. He offers to release hostages after he receives what he is asking for."

Two men stopped to peer in the window. Kitty ignored them, and looked busy with combs, the broom, whatever she could grab. They tapped on the window and she ignored them. They knocked harder. She looked up, scowled at them, pointed at the sign in the window, and walked away, hoping that her three o'clock appointment wouldn't show up early. The men turned away.

Chieko was busily dialing the police number, her back to the door.

"We are trying to get the names of the hostages and the identity of their captors." The television reporter announced.

"I am locked in a beauty shop at the Kam Hotel," she told the person who answered her call. "I was followed all afternoon. Can you send a police car to get me, please?"

"Ma'am, are you safe right now, and will you be safe until we get a chance to send a patrolman for you?"

"Yes, I guess so, but the shop owner will want to go home soon."

"Give your name, phone number, and address to our office manager. She will keep in touch with you."

Someone else took the phone and copied down Chieko's name and other necessary numbers and details. "All of our officers are on special duty. We are understaffed. Stay right where you are. I'll call back soon."

Kitty had heard Chieko's side of the conversation. "Well, that's fine service for you. Don't worry, honey. My client is at the door now. We'll keep it locked while I do her hair."

She turned the volume on the TV higher.

"There was a police raid on the Perkins House this afternoon. The police are not revealing any information yet. They are in communication with the renter of the house, who is demanding they provide him with a means of escape. He is not saying what he intends to do, if his instructions are not followed. The hostages appear to be women who were forced into vans at gun point and transported a short distance to the Perkins house off Williams Street."

As soon as Ross Ota heard the sirens and saw smoke coming from the Perkins property, he was on his way out of his office. As an afterthought, he phoned Chieko. No answer. He rushed to Noah's desk.

"Did Chieko say she was going out today?"

"No, isn't she at home?"

Ross shook his head. "All hell's broken loose over at the Perkins House. The raid must be in progress."

Noah was on his feet, running. They left the office together. Outside, he shouted back, "I'm going to her condo. You're not going to get involved in the raid, I hope?"

"I'm already involved. I'm the landlord, remember? Hope they aren't going to burn the place down or riddle it with bullet holes."

The excitement and big equipment from police and fire departments had attracted the curious. Traffic was tied up. Streets were blocked. Noah had trouble getting through. When he arrived at her condo, he leaped from his car and ran to the parking space she used under the building. The car was there, unlocked.

He had told her to keep the car locked. He looked front and back, and then noticed her cell phone on the passenger seat. She would have carried it with her if she had walked. He opened the trunk, holding his breath. Nothing. He closed the trunk lid, and greatly relieved, ran up to the lobby. He was grateful that she had given him a key. He fumbled with the key when he reached the door of her condo, calling her name aloud, and knocking on the door until the key turned. The open door revealed nothing alarming. Everything was in place. No signs of a struggle. Noah reached for the remote, and turned on the television.

The announcer was struggling to say something of interest, to hold his audience, even though he had been given no new information. He repeated everything he had already reported. It was news to Noah.

"The identities of the hostages have not been released, nor do we know who their captors are. They threaten to kill the women hostages one by one if the police don't get a helicopter to them within fifteen minutes. I have been told that the hostages are shoppers brought across the avenue at gunpoint by thugs. We are returning now to our regular program until we have more information." He identified himself and the channel.

Noah ran from the condo without turning off the television. Word must have leaked out about the raid. Why else would they have kidnapped the women? He couldn't face his fear that Chieko was one of them. In ten minutes, he was standing in the entry to the police station, explaining to the civilian employee in the office that his girl friend was missing. Had they received any calls concerning a young woman? The clerk was busy answering another phone call. She handed him a missing person form and a pen.

He pushed her hand aside. "No, no, no! You don't understand. Have you received any calls about a young woman?"

The clerk glared at him and turned to finish her call. She hung up, again handed him the form, and urged him to fill out the information. Noah's hand was trembling so that he could hardly write. His mind was unclear, as he stared at the blanks. Height? Body type? Hair? Long, short, medium, black, brown? Caucasian, Asian? Any scars?

The woman didn't return to the window that separated the station office from the foyer. A locked door connected the two areas. Noah shouted to get someone's attention. The woman returned, looked at him over her glasses. She took the ID sheet and examined his description of Chieko.

"Hey, Kelly." The woman turned to look at someone working in the corner. "Where's the report about the beauty shop?"

"Look, lady, you don't understand. I am trying to find someone. This has nothing to do with a beauty shop!"

The report was being shoved under his nose.

Chieko Ota locked in a beauty shop in the Kam Hotel. Noah muttered something between an oath and a prayer. He scribbled the number down to call it from his cell phone and ran out of the door, leaving the woman sputtering about the way the public treated them.

Chapter 57

Tense Times

As Noah was leaving the driveway from the Police Station, he called his boss's cell phone."Ota," he shouted,"I think she's okay. I'm on my way to pick her up right now."

"Oh," Ross breathed, as if great pressure was lifting off him."They still don't know who the women being held in the Perkins house are. Call me as soon as you have her, and thanks, Noah."

Noah dialed the number of the beauty shop. Busy signal. He was in the hotel parking lot in less than five minutes.

Kitty was eying the clock, wondering what she would do with this girl when it was time to close shop. She didn't like the idea of putting herself in danger. What was it all about anyhow? She was putting the final touches on the hairstyle of her last appointment of the day.

Chieko was the name she had given to the police department. She hadn't said a word after that. Just sat, glancing at the television, and turning pages of a magazine that she seemed not to be reading.

"I've got to make another call," Chieko said to the beauty operator.

Kitty had not mentioned what was going on to the client she was working on. She would rather that the girl not call the police now. It was not good business to have customers become alarmed.

Chieko was reaching for the phone just as Noah tried to open the locked door. He knocked on the glass."Chieko," he called loudly, unable to see her. The phone fell to the floor. She pivoted her chair, and in one motion was there reaching for the key ring dangling from the lock."Noah. Oh, Noah," she cried. The seconds it took to open the door seemed endless. Kitty and her customer froze, bewildered. Noah pushed the door open as soon as the key turned. The towel, wrapped as a turban around her head, fell to the floor. They held each other close, each repeating the other's name, Chieko gasping and sobbing.

Chieko pulled him into the shop. So much to say, but not here. Chieko removed the cape and searched in her purse for something to show

Kitty her gratitude. She pressed a fifty dollar bill into the woman's hand and kissed her cheek.

"Thank you. I'll be all right now." In seconds she and Noah were running toward the back exit that opened into the parking lot. They stopped to embrace again before going outside. Tears were wetting her cheeks.

Safe. Snuggled together in the car, Noah called Ross again. "I have her here. She's all right. You are, aren't you, Sweet?" He handed the phone to her as she nodded.

"Uncle Ross, I was so frightened, but I hid from them. Noah found me. I love you. Come over to my condo so we can talk, please."

Noah took the phone back. "Where are you, Ross? Is everything okay there?"

"Outside of the Perkins House on the driveway. It is still in a state of confusion. They are trying to calm the guy by offering him anything and everything. Meanwhile I think the SWAT team is going in. They've got to get those women out of there. God, Noah, I don't know what to say to you. I was so afraid that Chieko was one of the prisoners."

"I'll be there as soon as I get your lovely niece safely settled down in her condo."

Chieko looked at Noah in shock. How could he leave her now . . . for anything?

"Absolutely not, Noah. You stay there with her. I'm fine. I'm surrounded by what appears to be the whole island police force, firemen and all. They're doing a good job. They are letting me stay here because we are concerned with the property, and until now I was so scared that they had Chieko. Stay with her, Noah!"

"Okay, Boss." Noah was relieved that he wasn't needed elsewhere. With Chieko was exactly where he wanted to be.

They were settled in the condo. Time and again, they had embraced and kissed. Then she began to spill her tale of the suspicious-looking young men following her. She couldn't figure out why. Noah was piecing it all together, but did not think it was timely to tell her. He waited on her, seeing to her comfort, the temperature of the room, her needs. He wanted only to make her feel better.

He made tea for both of them, then puttered in the kitchen making a simple light snack. Cream cheese on some bread. He even cut the bread in sections after trimming off the crust, as he had seen her do. She smiled at his hands working over dainty fare to please her. He filled a plate with condiments, olives, small pickles, some celery. Everything he could find until she stopped him.

Noah made sure the fan was turned on, the windows and shades open, then got her a light shawl to throw across her body.

"Will you stop bustling around like a mother hen?" She laughed. "All I want is you, and I want you right here beside me." Instead, as soon as he placed the tray on the table at her side, he sat down at her feet, and began to massage them. She didn't argue. He was relaxing her.

Noah wanted to turn on the television to keep informed about the drug raid. But Chieko was not yet aware of all that. It would only add to her confusion and tension.

"Noah, isn't the Perkin's house one of Uncle's accounts? Were you working on it?"

So, she does know. The sound of a helicopter interrupted their conversation. "Yes and no. It is a company account, a big one, but your uncle handled that himself. He knows old Perkins from way back. Why do you ask?"

"There's a lot going on there today. I saw it on television while I was in the shop. Do you know about it?" A considerable pause ensued. "Noah. Is that where you told Uncle Ross you were going to meet him . . . after you settled me down," you said.

"Yeah. That's where he is. He's concerned about the property. There were hostages taken." The roar of the helicopter was becoming louder, as it passed over their heads. They were only about two miles from the location under siege.

"Hostages. Yes, I heard something about that, but I was so concerned about my own safety that it didn't really soak in. Are they safe? Are they getting them out safely?"

"Not yet, Sweet. Don't you worry about them now. They'll be okay."

Chieko was so tired, and now her mind was putting the small pieces all together. "Noah, those poor women. Does that have anything to do with what happened to me today? Were those creepy hoods trying to kidnap me to make me a hostage, too? Who is it holding those women prisoner?"

There was no use trying to keep her from knowing the whole truth. She had worked it out. "Clever lady. Maybe you and I should start a private investigation service. You are very smart."

"Don't tease me, Noah. How awful for them. And I heard that their lives are threatened. Oh, Uncle Ross isn't in the middle of it, is he?"

"No, no, no. Lie back, calm down. He's safe. They won't let him go into the property. Only the police know who the guy is. He's a drug dealer. Your uncle knows the alias he used to rent the place."

"Turn on the TV." She had to know.

He did as she wished, knowing that there was no way to calm her now. Even though she's safe, she identified with the others. Noah knew she probably would have been with them right now, if she hadn't outwitted the jerks who were following her. They must have seen her leave her condo, but there were too many people in the village, unlike the large parking lot where the other women were accosted and taken prisoner.

The local news station played music, then interrupted it to repeat or add to the information. The helicopter roared overhead again and again. An unnerving sound.

"We return with an update. The noise from the Perkins House sounds like a war zone. Some of the henchmen have surrendered to the police. The man who has been in communication has not been available for about twenty minutes. The police and a psychiatrist had seemed to be getting him to cooperate. Then he reversed his behavior.

"We do not know what is happening inside. There are flames in or near the house and sporadic gunfire. Now the sounds are like rapid-fire machine guns. One moment. Something is happening at the front gate. Several vehicles are rushing in. One is a fire truck. We are showing you the scene of what we are now hearing was a drug raid. We will keep the camera fixed on the property, and will inform you as we receive more information.

"Just a moment. Two vans are entering. One police car is leaving with the driver and three passengers. We can't see who they are. Our reporter at the scene says that they may be the hostages. Three of the seven hostages appear to be free. An ambulance is driving through the gate. Apparently there are wounded in there."

The television showed the scene with no more comments from the announcer. He promised to advise the viewers as soon as more information was available.

Noah and Chieko thought they could see Ross Ota near the front gate.

"They must have solved some of the problems since things are quieting down. No fire. No shooting. A lot of traffic in and out." Noah said and Chieko agreed.

The phone rang. Chieko grabbed it off its cradle. "Hello? Thank God." She smiled at Noah. "He says it's over. He's going in to look around. He'll be here as soon as he can," she said as she hung up the phone.

"Turn it off, Baby, and settle down. There isn't likely to be any more on the television news that Ross can't tell us when he gets here."

Chieko agreed. She was still anxious about the hostages, but she could use some peace and quiet. She turned on some music. They curled up on the couch together, happy to be in one another's arms.

They were nearly asleep, exhausted, when Ross phoned from

downstairs. As he came into the condo, Chieko was at the door to hug him and kiss both cheeks as was her custom. Noah was beside them, ready to shake his hand. They had become warm friends since the morning Ross had dropped by unexpected.

Chieko had the tea ready with some cookies Uncle Ross was fond of. They gathered around the coffee table, Ross in his favorite chair, and the two of them side by side on the couch. Ross noticed that they were holding hands as they waited to hear his account of the day. First, he phoned to have some Chinese food delivered. Chieko got up to light several candles to add to the warmth created by their mutual love and thanksgiving. She was pleased with the response of her favorite men toward each other.

"Now, tell us everything," she said.

"And you, my dear, I want to hear everything about your disappearance today. It scared us to death."

So Chieko and Noah allowed Ross to enjoy his tea while they told him about their day.

He listened carefully, recalling his fears as they related it. Then he began with the final hour at the Perkins property. They asked him to tell them about the hostages questioned.

"That's the good news. Some were roughed up a bit. I think he did that to convince the police that he meant business. But they all got out all right, and to be sure of that they were taken to the hospital where their families and friends picked them up. I am so grateful that you were not one of them, Chicadee."

"Who was the fool who caused all this trouble? Who masterminded it?"

"I wouldn't call him a mastermind. A fool, yes. It was a huge drug operation. The mastermind is someone still in South America. The police know who, and where he is. With time and luck he'll fall by the wayside, but others will be tempted by big money. We must fight drugs from within. We are not winning because it is our own people who buy drugs. They keep the drug peril a threat to us all. We must nip it in the bud here in our own culture, here on our own island.

"But yes, he was just another fool looking for easy money. He thought it would be easy anyhow."

"Was? Is he dead?"

"He killed himself when the SWAT team surprised them. They used guerrilla tactics to make their way toward the house. They overcame the guards of the hostages. Most of them ran down the driveway to surrender. A few escaped through the brush and tried to get over the wall to the highway, but the police picked them up. And Mr. Mastermind killed himself. Did a messy job of it, too. Tried to set the house on fire, but it did little damage, he didn't do anything right."

"So, it's over," Noah said. "Have you been in contact with Perkins yet?"

"Yes, he and I were talking while this was going on. We may have some surprises about the house. I have wanted to buy it for a long time, but he wouldn't sell. Well, he's getting old, and tired of the bother of it. I don't think he has the heart to put time, money, and thought into it anymore. I'm going to present some alternatives that I think would be advantageous to him and to Kona."

"Want to tell us about them, Ross?"

"No, I hear a doorbell. Must be our dinner. Let's eat, that is if you two can keep your hands off each other."

Chapter 58

Transition

It rained all night. Noah and Chieko had enjoyed listening to the rain together, lying on the couch snug in each other's arms. Noah awoke to the new day just as the darkness was being laced with the first light, just enough to change nature's backdrop from black to gray. Could there be any more happiness than he felt this morning? Could there be any more love than he felt for this woman sleeping in his arms? He had never experienced more elation than he was feeling at this moment.

She stirred but did not wake up. He lay there, content to gaze at her. He recalled what Ross had said as the two men were getting ready to leave last night.

"I think you should stay here with Chieko."

Noah and Chieko both looked at him, surprised, and then looked at each other, both trying hard to conceal a smile ready to light up the closing of a most difficult day.

"You can sleep on the couch," Ross said to Noah. He was chuckling inside while keeping a serious expression on his face.

"Is that all right with you Chieko?" Noah asked politely.

"Yes, that would be fine," she said, trying to appear disinterested.

They both heard Ross specify the couch for Noah. As soon as Ota had closed the door behind him, Noah proceeded to obey. He was removing his shirt. Chieko had slipped out of her garments, smiled and stretched out to wait for him, pleased that she had bought such a roomy couch. Not, what her uncle had in mind. She giggled. "You're a hussy," Noah teased, but did nothing to discourage the move as he slid in beside her.

Noah didn't dare misread Ota's mind. He realized that he was in Ross's good graces, but he had never expected him to give his employee this much rope. One thing for sure, he would hang himself with it if Noah took advantage of his boss's trust.

Not to worry. Chieko had snuggled up tight against him and was already asleep. Another night with no discussion. No nothing.

Now in the quiet of morning, with the small zebra doves cooing on the windowsill, Noah's mind toyed with ideas for their future, when suddenly, an unexpected thought gnawed on the sweetness of the moment. She must be about twenty-three years old. He'd never thought about an age difference. That made him more than twenty years older. He winced at the thought.

Lying there drinking in her beauty, he was glad at that moment for the age difference. If he were in his teens or early twenties, his hormones would never have permitted the kind of control he was exercising.

But has Chieko considered the span in their ages, he wondered? Of course not. They had discussed no more intimacy than that of a friendship. Yet they had permitted themselves to balance their relationship while walking on the edge of a saber. A titillating desire was always present, wanting more. Maybe they were both crazy. People don't exercise this restraint anymore.

His gaze was now riveted on the light streaking through the curtain onto the wall.

"What are you thinking about? You look so serious." Chieko's voice filled the room and scattered his troubling thoughts.

"Things we must discuss as soon as our lives return to a comparatively normal pace."

"And what are those things?" she asked. As if completely unaware of his struggle to contain his passion, she snuggled up closer to him.

"Chieko, we . . ."

She smiled, her eyes closed, her cheek resting against his chest, "We what?"

"We have to get up. I have to get to work, much as I would prefer to stay here with you." He detested his cowardly reluctance to discuss their future together and their age difference. His excuse? There wasn't enough time.

Then, there was the artist, the one who had been at the picnic. Also older than she is, but about ten years younger than he was. But Noah knew somehow that he could dispense with that concern. He threw his legs over the side of the couch and got to his feet.

"No kiss?"

He bent to kiss her. "Good morning, my beauty." He grinned, but returned to his mind-wrenching mental exercises as he wandered the room getting dressed. "Impossible," his mind reasoned. I've been with her so much that I'd be aware if there is an attraction between them. There had been no opportunity for the two to have been together. Or had there?

After all, Chieko had disregarded orders from both Noah, and her uncle to not leave the condo without one of them being with her. Noah had not believed Chieko would deceive him, but she had gone out at least twice without notifying him or Ross.

"And the man, yes. He was attracted to her. I remember the way he looked at her, and touched her. That guy knows how to handle women. Handle. He regretted his choice of words. But if there was anything to it, there would be signs.

"Surely it's all in your imagination, you fool." Noah silently addressed the image in the bathroom mirror. He buried his face in the towel.

The phone rang. "Yes, yes. This is Chieko. Of course I remember. How are you? Did you enjoy the picnic? And did you get all the information you needed? . . . No, I'm afraid I can't today. I must work on my plans. Now that I have the specifications for the contest entry, I'll be able to forge ahead at great speed. Another time, perhaps?"

Noah resisted his desire to slam the partially open door. He closed it carefully so he could not hear any more of the conversation, though he was well aware who was speaking at the other end. "Another time, perhaps." Noah mimicked her sweet voice. Why didn't she just say, "NO!"

For a moment, he stared at himself in the mirror. Not the face of a young man. Mature, he preferred to think, but the beginnings of wrinkles were there. Soon the gray would be showing in his thick wavy hair. I'll bet Joaquin "What's-his-name" would not play the gentleman if he were in bed with her. Would she care . . .?

He went through the living room at lightning speed, putting on the shoulder holster, his shirt, and examining the 9 mm automatic before he put it under his clothing. Obviously, she wasn't going to mention the phone call.

"Well," he said. "Have a good day. I won't be seeing you for a few days. Got too much work to catch up on."

Chieko sensed a change of mood. Had he heard her talking on the phone? So what if he did. She had nothing to be ashamed of. She would have told him if it was of any consequence. "All right. This is the second time this morning I've had to beg for a kiss. But run along, I hate the feel of your body with that thing strapped on you. Call me?"

"Of course." He smiled at her. It was a weak effort, hindered by waves of jealously, and frustration.

Chapter 59

Confusion

Noah stayed away for days, then weeks. They spoke on the phone, but both were immersed in demanding work. Their conversations were polite, and interested, but remote and cautious.

After the drug bust and the attempt to kidnap her, Chieko refused to be confined like a prisoner. She, Noah, and Ross agreed that she could go out alone if she took care to be cautious. Noah would not need to chauffeur her anymore.

The day after the police raid on the Perkins house the local newspaper headlines proclaimed "LARGEST DRUG BUST SUCCESSFUL." Chieko scanned the article, which listed the drugs confiscated. Ecstasy, heroin, ice, cocaine, some she had never heard of. A Multimillion-dollar drug bust. The ring had been operating mainland coast-to-coast, used Hawaii as a distributorship location, after the drugs arrived from Columbia. It was a long article with companion pieces.

Chieko concentrated on those articles and how they related to Hawaii's children. "All signs suggest the taboo against marijuana is fading. Marijuana use among teens is up." She noted that shockingly high percentages of children use marijuana and that their use increased from grades eight to ten, and by twelfth grade, twenty-three percent had used within the past thirty days. [1]

Here's a good one. Chieko read that the Department of Education is receiving $5.4 million from the state tobacco settlement windfall. The state health director believes that schools with vending machines that sell soda should not receive a share of it.

"Good for him." What better way to cope with greed than to withhold large funds? Chieko shook her head in response to the hopelessness of a society that wanted to include ethics in education while the adult world has double standards.

"'More than half of the public schools in Hawaii have vending machines. Revenue from the sales provides much needed funding for student activities and supplies.' How can we justify receiving income from a product we have known to be harmful to our health? Our government has benefited financially from years of taxes on tobacco products. All the while our citizens were dying from the use of it." [2]

Sandy had said that her students drank soda all day long, starting with breakfast. And where do they get that much money? She asked herself.

She turned the page. Tobacco stings are becoming a regular target against the retail outlets that sell tobacco products to anyone younger than 18. She recalled reading about many recent stings.

The police have unfairly served as the whipping boys for offences committed by only a few officers on the force. Maybe this recent raid, as well as others ongoing, will make the public more aware of the good they do. Chieko was disturbed by the lack of respect shown in blaming the law, all else, and everyone outside of oneself. Especially the practice of grinding down all authority. She closed the newspaper in disgust.

Noah's mood, since he and Chieko had not been seeing one another, had cut into his productivity, yet, his responsibilities were increasing. Ross Ota assigned him to take charge of the Perkins property. There was a lot for him to do, make the property ready for whatever the owner would direct them to do. Noah was to supervise the renovation of the house and grounds.

The police and fire inspectors had completed their search for evidence. Those arrested were punks, but the officials wanted the ringleaders. It was a bad break that the drug dealer communicating with the police had killed himself before they could get useful information, specifically names, from him.

Well, it was clean-up time now. After the police removed the yellow tape, Noah could enter the house and surroundings.

Noah struggled to eradicate the worries he had planted in his mind the last time he had seen Chieko. How long would Chieko keep him dangling? Why did they never discuss a future together? The word "marriage" was not one he chose to use. Why? What was holding him back? Obviously they both had evaded the subject.

Chieko detested the fact that most people seemed to harbor anger and to take delight in getting even. She closed her eyes attempting to recall words of wisdom she hoped to live by: *It is arrogance to believe we can change the course of someone else's life. It is wisdom to know that we can change the course of one's own life.*

Sensible words a respected counselor had shared with her, but did she believe that? Would marriage hazard her career? Can a woman really have it all? She had worked so hard to arrive at this stage of her life.

The morning hours had drifted away with few results. Usually they were the most productive parts of the day for her.

Another saying she had copied from the Oprah Winfrey show:

"Tragedies and crisis lead you to experiences that open you to life, if you allow them to."

She was not ready to contemplate that one.

She searched for her books of wise quotations. Then recalled that she had lent them to Noah. It was an excuse to phone him. She happily grasped at it. Tonight maybe. So much to do now.

---

[1] *Indianapolis Star*, Editorial: *Marijuana* taboo? June 2000.

[2] *West Hawaii Today*, from Honolulu (AP) No tobacco money for some schools. 6-15-00.

Chapter 60

Winding Down

In spite of the confusion about her direction in life, Chieko's mind was churning with ideas for her architectural drawings. Who to test them on? Joaquin, of course. She had targeted him as her artistic adviser. She had her own ideas, but could use his opinions for artistic touches.

She wished she had a real office in place of the one in her condo. Too intimate to invite him here, but better this than to go to his secluded home. If only she had a definite property in mind. It would be so much easier to plan the Community Learning Center.

She balanced the phone receiver on her shoulder. Her hands held a page of her plans. The phone rang. No answer. She slammed it down.

She returned to her worktable. Where did she leave off? The location of the property. Well, her imagination would have to suffice. Land on the Kona side of the island was all pretty much the same. Most of it was on a slope, the steepness would vary somewhat. So, there would be the mauka area, (upland), and the makai area toward the sea, (down slope).

The shape could differ. Some properties were elongated parallel to the coast, but most were laid out from a mauka / makai direction. That was the way the early chieftains had divided their territories, as though they were cutting slices of a pie out of the island, the crust being the seacoast.

She pictured a stretch of land that varied from about 500 feet elevation to 700 feet if they were fortunate enough to have that much territory. Never mind trying to estimate how many square feet would eventually be allotted to the Center. That was impossible to guess. She would just have to design all of the major buildings to surround the central library. No way to know how much space there would be between them.

She picked up the phone after it disturbed her concentration. "Oh, Joaquin. What? You knew I called, caller ID. I figured that you were working at your kiln. That answers my question as to your availability today. You are not available, right? Yes, I could cover some things on the phone, if you have the time. It concerns the framework of ideas I'm considering. May I read them to you?" Affirmative.

"I envision the library in the middle. It will include history, psychology, philosophy, science, the arts, and technology. It's a library for students of all ages. They'll need computers, copy machines, videos . . . you get the idea.

"There is to be a culinary arts center near the entrance, just inside the property, so the students can prepare meals, catering, and baked goods for the public at a reasonable cost to cover expenses, not labor. They'll need a kitchen, classroom, carrels, and restrooms. Other buildings will have the use of separate outdoor restrooms spaced throughout the center.

"Oh, you don't like that? I'll consider toilets and sinks in each building, but remember that I'm trying to keep costs low, including maintenance. This is Hawaii after all, we don't have to troop through snow and very seldom through rain. Okay, I'll think that over. What? Yes, I'll put a sink in each building, for coffee, clean-up, and such. Let me continue.

"At the highest elevation of the campus, a green nursery. Room for growing plants by several methods, aqua culture, raised beds, Koi ponds, and waterfalls, whatever. They can supply plants and care for the landscaping as part of their course work. They can also work with the Department of Agriculture agents when they need to control infestation. Botany, horticulture and chemistry departments will need special equipment, inside and outside.

"An art building, of course. A large building, perhaps two stories, to provide students classrooms for painting in oil, watercolor, acrylics, etc. Pottery, sculpture, metals, wood, and rock all possible forms. And technical art such as graphics. The machines will be terribly expensive.

"Yes, there will be opportunities for most departments to earn money and to cooperate by sharing with other schools in the area."

"It sounds spectacular, Chieko, but I thought this was for high school classes, and later for the lower grades."

"Oh, of course, I was just telling you about the frosting on the cake. All of these buildings are for high school students and adults. Classrooms in separate buildings will be large enough to provide for three separate classes within one structure. Partitions that open up can double or triple the size for very large groups."

"I have dozens of questions to ask you, Chieko, but my kiln requires my attention. I'll want to know about the structure, plumbing, the electricity, the staffing, and more. It sounds great. Gotta go. We'll talk later." He hung up. Left her listening to the buzzing phone, which she slowly set down in its cradle.

Well, that was abrupt, she thought. Then, she was embarrassed that she had monopolized the conversation. It's just that there is so much to share, and no one to share it with. Everyone else is too busy to want to listen. I need to bounce my ideas off someone.

She worked on the placement of her buildings on the envisioned land. She could move them around, until they secured a specific property.

Chapter 61

Time Out

Chieko touched the button on her cell phone. "Noah? Hi. Hope I'm not interrupting . . . I'm at home. Been working hard all day. Thought maybe we could both take a break and have dinner here tonight. Interested?"

"Oh, you're acting as overseer at the Perkins house? How long will you have to be caretaker there. Sounds like a very dull job. Yes, I'll hold."

"Chieko, are you still there? Can't say how long. Honey, I have to hang up. Something is going on at the gate. I'll call back."

Chieko got on the phone to her uncle. "How is Noah going to eat if he stays at the house? I'd like to drop off some food for his dinner tonight . . . It's all right? Thank you, Uncle."

Ross Ota took a few seconds to consider before he picked up the phone. "How are you doing, Noah? Are you comfortable there?"

"Well, it isn't very well furnished, Ross, but I'll manage."

"Do you want a bed and mattress?"

"No, I have my sleeping bag, I'll be fine."

"I may not be able to deliver your dinner as I intended. I was looking forward to a quiet evening to talk, but something came up. I'll have someone else deliver your meal. And, Noah, if you want to invite a friend over for company that would be okay. With no electricity, no television, no radio, well, I hope you're a nature lover. Call if you need anything. The police will patrol periodically."

"Noah, it's me, Chieko. I'm at the gate. Can you let me in?"

"I'll be right down." He hurried makai to let her in, surprised and pleased to see her there. He got into the passenger side, and she drove up the road to the house. He could smell something delicious. Bags of food rested on the back seat. Fried chicken? His mouth watered. But best of all was the joy of seeing her there.

They carried the packages upstairs where he had chosen to sleep. There was one chair, his sleeping bag spread out on the floor, and a window seat surrounded by the bay window in an otherwise bare room. She put the packaged food on the surface of the window seat.

"I don't suppose there would be another chair somewhere in the house?"

Noah tore his eyes from this vision that had just appeared. He raced to another room and returned with a straight back chair.

"Well, aren't you talkative!"

"I'm just in shock. Never realized that it would be so lonely here. Thought it would be restful." He should tell her how pleased he was just to see her.

"Right here." She pointed to her cheek. "Just a little peck will do, Noah. If it's not too much to ask."

"I'm sorry, Baby," he whispered as he took her into his arms. With her here, this dismal place seemed lit up with firework displays. Actually, the stars overhead danced like diamonds in an ebony sky. How easy it had seemed to distance himself from her. Yes, easy, until he saw her dark eyes catching the glint of candlelight. Just keep busy, not to allow thoughts of her to creep in. Easy?

He held her close, unable to say anything.

"Is that where we sleep?" she asked, pointing to the lump of cloth on the floor.

"Sleep? You're staying tonight?"

"Unless you don't want me."

Every gland in his body overreacted. He felt like a schoolboy. Damn, she was doing it again. He let go of her.

"Let's eat. It smells fabulous." He had broken her spell.

Tonight, he reasoned, tonight we are going to talk. There was nothing else to distract them.

They sat on the chairs and used the window seat as a table. Fried chicken, cole slaw, potato salad, but not as good as his. In the bakery box was a cheesecake she knew would tempt him. She had brought a selection of drinks. It seemed like a beer night, Noah decided. He did not want the romantic association of wine to influence him. He knew what they must do. Talk first, then who knows?

Food and the beer mellowed his mood. And she does look so lovely by candlelight, he thought. Chieko crossed the room to look out the south window. Moonlight burnished the edges of clouds, as it peeked through openings in the vapor. The waxy white plumeria blossoms competed with the moon glow.

"It must be a lovely garden in daylight," she said softly.

"It's overgrown, neglected," he replied.

Noah straightened his sleeping bag, unzipped it, folded it back, and stretched out on it. He stared at the patterns of shadows and light dancing on the ceiling. They gave the illusion of fabric billowing overhead. He wanted no more illusions. He wanted reality.

"Chieko." She turned to face him, unaccustomed to the brusqueness of his voice. "We must talk. Where shall we start? We scarcely know each other. We don't know what the future holds for us . . . if anything."

She didn't speak, but moved to his side and crouched down on a part of the sleeping bag he had opened for her to sit on. She leaned over to kiss his lips.

"Don't, please," he insisted. "Talk." She stared at him. Silent. "I'll start. Here we are . . . I would like to say 'two lovers,' but I feel that it is only I who am in love, and you are playing a game. Here is my question? Do we have a future together, Chieko? Do you see us as husband and wife? Do you long for a future with me, with perhaps a child or two of our own? . . . Chieko?"

"I'm not a soothsayer, Noah. I don't try to foresee the future."

"No. No! Chieko. You know what I'm saying. I'm asking what you want our future to be. Our thoughts are the seeds that start the plant growing. The seed must be planted first for it to flower. Planted in your mind and mine. What do you want?" No response. "Chieko, what do you fear?" Noah was pleased with his persistence, even though his questions remained unanswered.

"Don't badger me, Noah. You make me feel cornered, and . . . and under attack. You have no reason to treat me like this." She began to sob, quietly at first.

Noah clung to the lifesaver she had thrown him. It was a sign that she was on the verge of truth, of disclosure. He felt her pain, but he would continue.

"Do you remember these words, Chieko?" He closed his eyes and recited:

"When you walk to the edge of all the light you have,
And you take that first step into the darkness of the unknown,
You must believe one of two things will happen.
There will be something solid for you to stand upon or,
You will be taught how to fly." [1]

"If I asked you to marry me right now, would you say no? Is there anyone else? Listen to this one, Chieko:

> *"Falling in love requires risk,*
> *Staying in love involves balance,*
> *Being in love rewards vulnerability."* [2]

"Which of those do you fear? Risk, balance, or vulnerability? Or is it all of them?"

She was sobbing quietly now. He so wanted to console her, but he was on the road to truth.

"Yes, I am afraid. I'm afraid of a commitment. I'm afraid to have someone know me, truly know me. I fear the changes that come after marriage. Two lovers eventually become two entirely different people. Haven't you ever noticed?"

"Where did these fears come from, Chieko?" Her face glistened with tears in the dim light.

"Where are these people who changed so much after they married?"

"I don't want to be like my mother, Noah." It poured out, almost a wail.

Noah relented, his forceful manner dissolved into pity. "Come here, Chickie." His voice caressed her. She rolled over, nestling against him, her knees drawn up in a fetal position.

"Tell me about your mother."

"She died." Chieko's tone and speech seemed to have regressed to childhood.

"How old were you?"

"I was about four, four years old. He beat her. I saw her. Her pretty face was bloody. One eye was closed . . . She was weeping. After that she just sat, and stared. Stared at nothing. She didn't know I was there. I never saw my father again. Then, one day some people came and took me away. I remember a big building with lots of little kids. I stayed in bed except when they made me get up. Then Uncle Ross came. I was so glad…" A long contained sob, labored breathing. "…to see him. All I could do was cry. He took me away. Finally, after a long time, I was happy again, except when I thought of my mother. Uncle Ross wouldn't tell me where she was. I didn't know she was dead.

"One rainy day I was playing in my uncle's closet because I was afraid of the thunder. I was poking around, opening boxes and a newspaper photograph fell out of a dusty box. It was a picture of my mother, after she had been beaten. I put the box back, but I kept the newspaper clipping hidden. It took years before I could read it. It took more years to understand the horror of it.

"I was afraid to ask anyone what 'rape' meant. The dictionary said it was a crime. Then there were some words in the dictionary that I didn't know then: 'to carry away by force.' I understood that, but the other part, I didn't understand.

"When I did know the story in full, I wondered how my father could have hurt her so. She didn't file charges against him, Uncle Ross said, but she was destroyed by it. She killed herself. In the twisted way women rationalized abuse, I think she blamed herself. But I hate him.

"You are right about my fears, Noah." She dabbed at her eyes. "So, now you know. I had gotten over it, I thought I had, but you awakened it all. When I was attracted to boys or men, at the same time I really hated them, especially the macho types.

"You were so gentle . . . until tonight, when you reverted to kind. I want to go home now, Noah. I hope you're satisfied."

Noah was stretched out on his back on the sleeping bag. Her words stung. Chieko started to get up. He reached for her arm to pull her toward him, and she reacted in anger, or was it fear? He held on to her wrist.

"Lie here by my side, and listen to me, Chieko. I wonder why your uncle never took you for counseling. It could have helped. You still need help, because you keep so much anger hidden inside.

"Remember the books of quotations you lent me? When I was struggling with confusing thoughts that I couldn't cope with, I memorized those I thought I could use. Here's one for both of us:"

> *A wise man in the storm prays to God,*
> *Not for safety, but for deliverance from fear.*

"That's from Emerson. And another:

> *If you find yourself in a hole, the first thing to do is stop digging.*

"We were both digging holes that were getting deeper and deeper."

> *Angry people are those people who are most afraid. Dr. Robert Anthony.*

He framed her face with his hands. She closed her eyes to avoid looking at him."Chickie, come on. Can't you see that our feelings, the anger and resentment, insecurity and fear, keep us from getting on with our lives? These feelings are barring us from the healing we can receive from love. Here is another saying I recall:

Regrets look back, worry looks around, shame looks down, and faith looks up.

"Look up, please, Chickie. In the morning we will talk more. We are both worn out."

Noah held her close and inhaled the scent of her hair. He pressed his face against the silken strands. The moon slid through the vapors, as if playing tag with comets racing toward the dawn of a new day. Sleep came to calm their pain . . . temporarily.

[1] Dr. Patrick Overton, *Rebuilding the Front Porch of America,* (Essays on the art of Community Making).

[2] Glenn Levinson, *Introspection,* Oct. 1999.

Chapter 62

Breakdown

Noah awakened in the barren room he had come to know too well. But something was different to the unfamiliar bleak surroundings. How long had she been awake? How long had she sat there staring at him?

"Good morning, sweetheart." He would try to be cheerful. If only the sun were shining, but it was to be a rare cloudy, rainy day. He had never seen her look so forlorn, her hair tousled, her clothes rumpled, her eyes . . . empty. She had weathered the library bombing better than last night's ordeal. He felt shamed.

What a terrible experience for a four year old. No wonder she had stored that all inside of her. And Ross. It had surely been painful for him, too. His own brother had driven his wife to suicide and deserted his own child. Now Noah saw both Ross and Chieko in a different light.

Chieko continued to stare. Noah blamed himself for reawakening Chieko's long buried pain and anger. She had been fine until last night, when he had meddled. Noah recalled how he had urged her to tell her hidden, well-buried fears. Who did I think I was? How much damage have I done? And what do I do now. "I love you, Chickie." Her eyes filled with tears. They had the look of glass behind a waterfall. "Shall we go get some breakfast?" She only stared.

Noah could not leave her until she came out of this. He would have to bring Ross into it.

"I forgot to put on the bathroom light last night. Did you find it?" She sat. Rigid. Unresponsive . . . He rolled to his knees, and stood, stretching his muscles. He bent over to pull her to her feet. She resisted, but he forced her to stand and held her in his arms, a limp bundle. He felt the damp clothing she wore. She had wet herself.

"Come on, Sweet. We'll get cleaned up." He took her hand and led her into the bathroom. Something has snapped, he told himself.

"Do you want some help?" No response. He took the washcloth and wiped her face. Its coolness seemed to revive her somewhat. Noah held her small hands under the cold water and then wiped them dry. He was getting frightened. He held his cupped hands under the faucet and lifted the cool water to his own face. He ran his wet fingers through his hair.

"Come on, Honey. Do you want a bath?" Then he remembered that there was no hot water. "Do you want me to carry you?" He swooped her up in his arms and returned to the bedroom with her. He set her down on the window seat.

She continued to stare. If he spoke she turned her attention from the floor to him and then back to the floor. He touched his hand to her cheek, her forehead. Normal, no temperature. All seemed normal except . . . he fought back a sob.

Noah grabbed his cell phone. Without any greeting, he said, "Get over here right now. Bring your key to the gate."

Five minutes later Ross Ota walked up the stairs. He saw the agonized look on Noah's face, and the rumpled sleeping bag on the floor. Then he saw Chieko in the window seat.

"Chieko," he croaked. "Are you all right, Chickadee?"

Her sob had a mournful sound. When Ross knelt on the floor in front of her, she put her arms around his neck. This seemed like a good sign to Noah.

Ross looked back at the sleeping bag. "My God, Noah, you didn't . . ."

"Of course not, Ross. You know better than that. I got her talking about her childhood, her mother . . . did you know she was carrying all of that pain inside?"

"I've got to get her to a doctor. I haven't seen her like this for a long time."

"Why didn't you tell me? I would never have questioned her."

"I intended to tell you, soon. I thought you would be right for her, that you would provide the balance she needed."

Noah leaned over to pick her up. She recoiled from him. He soothed her with soft words of assurance. "I'll take her to the car. Bring her purse, and anything else you see of hers. Shall I go with you? I don't think I can bear waiting here."

Ross was already in the driver's seat as Noah was getting a seat belt around her. "Stay here. I'll call as soon as I have anything to tell you. Go on with your work, Noah, and keep your phone handy. It will be easier on you to keep busy."

He scribbled some numbers on a scrap of paper. "Call this doctor, and tell him I'm on my way to the hospital with her. Tell him to phone the emergency room and to be there as soon as possible."

"Ross, you know I didn't harm her. I didn't touch her. I never have. I had no idea, Ross. I wish I had known."

"I'm sorry, son. It isn't your fault."

Noah stood watching the car going through the gate. The gate closed. He dropped to his knees, exhausted and bewildered.

Chapter 63

Upbeat

C hieko's stay at the hospital was brief. Her doctor, a psychiatrist, had confirmed what Ross already knew. And Ross passed on the information to Noah.

"She suffered a nervous breakdown, not her first. While she was studying for her degree, stress triggered what the doctor describes as 'an acute onset that interferes with normal function, thought, or action.' It came on rapidly.

"Acute is the opposite of chronic. If this were chronic, it would be long lasting, and recurring. Acute indicates that this will be of short duration and will require a day or two in the hospital. If all goes as well as expected. She'll have some sessions with the psychiatrist, like a counseling session, only higher-priced." Ross was able to joke, and Noah relaxed . . . somewhat.

But he later did his own research. Guy Benson likened Noah's study to a lawyer defending himself in court. "You are too emotionally connected, Noah," he said. "Get your information from a doctor so that you don't misread the condition."

Nevertheless, Noah went to the medical section of the library and learned that "patients experiencing trauma may produce disordered feelings or behavior. Trauma is an emotional or psychological shock. Sometimes there is regression to an earlier reaction, characterized by mental state and behavior inappropriate to the situation."

He was satisfied that all of that fits. Then he read on:

Schizoid personality disorder. A disorder of the personality. (So far, it was clear!) *Persistent indifference to social interaction and a limited range of social experience and expression. Begins in early adulthood . . . neither seek nor enjoy close relationships nor do they want to be part of a family. They lead lonely lives; have no close friends or confidants; sexual interests and activity are almost nonexistent; rarely do they experience strong emotions such as anger and joy. They appear cold and aloof and rarely reciprocate gestures or facial expressions such as smiles or nods.* [1]

He already wished he hadn't gone looking for information. Should have listened to Guy. The description sounded a lot like him, or how he had been during part of his life, how he was afraid of becoming again. Come to think of it, that reads like a description of many people he had known. He slammed the medical dictionary shut before he realized that the doctor had not included *Schizoid personality disorder* in Chieko's diagnosis. Guy had been right: he had gotten carried away with his research and had only confused the issue.

Chieko's sessions with the doctor were encouraging. He was satisfied that her work on the plans was good for her, not stressful. If her relationship with Noah was serious, in fact, he said, even if it was not, they could both benefit from counseling, either from him, a qualified psychologist, or a wise counselor.

Chieko was embarrassed and shy when she returned home from the hospital. Noah sent flowers. Both Noah and Chieko communicated through Ross. Chieko sent her thanks for the roses he sent, but said that she did not feel well enough to see him. She also requested that he not call her because it made her nervous to talk on the phone. Noah was willing to abide by her wishes, but he felt rejected. She wasn't even giving him a chance to apologize or explain his intentions.

Actually, Chieko felt quite strong. She was capable, even eager to return to her work on the Learning Center plans. Her uncle was coming by regularly. She was grateful to be able to have him as a sounding board and to ask him about the availability of materials on the island.

To begin with, Ross scoffed at her plan to use cement, with a steel framework for her buildings, but she won him over. Together they researched the use of those materials in the building industry, and discovered that we lagged far behind other countries in their use.

"But Chieko, we have no one on the island to supply this, especially in the quantity that we'll need."

She would only say, "Then how do we start a cement business that would be able to make forms and have the heavy equipment to handle and deliver the tilt-ups for the siding?" After all, the volunteers cannot do everything. People in Kona are wonderful about turning out for volunteer work. Many people in the islands already work at two jobs to survive here.

"Chieko, Chieko. I cannot work miracles. Solar-Voltaic roofing, steel framing, and concrete siding. This is becoming a very expensive undertaking. The judges of the contest will rule you out on that alone."

"I don't believe that, Uncle Ross. They are looking for new industry here. We have to import most of our lumber. If we can develop a means for cheaper, more practical housing, more of our people will be able to own their own homes. Insurance costs will tumble. Yes, voltaic panels are more expensive at first, but electricity on our island costs a lot. Generating our own electricity is the answer. It will pay for itself in between five to ten years. Then, think of it. We will be selling it back to our island supplier."

He could not argue with the practicality of her plans. If the judges had an entrepreneurial streak, she could win on these ideas alone. However, he remained dubious that the judges would agree.

"They are great ideas, Chickadee. I'll not discount them until I check on the plausibility of it. This is Hawaii, you know, not New York."

Within the week, Ross had talked to the owner of a cement company on this side of the island; he discovered the man had been trying to enlarge or sell his interests. Ross contacted a banker who knew an investor on the mainland. The investor located a grant available in Washington that fit their needs to perfection. Then Ross was on his way to the airport to meet the investor who was flying in on his own plane.

A few meetings within the next few days, and Ross and the cement company owner were in business working out the snags, which were numerous. Fortunately for them, money does talk. Experts in the field were flown over. More planning. Heavy equipment was ordered, and Ross had another enterprise to keep tab on.

He saw very little of Chieko during that time and phoned her often to apologize. Since her ideas had sparked this new investment of his, she could not complain. Ross knew he had been bulldozed into this, but he never could argue against quality. It would win out every time.

Chieko was able to lose herself in her drawings. Nothing else seemed important. She worked hours on her plans.

Ross Ota had carried out his instructions regarding the Perkins house and land, but he was having no success in communicating with the owner. Ross called Noah into his office. "I'm going to be gone a few days. I'll be in Monterrey, California. It's the Perkins account. I've got to get the old man to make some decisions. Not good for a property to sit idle. "I wish Chieko would not turn her back on you. She's being awfully stubborn."

"She's hurt." Noah knew this was true, though it was hard to admit.

"Well, she ought to get over it. She works all day."

How's she doing?"

"She's a perfectionist, all the way, but she'll have them done before the deadline next month."

"Is it putting pressure on her? Stress?"

"Not at all. She's loving every minute of it."

"You want me to watch over her, don't you?"

"I don't know who else to ask. She has stopped tutoring the kids at the library. She doesn't have any close friends. I'll take her with me if she can afford the time. I'll ask her."

As Ross had expected, she was adamant in her refusal to go with him. "Certainly not, Uncle. I don't have a lot to do on the plans, but I'm not going to leave it all until the last minute. You go. Don't worry about me. I'm fine."

Noah called her every day while Ross was gone. Their conversations were polite, and they both tried to sound casual.

Ross stayed in California only a week. Old man Perkins was very ill. Ross made sure that he was of sound mind when they talked and that his attorney was in the room.

"Hell," the old man said. "I'm busy a dyin', Ross, and you 'n' Harvey here are botherin' me with stuff I don't care about. I'm the last of my tribe. Ever'body's been after me ta give my money away. I shoulda planned better . . ." and he fell into a fit of coughing that sounded like his last.

"J. J., I'm glad your lawyer is here. Do you trust him?"

"With my life . . . course that's only cause there ain't much left of it." At this he broke into spasms of laughter that made Ross think death was just moments away, but the old man rallied.

"J.J., do you trust me?"

"What're you gittin' at, Ross? You've had my trust fer years, and never let me down."

"I came over here to help you make a decision on the Kona property. I didn't know that you were sick. Just wanted you to tell me to rent it, lease it, or sell it. I swear to God that was all I had in mind till a few minutes ago."

Ross explained as briefly yet as clearly as possible about the Community Learning Center. He explained their goals, their philosophy, and their belief that students could accomplish more by taking responsibility for their own education. He told about the buildings that would make up the Center: the library, the green nursery, the culinary arts building, and other classrooms. He knew that he had to get to the point, in spite of the fact there was so much to tell.

"The group behind this plan is well organized. They are citizens of Kona who want the best educational opportunity for their children. They have already received some grants, but so far they have not been able to purchase land to build on."

"Well, get on with it. You want me to sell the Kona property to them?"

"No, I want you to give it to them. Your house could be their hospitality and office center." He paused. "If you don't or if it is sold, the State of Hawaii will take at least half of its value."

Perkins squinted through his bushy eyebrows. "Good God in heaven, man, I ain't dead yet, and I ain't daft yet. Close to it on both counts, I'll admit, but I ain't never given that much away in my whole life."

"That's the point, J.J. This is your opportunity to leave something you'll be remembered for, as long as it stands. And it will be standing for a long, long time.

"There's one thing I must tell you, because you and others may misconstrue my interests in this. My niece is an architect. She entered the contest to design the buildings and overall plan of the community center."

Both J.J. and the lawyer scowled at him.

"She has just finished six years of training. I'd like for her design to receive the consideration it deserves but I know how it would look if people thought I swayed the judges' decision. Neither Chieko nor I want that kind of acclaim or blame. If she should be disqualified she would yield her prize to the runner up."

His listeners looked relieved. The lawyer had been scribbling some figures in his notebook. "J.J. your friend here has hit on something I wanted to talk to you about. I had other organizations that could do much good with money from the sale of that property.

"I've heard you rave about the greed of government, not to mention its stupidity. If you give the property to be used for a Learning Center, you'll keep it out of the hands of the 'bureaucratic bastards' as you so colorfully refer to them. If it is sold and the proceeds go to any charities, the U.S. Treasury and the State will get a whopping big share of it.

"We need to look into this more thoroughly, J.J. If it looks good to you I can do some research this afternoon and draw up a paper tonight for you to sign tomorrow. I know how much you have loved Kona and your home there. Your generosity will give opportunities to the youth, thus to the community."

J.J. was showing the strain of his final business dealings. He was pale and had slipped off the pillows that had propped him up.

"Ed, I don't know if I'll be here tomorrow to do any signing. Ya got some paper and a pencil? Start writin.' As clear, and brief as possible, and I'll sign it right now."

Attorney Edward G. Cohen and Ross Ota stared at each other for a few moments. Then the lawyer said, "I'll have it ready in a few minutes, J.J." He did.

J.J. had his eyes closed. "Are you asleep, old friend?" Cohen said. He placed his hand on the thin, bony arm lying on the sheet, its skin white as ocean spray.

"Read it to me Ed."

It had taken ten minutes. "I, John Jacob Perkins, do bequeath my

Kona property, including land, house, and anything attached to house or land, to the organization known as Apple A Day, Incorporated, to be used for the intended Community Learning Center within the boundaries of Kailua-Kona, Hawaii.

"As trustees for this property, I assign Ross Allen Ota and my attorney, Edward G. Cohen."

"Sounds real good, Ed. Where the hell is a nurse when a man needs one?" He tried to roar like a lion, but the sound was more cub-sized. "Nurse, we need a witness."

"No. Two witnesses, J.J. Do you want blondes or brunettes?"

"Hell, I'd take one of each if I could lift my head off this piller."

Ross raised the pillow that cradled the old man's head. Ed placed his hand on the right line, and J.J. signed the paper with almost his last breath.

Ota and Cohen signed, then the two nurses signed as witnesses.

The two men sat with him, one on each side, their hands on his, until he slept.

In the morning, Cohen got the phone call he had been expecting. "Mr. Cohen. This is Mr. Perkins's nurse, at the hospital. Mr. Perkins passed away during the night as he slept. His instructions are to call you."

[1] Taber's Cyelopedic Medical Dictionary, Edition 17, F.A. Davis Company, Philadelphia, p1759-1760, 1989.

Chapter 64

Gift from the Angels and J. J. Perkins

W hen Ross's plane touched down, there were two people at the airport to meet him. They converged on him from both sides as the passengers walked into the Kona International Airport. He was happy to see both of them. "Dinner is on me, but I have to stop by the Perkins Property before we go to eat," he said.

Noah and Chieko were helping Ross carry his small bag and brief-case. They all chattered at once. So glad to be together. Everyone had much to share about things that had been happening, but Ross kept all of his news to himself. There must be a perfect time to reveal it. He wanted as many of the founders and early members as possible there to receive the news.

When Noah drove Ross's Cadillac through the Perkins property gate, it was early afternoon. Ross was in a quandary. What could he say to avoid giving it away? He had to express his joy. Some little white lies would be the means to the end. Noah's question gave him the opportunity he needed.

"Was the trip worth it, Ross? Did the owner give permission to sell it, or is it still going to be our company account?"

"Well, yes. It was a very worthwhile trip. Mr. Perkins was in serious condition in the hospital. He was lucid up to the very end, the night before he died . . . well, to make a long story short, the property was sold intact, with the new owners already determined. Old J.J. Perkins was a fine fel-low, one of the old-timers who worked hard to earn every penny. He was smart and learned how to use money, rather than how to lose money, the way most people do when they get some of it. Sorry to see him go, but he will be remembered, and honored. I'll see to that."

They had gotten out of the car and were under the canopy of trees. "He must have kept it very nice when he lived here," Chieko said. "I hope the new owners will remodel this or build something beautiful here."

"I am sure they will. He and his wife loved it here. Yes, he died with fond memories of the past and with high expectations for its future. Well, let's go eat."

It was the first relaxing evening they had enjoyed together for a long time. Ross watched the two young people. Two wonderful human beings, he thought. They need each other and don't know it. And I need them. I would hate to die the way Perkins did, leaving no one behind to enjoy what I have to leave them.

"One question, Chickadee. When will the contest winner be announced? Are you shrugging your shoulders? You mean that you don't know? Well, I know who it will be. Don't you, Noah?"

"Without a doubt," he grinned.

"Please, you two. I don't want you to be disappointed if I don't win. I'm up against tough competition. Some experienced and renowned architects are entering."

"Will you be terribly disappointed if you aren't the winner, Chickadee?"

"No, I really wouldn't. I have enjoyed the work so much. I'll find a way to use the plans I've drawn up for the Learning Center."

Ross took her two tiny hands in his. "I am so happy to hear that, my dear. I was worried because once I started getting involved with the cement company, I realized that people might make accusations if you win. You know, they might say the contest is rigged. If that happens, maybe you could accept the honor and refuse the prize, or . . . It would be so unfair if we are accused, but it might be good to have a plan because, it could happen. Do you know what I'm saying? I mean for you to enter, and be happy whether you win, you don't win, or if you have to give it up. I'm babbling, but I hope you understand."

"Uncle, I am afraid you will be the most disappointed if I don't win, and you mustn't be. Whatever comes, it has been wonderful."

Chapter 65

Conclusion

On an island in the middle of the Pacific Ocean there is a village named Kailua on the Kona Coast. In Hawaiian "Kai" means sea, ocean, or water. "Lua" means a hole, a pit, a grave, or a cave. As a diver, I have seen caves one can enter from the ocean. Therefore, I like to translate Kailua as sea cave. Whatever the source of the name, it has a lovely sound, Kailua, and it is a lovely place.

I have seen miracles occur in Kailua, for there are wonderful, loving people here who care and who make good things happen. I have seen volunteers turn out to accomplish all kinds of good for the island and its people. I have seen Kona residents contribute time, muscle, tools, art and such to make a dream reality.

The island has Habitats for Humanity, and many active Service clubs. People contribute to help those less fortunate than themselves through yard sales, auctions, or collection jars kept on store counters. Owners of businesses donate to the community. The youth serve as volunteers. For Kona has a heart.

The building of the Community Learning Center began with the originators of Apple A Day, Incorporated. They were determined to find the best ways possible to educate our children. Despite complaints, confusion and attempts to place blame on anyone and everyone, no one had solutions until AAD began at ground zero to analyze and reconstruct education one step at a time.

First, the brightest children, those who had goals, were challenged. The dream grew to encompass all ages, including adults. Adults and children together in a never-ending search for knowledge and wisdom. Knowledge intertwined with wisdom, powered by gut-level intuition that sparks the joy of self-searching and instills confidence. A community composed of all ages, colors, ethnic heritage, and religions woven into a tapestry of aloha.

Two years ago, the construction of the first buildings of the Center started. The grounds are now exquisite. Ecologically co-habitable plants, lava rock, gravel, and sand. Koi swim in ponds. There is no lack of sun, so there is no lack of solar electrical energy to power the pumps that keep the water moving, and to light the lanterns that grace the gardens at night.

Trees at some distance from buildings were saved, and pruned. New planting near the buildings had to be limited to shrubs, succulents, and drought-tolerant varieties, for the sun must not be blocked from the solar and photovoltaic panels.

The first building was the green nursery at the highest elevation of the property. The first students enrolled to study botany while landscaping the grounds. Then, a library, a roomy, comfortable, well-equipped place for research, study and relaxation. Its central location generated calm within its walls, and its perimeter. Only the library, the culinary arts building, and the Perkins house have indoor toilets and bathroom facilities. The other buildings have only a counter, sink, cold water and electricity. The partially enclosed restrooms located between buildings can be hosed down for regular cleaning.

The high school classrooms were constructed early. The first students were the ones who would be graduating this year. Their motto: "Given the responsibility, we will lead." They are proof of the effectiveness of an education planned around each child's main interests. Given full rein, and guided by parents, mentors, and dedicated educators, the children's interests broadened and bloomed until nothing held them back. They, the students, taught others as they learned. Through their efforts to teach, they extended their own knowledge. Their mentors likewise were inspired to continue their own education while guiding and encouraging their charges.

The first graduation this June will be memorable. The school has gained international renown. Similar schools have grown up in this region, and in remote places on our globe. The students have impressive scholastic records. They have made themselves eligible for the best colleges, and now the younger students are following in the path of their older brothers and sisters.

"The power of aloha reigns here. It is our key to humanity." These words span the arch over the entrance gate. The ethnic diversity of Hawaii's citizens is boundless. People on these islands have known, long before the understanding of DNA, that there is only the human race. This knowledge brings us together

The small CLC buildings resemble the early thatched-roof huts. They were built to be durable and virtually maintenance free. They blend with both indoor and outdoor environments. The concrete siding reflects the colors of nature. Inside, local artists painted trompe-*l'oeil* scenes that reflect the subjects being studied at each location or the local flora and fauna.

At the entry, just inside the gate, gourmet luncheons are served. We can purchase baked goods or arrange for catering there. All of these are prepared, sold, and served by the culinary arts students.

As one enters near the makai border of the property, a fountain sculpted by a local art student stands guard. The fountain is a monument to John Jacob Perkins, whose gift of ten acres of land made this Center possible. Mr. Perkins died four years ago. A grave in a quiet alcove of the garden contains the ashes of Mr. Perkins and his wife. A plaque bears their names and pays tribute to his generosity.

Near the library, a metal and lava sculpture honors the work done by volunteers who gave generously of their time, energy, skills, and money to complete the Learning Center. The Center is intended for all ages. It is for all who seek knowledge. How fortunate we are to live in a country that provides freedom and opportunity to find our own answers to questions for which there is no one simple answer. Classes are offered here mornings, afternoons, and evenings for any subject of merit.

The Perkins home is a hospitality house and provides business offices for the property caretakers. The designs have improved life on these islands. The buildings have no air conditioning, except in the library to preserve books and documents. Fans are used overhead in other buildings. Louvers in the ceiling dome draw the warm air upward and out.

The photovoltaic panels on the roof supply more than enough electricity for lighting and other electrical requirements. Floor-to-ceiling metal gates frame the entrance and the view of the garden. Shutters fold inward to cover the entry on rare stormy days. The openings capture the Kona breezes as they move makai in the morning and mauka in the evening.

Students in the metal shops, guided by their devoted teacher, did the ironwork. Likewise, the inside shelving, door, and window frames were built by high school students in advanced woodworking classes.

The radio station KABC was relocated on the property and continues to serve the community. It also provides opportunities for students to gain broadcasting skills. Igor Connifer, who played a major part in unifying the community in the early stages of Apple a Day, manages the station. He now trains students interested in communication and journalism. His first student and co broadcaster, Kirk Collins, received a scholarship from Yale. He will be graduating with a Bachelor of Science degree next year.

Today there is a celebration at the Perkins House to commemorate the first year for Kona's Community Learning Center. Some student reporters have been assigned the honor of interviewing key people who started with a dream, and who are now enjoying the reality of a dream come true.

"Good afternoon, friends, students, and families. I am Barry Benson. I am a student here. I have completed my first year. I started with the first elementary class formed. We do not classify ourselves by standard grade levels. I am now almost eight years old. In our school, we like to gobble up information as fast as we can, in areas of our greatest interest.

"I would like to introduce my mentors, who try to keep my education balanced and progressing in directions that will benefit me in the future: My dad and mother, Mr. and Mrs. Guy Benson." They smiled, trying to contain their pride. They had coached him well.

Noah took the microphone. "Thank you, Barry. This Community Center started with a dream. Barry's father, Guy Benson, initiated the ideas for improved public education. Guy Benson spread his ideas until he had a following of like-minded people willing to work to make the dream come true. Thank you, Guy, for the dream and the persistence to win others to the cause."

Guy took the mike Noah handed to him. "I would like to introduce several people who dedicated themselves to the fulfillment of our dreams. My dad, Alf Benson, a distinguished educator from the traditional schools of Scandinavia. Dad is eager to move into one of the guided care residences being built on this property so you are likely to see him strolling through the center, the library and the classrooms every day.

"The following people did whatever was necessary, wherever they were needed. Many of you will recognize Noah Solomon as the president of Apple A Day, Incorporated for the past three years. Under his leadership membership started increasing." Guy handed the mike to Noah.

"Apple A Day grew fast when a new resident moved to Kona. Igor Connifer. Everyone knows Igor. We don't know how we got along before KABC was licensed here in Kailua. Everybody hears you, Igor, at least twice a day if they drive to or through Kailua." Igor just popped his gum and grinned, his ponytail waving in the breeze.

"Mrs. Gail Sanders-Collins now teaches the high school students with four other teachers and a team of aides. She and her fellow teachers each have at least two major studies to fortify their expertise." Sandy stood only after the applause demanded it and then sat down.

"Mr. Ike Epstein." All of the students cheered and applauded. "I guess you need no introduction, Ike. I understand that you have delayed your retirement to oversee the custodial responsibilities here for awhile. I don't think you'll ever want to retire." Ike rested his hands on his stomach, nodded his head, and laughed.

"Well, folks as time went on more people than we can count or recognize individually contributed to this dream of an educational center and the adventure in learning that this school has pioneered. I want to ask everyone involved, who also bought one of our money-making T-shirts, to stand and be recognized."

Almost everyone in the audience was wearing a yellow shirt, standing, and applauding themselves. They sat down revived by their stretch and by filling center stage for the moment.

"Friends, I want to introduce you to a man who was a friend of our benefactor, J.J. Perkins. He is a friend of ours also, Mr. Ross Ota." Ross came forward and leaned into the microphone.

"Thank you. I wish J.J. could be here to meet you and to see what you have done with the property he willed to you for our Community Learning Center. J.J. was not highly educated through schooling, but he had educated himself as you are all doing. He had a quality that can be a byproduct of 'book learnin,' as he would have called education. The byproduct of which I speak is wisdom. You can gain wisdom through experience, 'book learnin,' and a third most important way which I'll call 'straight thinking.' Some people call it 'common sense,' and some say it's 'horse sense.'

"The world is too complicated now to limit education to experience, as could once be done. It takes all three, and the world is moving so fast that the 'book learnin' can never stop. We need to refer constantly to specialists in varied fields of study, just to keep up.

"I want to say just one more thing about 'straight thinking.' It has to do with integrity. You will notice that the word integrity includes g-r-i-t, 'grit' in the middle. Integrity is honesty. One definition of 'grit' is 'obstinate courage, or pluck.' I'm sure that everyone knows what 'integrity' means, but stay with me for just a minute. I like this word. Integrity. I don't think that education is worth a darn without integrity. It means: 'being complete, wholeness . . . being whole.' Here are some other synonyms: 'soundness; unimpaired condition; uprightness, honesty and sincerity.'

"If J.J. were here he would want to impart all of those qualities to you. May I repeat? May you in this place of education, of learning . . . may you become complete, may you be sound in body and mind; may you practice honesty and sincerity toward yourself, and others. 'To thine own self be true, And it must follow, as the night the day, Thou canst not then be false to any man.' [1]

"If all who enter here wield the sword of integrity and bear it honorably with those thoughts guiding them, J.J. Perkins will know that he used durned good horse sense when he left this property in your care."

At the end of the program, Ross walked over to the library plaque with his niece and his friend Noah Solomon at his side. Below Perkins' name, etched into the brass, was this inscription: *Architect: Chieko Ota-Solomon.*

[1] William Shakespeare, *Hamlet,* Act 1 Scene 3.

LEA MCCLURE's teaching assignments have included grades K through 12 and adult education in affluent and poverty-stricken, urban and rural locations. Now retired, McClure continues to educate.